THE
UNAUTHORIZED
STAR
WARS
COMPENDIUM

THE UNAUTHORIZED

STAR WARS

COMPENDIUM

THE COMPLETE GUIDE TO THE MOVIES, COMIC BOOKS, NOVELS, AND MORE

BY

TED EDWARDS

BOXTREE

First published 1999 by Little, Brown and Company, New York

This edition published 1999 by Boxtree
an imprint of Macmillan Publishers Ltd
25 Eccleston Place London SW1W 9NF
and Basingstoke

Associated companies throughout the world

ISBN 0 7522 1188 9

The author is grateful for permission to use the following contributions:
Photographs by Albert Ortega; 'Death Star = Death Trap' and 'Prequel Trilogy
Speculation' by Dan Vebber; 'A Critical look at the *Star Wars* Trilogy "Special Editions"'
by Mark Altman; 'Fifty Reasons Why *Jedi* Sucks' and 'Ten Reasons Why
Jedi Doesn't Totally Suck' by Dan Vebber and Dana Gould

1 3 5 7 9 8 6 4 2

A CIP catalogue record for this book is available from
the British Library.

Printed and bound in Great Britain by
Butler & Tanner Ltd, Frome and London

CONTENTS

INTRODUCTION

A LONG TIME AGO — in fact, much longer than an entire generation probably cares to think about — George Lucas transported audiences to a galaxy far, far away; a journey from which their collective imagination has yet to return.

More than two decades after its original release, *Star Wars* is very much on the minds of science fiction enthusiasts, as witnessed by the nearly innumerable licensees signed on to a property that hadn't — until the prequel began shooting last year — been in production since 1983. Among them are Bantam Books, which is in the midst of a best-selling publishing program, and Dark Horse Comics, which has continued the saga in numerous miniseries.

Star Wars, it would seem, is here to stay; its impact is as powerful as ever, a point emphasized in a *New York Times* article that noted, "The unprecedented success of *[Star Wars]* turned Hollywood's attitudes toward science fiction upside down, changed the industry's definition of summer, re-established symphonic music in films, exploded the boundaries of special effects, gave new importance to sound, created a pop mythology, and made merchandising the characters from a movie as important as the movie itself."

The book you're holding is designed as a complete overall guide to the *Star Wars* phenomenon, from George Lucas's inception of the concept through production of the original trilogy, the radio dramas, the novels, the comics, the revised Special Edition trilogy, and the franchise's resurrection, including a look ahead to the new trilogy, beginning with the recently wrapped *Episode One*.

I could conclude this introduction with the words "May the Force be with you," but, hey, that would be a cliché.

TED EDWARDS

June 1998

THE UNAUTHORIZED

STAR WARS

COMPENDIUM

THE MAKING OF
THE STAR WARS
TRILOGY

EPISODE IV: A NEW HOPE

EPISODE V: THE EMPIRE STRIKES BACK

EPISODE VI: RETURN OF THE JEDI

FROM A 1998 PERSPECTIVE, it seems impossible to believe that as recently as twenty-odd years ago the words *science fiction* were whispered by Hollywood executives and *not* shouted from the highest soundstages. It was hard to argue their point, because for the most part the genre equaled death at the box office.

Certainly there were exceptions, most notably Stanley Kubrick's *2001,* Fox's *Fantastic Voyage,* and Franklin Schaffner's *Planet of the Apes,* as well as the small-screen *Star Trek* phenomenon of the 1970s that defied all explanation. In general, the perception was that the genre was a leftover from the 1950s, when our planet battled mightily — over and over again — against aliens from other planets who had nothing better to do than plot our destruction. The bottom line is that no one but the diehard fans was taking science fiction seriously.

One of those people was a young filmmaker named George Lucas, who, in the early 1970s, wrote and directed both the cult (read: critically acclaimed, box office empty) classic *THX-1138* and the blockbuster hit based on his youth in Modesto, California,

American Graffiti. According to Lucas, he was interested in creating a space saga back in 1971.

"Originally, I wanted to make a Flash Gordon movie with all the trimmings," he said, "but I couldn't get the rights to the characters. So I began researching and went right back and found where Alex Raymond (who had created Flash Gordon) had gotten his ideas. I discovered that he'd gotten his inspiration from the works of Edgar Rice Burroughs, especially from his *John Carter of Mars* series of books. I read through that series, then found that what had sparked Burroughs off was a science fantasy called *Gulliver on Mars,* written by Edwin Arnold and published in 1905. That was the first story in this genre that I have come across. Jules Verne had gotten pretty close, I suppose, but he never had a hero battling against the space creatures or having adventures on another planet. A whole new genre developed from that idea.

"I had the *Star Wars* project in mind even before I started shooting *American Graffiti,*" he added. "On our first vacation after I'd directed *American Graffiti,* my wife, Marcia, and I went to Hawaii. That was great except that I wrote the whole time I was there. I'd already started thinking about *Star Wars.* A director can leave his work at the studio; a writer can't. There's always a pen and paper available. A writer is thinking about what he's supposed to be doing, whether he's actually doing it or not, every waking hour. He's constantly pondering problems. I always carry a little notebook around and sit and write in it. It's terrible, I can't get away from it."

Throughout his pondering, Lucas realized he was certain what he wanted to create. "I wanted to make an action movie — a movie in outer space like Flash Gordon used to be," he said. "Ray guns, running around in spaceships, shooting at each other — I knew I wanted to have a big battle in outer space, a dogfight thing. I wanted to make a movie about an old man and a kid. And I knew I wanted the old man to be a real old man and have a sort of teacher-student relationship with the kid. I wanted the old man also to be like a warrior. I wanted a princess, too, but I didn't want her to be a passive damsel

> I'm trying to make a classic sort of genre picture, a classic space fantasy in which all the influences are working together. There are certain traditional aspects of the genre I wanted to keep and help perpetuate in *Star Wars.*"
> — GEORGE LUCAS

in distress. What finally emerged through the many drafts of the script has obviously been influenced by science fiction and action adventure I've read and seen. And I've seen a lot of it. I'm trying to make a classic sort of genre picture, a classic space fantasy in which all the influences are working together. There are certain traditional aspects of the genre I wanted to keep and help perpetuate in *Star Wars*."

The *Star Wars* trilogy, comprising episodes four through six of George Lucas's overall saga, did not begin as one fully developed, high-concept pitch but rather evolved over a five-year period through a variety of scripts and story treatments. In fact, the origins — the original story lines and development of the characters — are just as fascinating as anything that has appeared in Lucas's final vision. But as with all great sagas, one must go back to the beginning, back to that first spark of the imagination.

As Lucas explains it, his original goal was to create a modern fairy tale. While studying film at the University of Southern California, he became fascinated by the way culture is often transmitted through fairy tales and myths. Fairy tales, he determined, taught people basic lessons in good and evil and how to conduct themselves in society.

"Mythology," Lucas said at a press conference, "in general is used to convey certain social values and social precepts from one generation to the next. In the beginning, it was an oral tradition designed to give the community a cohesive set of thinking modules that allowed them to be a society. And these were told in story form because that was the best way to teach them. In modern society, where there's competition from lots of media, better communications, larger masses of people, the conscious use of mythology has gone by the wayside.

"The film industry," Lucas continued, "picked up a lot of classic works, a lot of classic motifs. Many of those movies, when I was growing up, were Westerns. When I got into college and started studying anthropology and got into this stuff, an instructor said that Westerns were the *last* American mythology, probably the last world mythology, to develop. In the sixties, that all fell apart. Westerns went by the wayside, especially film Westerns. We were sitting there with nothing specifically mythic. One of the reasons I started doing films was to create a new kind of myth — using space because it's the next frontier. It's more motifs than anything else. The messages that you impart, the themes, the dramatic issues that you're dealing with like good and evil and friendships, are pretty classic. The structure of mythology in terms of the hero's journey is also fairly classic. It has been said that there are only thirty-two plots in the world, and everything is a variation of them. Mythology takes those thirty-two plots and puts them into a slightly more structured context, especially when it comes to the heroic part of it."

After failing miserably to satisfy the corporate executives at Warner Brothers with his first feature film, *THX-1138* (1970), Lucas began submitting ideas for two motion pictures to several of the other studios. One of them eventually became the hit movie *American Graffiti* (1973). The other was the aforementioned intended remake of Flash Gordon. Eventually he obtained tentative approval from David Picker at United Artists for a completely original story.

As Lucas explained to the *New York Times,* the intended audience for *American Graffiti* was sixteen-year-olds, whereas *Star Wars* was designed for those about two years younger. His reasoning was that youngsters at the time no longer had a fantasy life in the same way that he and his contemporaries had had. Heroes of the time were people like Kojak or Dirty Harry. "There's all these kids running around wanting to be killer cops," said Lucas. His hope, in response, was to open up the realm of space for those kids, at the same time putting a sense of adventure back into the science fiction genre and moving a bit further away from the genre's growing preoccupation with science. As a result, *Star Wars* was an attempt to give young people a faraway and exotic environment to unleash their imaginations in. "I want them to get beyond the basic stupidities of the moment and think about colonizing Venus and Mars," he added, noting that the only way for something like that to happen would be for kids to forget about reality (to some degree), pick up a ray gun, jump into a spacecraft, and take off with a Wookiee in outer space. Noted Lucas, "It's our only hope in a way."

While he was adding the final touches to *Graffiti* in February 1973, Lucas started sketching rough ideas for his film. He wrote every morning and spent his afternoons and evenings researching fairy tales, mythology, and the writings of Joseph Campbell (in particular, *The Hero with a Thousand Faces*) and Carlos Castaneda (notably, *Tales of Power*). He also consumed every work of science fiction, from the classics of the genre by Edgar Rice Burroughs and Alex Raymond to the more contemporary tales of Isaac Asimov, Frank Herbert, E. E. "Doc" Smith, and Arthur C. Clarke. But Lucas knew that he was much more of a conceptualist than a writer and admitted to having great difficulty getting his ideas down on paper. He was still struggling with those ideas when he first met Ralph McQuarrie, an illustrator for Boeing aircraft who had also worked for NASA, and asked him for suggestions on how to visualize his concepts for the screen.

By May 1973, Lucas had completed a ponderous thirteen-page story treatment. Handwritten on notebook paper, it told "the story of Mace Windu, a revered Jedi-bendu of Ophuchi who was related to Usby C. J. Thape, a padawaan leader to the famed Jedi." His agent, Jeff Berg, and attorney, Tom Pollack, didn't understand a single word (understandably not) but nonetheless agreed to help him submit the idea to United Artists, which still held first option on his "big sci-fi/space adventure/Flash Gordon thing." David Picker reviewed Lucas's treatment for *The Star Wars*, as it was then called, and passed on the project, fearing how much it would cost to make. Universal Pictures, which also had an option on Lucas's next picture as part of the *Graffiti* deal, was equally cautious and eventually declined to develop the project.

In the pages of *Rolling Stone,* Lucas explained that he thought *Star Wars* would be a fairly viable project. Initially, he thought the film could pull in roughly $16 million at the national box office (foreign wasn't much of a consideration at the time). If the film could be produced for roughly $4.5 million, with the same amount being spent on prints and advertising, there would be a decent amount of profit left over for a studio willing to take a chance on him and *Star Wars*. When he went to United Artists, he pitched the film as a Flash Gordon–like adventure with a healthy dose of James Bond thrown in for good measure. But the studio didn't see it the same way he did, halted by perceived limitations at the box office. From there he went to Universal, which wanted to pay him $25,000, which was "half of what my friends were asking, and the studio thought I was asking for twice as much as I would get," mused Lucas. They turned him down as well and he proceeded to Fox, which climbed aboard.

It was Lucas's opinion that Fox agreed to do the film for a couple of reasons. First of all, they had had great success with the *Planet of the Apes* film series, a forerunner in some ways of *Star Wars* (though comparatively much smaller) and the only truly successful science fiction film series in Hollywood history up until that time. Second, Alan Ladd Jr. understood the appeal of the film and got Fox to give it the green light. "I kept doing research and writing scripts," Lucas explained. "There were four scripts trying to find just the right thing, because the problem in something like this is you are creating a whole genre that has never been created before."

Lucas understood the problem, rhetorically asking how you could explain a Wookiee to an audience, or how to determine what the film's tone should be so that it wasn't a children's film that played down to the audience but would be, instead, an entertaining movie for all ages. Essentially the story maintained a wholesome, honest vision about the way he wanted the world to be — and how he hoped kids would want the world to be. He felt that many of the themes he was dealing with were carryovers from *THX-1138* and *American Graffiti* in terms of accepting responsibility for your actions and things of that nature. Lucas admitted that it took him a long time to get the story and script right, and that once it was completed a preproduction budget of $16 million was the result. Knowing there was no way so expensive a film would be produced, Lucas began slashing, first the hoped-for new equipment (" 'Okay,' " he reflected, " 'we'll cut corners and do a lot of fast filmmaking,' which is where I really come from. *Graffiti* and *THX* were nothing, both under million-dollar pictures"), and then some of the scope of the story. Eventually the budget got down to $8.5 million, which was pretty much as low as he felt it could go.

As noted above, upon hearing the complicated scenario, Ladd agreed in principle to a deal even though he didn't really understand the concept (Lucas later relied on production sketches from Ralph McQuarrie to further cement Fox's offer to back a big-budget space fantasy). Less than two weeks after Universal had turned *Star Wars* down, Fox agreed to pay Lucas $50,000 to write and $100,000 to direct a film that would, ultimately, become the highest-grossing movie of all time (replaced in 1982 by pal Steven Spielberg's *E.T.* before taking back the crown after the release of the Special Edition, and ultimately giving it up to James Cameron for *Titanic*). Universal undoubtedly kicked itself in its corporate behind when *Graffiti* turned out to be a blockbuster and they had turned down its auteur's follow-up film.

Lucas was reportedly told by his agent that he could renegotiate his deal with Fox for upward of half a million dollars. Instead, he sought control. He wanted to supervise all merchandise and receive a percentage of the profits, retain all literary and music rights and all sequel rights, although Fox would have first crack at distributing said sequels. The studio, not having all that much faith in *Star Wars*, gave in to Lucas's demands, believing it was saving more than $500,000. This would, of course, prove costly, particularly in terms of merchandising.

Charles Lippincott, formerly a vice president of Lucasfilm, isn't surprised that Fox gave Lucas such leeway in terms of licensed products.

"Merchandising on films had not been very successful," he points out. "The last big merchandised movie was *Doctor Doolittle*, which was also from Twentieth and had been a disaster. People looked at TV as a thing to merchandise. We were up against *Charlie's Angels* — posters were very big for that — and *The Six Million Dollar*

> **M**erchandising on films had not been very successful. . . . People looked at TV as a thing to merchandise. We were up against *Charlie's Angels* . . . and *The Six Million Dollar Man*. . . . You were looking at an era that had nothing to do with movies."
> **— CHARLES LIPPINCOTT**

Man, which was very successful in terms of merchandising. Then there was all of the postmerchandise on *Star Trek* after the series was over. You were looking at an era that had nothing to do with movies."

And while all of this was going on, Lucas was still without a workable script — but not for long.

SCRIPT DEVELOPMENT

MAY 1973: The original story synopsis for *The Star Wars* begins "Far above the blue-green planet of Aquilae, a silent battle takes place. Six sleek, fighter-type spacecraft rocket toward an orbiting speck, which is a gargantuan space fortress, and fire their laser bolts. The small ships are no match for the fortress, and are easily dispatched. The explosions echo across the vastness of space, and a roll-up explains that 'it is the twenty-third century, a period of civil war.' "

Though somewhat crude and unpolished, the thirteen-page story treatment sketched out most of the action that would follow in the series. The group of characters' adventures on Aquilae (in the desert and the cantina), Leia's rescue from the prison complex, the dogfight in space, and the awards ceremony all survive to the final draft of *Star Wars*. A chase across space and in the asteroid belt, and the intrigue on the city-planet of Alderaan, form the basis of *The Empire Strikes Back,* and the featured jungle battle finds life in *Return of the Jedi.*

The characters also remain surprisingly faithful to their first inception, even though certain changes do occur. Leia continues as princess, while the character of Luke Skywalker, here a veteran general, would ultimately be made a teenager (replacing a rebel band of boys). The aging general becomes Ben Kenobi, the desert hermit and aging Jedi Knight. A pair of bumbling bureaucrats would be transformed into C-3PO and R2-D2; furry aliens evolved into Chewbacca, the Wookiee, and the Ewoks; and the Sovereign ultimately becomes the Emperor. The only central character missing from this early screen treatment is Darth Vader.

MAY 1974: After working for more than a year, Lucas completed a first-draft screenplay. The story introduced the Jedi Bendu, who were the chief architects of the Invincible Imperial Space Force and personal bodyguards of the Emperor, and pitted them against the evil Knights of the Sith, a sinister warrior sect. The hero, Anakin Starkiller, eighteen; his younger brother, Deak; and their father, Kane — the last of the Jedi Bendu — have been hiding out on the desert planet of Utapau for many years. When Deak is killed by a seven-foot-tall black knight who comes looking for them, Kane decides that it's time to end their exile.

GEORGE LUCAS

While the first-draft screenplay alters and expands much of the original material, it's still very crude and bloated in cinematic terms. Lucas's year-long effort introduced two villains: a sadistic general named Darth Vader, and Prince Valorum, a Black Knight of the Sith. The characters are both interesting but, at this point in the saga, somewhat one-dimensional. By making them into one person who starts out as the embodiment of evil, then changes in reaction to another's evil deeds, Lucas has the essence of the space fantasy's tragic figure. Additionally, he seems to transpose Kane Starkiller's disability (he must remain in protective cybernetic armor to maintain his life systems) onto later conceptions of Vader. Han Solo, the huge green-skinned smuggler, remains somewhat unchanged (except in appearance) by the final draft. Owen and Beru Lars would eventually become farmers (not anthropologists) and play a much more important role as Luke's uncle and aunt. Of course, the two bumbling bureaucrats are now bumbling robots.

The earlier sequences (on Utapau and in the capital of Aquilae) also provide interesting clues to characterization: for example,

Grand Moff Tarkin appears not as a governor but as a religious leader; and Kane's decision to leave his son in the hands of a master is similar to that made by Ben Kenobi, surrendering Luke to the master Yoda. But there was still much work to be done before the script could be a film.

JULY 1974: Two months later, Lucas produced a slightly revised version of the first script. Although the central action remains the same, several names and concepts had been reworked (for inexplicable reasons). Luke is still an aging general, but now he is identified as a former Dai Noga who masters the great space Force. *Force* is used for the first time to identify a metaphysical power that only Dai Nogas can utilize. Princess Leia has become Zara, Anakin Starkiller is now Justin Valor, and the Wookiees are referred to as Jawas.

Captain Dodona replaces Prince Valorum as a member of a warrior sect known as the Legions of Lettow. He has been given the task of hunting down and destroying the remaining Dai Nogas, but he, like Valorum, undergoes a change of heart. Other changes, for the most part in name only, appear throughout the story and provide a surface, somewhat cosmetic change to the whole saga. Lucas knew the script was still a mess and worked hard to produce another version.

JANUARY 1975: The second screenplay was finished, with the title *The Adventures of the Starkiller, Episode One of the Star Wars.* The new story was set in the Republica Galactica, which was ravaged by civil war, and focused on a quest for the Kiber Crystal, a powerful energy source that controlled the Force of Others. (Fans of Alan Dean Foster's *Star Wars* novel *Splinter of the Mind's Eye* will no doubt recognize this reference to the crystal.) The roll-up concluded with a prophetic promise: "In times of greatest despair there shall come a savior, and he shall be known as 'The Son of Suns.'"

This screenplay had finally brought Lucas's epic vision into focus. While the story remains consistent with his original synopsis, the action, broken into three distinct locations, was certainly manageable from both an aesthetic and a technical point of view. He

> **W**hen you arrive in the middle, you miss all the tedious exposition and jump right into the action. We wanted that effect with *Star Wars* — the feeling that you had come in after the movie had started."
>
> **— GARY KURTZ,**
> producer, *Star Wars*

had pared his story down, blended characters, and discarded material that would eventually comprise the other two films. Lucas had also transformed the two most endearing characters into their final form. Darth Vader was now Dark Lord of the Sith and the chief adversary of Luke and the forces of good. Han Solo is no longer a green-skinned alien (like the bounty hunter Greedo) but a young Corellian pirate. In fact, Solo's character is drawn as a thinly disguised version of Lucas's own mentor, Francis Ford Coppola. And although the Kiber Crystal would ultimately be dropped from the series (as the physical embodiment of the Force), Lucas had found the central impetus (Hitchcock often referred to it as MacGuffin) upon which the action would turn.

Lucas now also knew that this story was only part of a much greater whole. In May 1975 he retitled *The Star Wars* as episode four in *The Adventures of Luke Starkiller* and sent a synopsis of the screenplay to Alan Ladd Jr. The Fox executive greeted the draft with much enthusiasm but questioned Lucas about the other episodes. It seemed strange to everyone (but Lucas) to start a motion picture in the middle of the action.

Gary Kurtz, who would ultimately serve as producer of both *Star Wars* and *The Empire Strikes Back,* mused to *Starlog* magazine, "Certain kinds of movies just work better — or seem to work better — when you come in in the middle. I know that was the case with a lot of the low-budget films I made with Roger Corman. When you arrive in the middle, you miss all the tedious exposition and jump right into the action. We wanted that effect with *Star Wars* — the feeling that you had come in after the movie had started."

Recently, Lucas described the process: "What actually happened is that I wrote this big script, and in writing that script, I wrote a back story to go with it. The script was vast, and I knew it was going to be difficult to film. So I said to myself, 'Well, let me take this first act and I'll expand it.' I knew it had to be fleshed out, so I took the other two-thirds of the script and put them on the shelf. I told myself, 'Someday I'm going to get back to those.' This is partly what a writer does; you get an idea that's too big for one book, so you put the rest over there and you concentrate on this one part. That's what I did. I finished the first one. Some have said I showed wisdom in retaining the sequel rights, but the reason was I didn't want some clause in there that would make it virtually impossible to take the sequels anywhere else. I decided that even if the first one did not do well, by hook or by crook I would finish the other two.

"The first film came out and was a giant hit," he added, "and the sequels became possible. Then people suggested we could do more than three, so I thought, 'Gee, I can do these back stories, too.' That's where the 'Chapter IV' came in. Then everyone said, 'Well, are you going to do sequels to the first three?' But that was an afterthought. I don't have scripts on those stories. The only notion on that was, wouldn't it be fun to get all the actors to come back when they're sixty or seventy years old and make three more about them as old people. That's how far that has gone, but the first six will definitely get finished."

While writing and revising the various drafts of the screenplay for *Star Wars,* Lucas had kept changing his mind about the focus of the story. He scribbled out in longhand on specially selected blue-and-green lined paper various story synopses. Between drafts one and two, he wrote a prequel of sorts that dealt with Luke's father and his relationship to Darth Vader and Ben Kenobi. Lucas decided he didn't like it and wrote a completely different treatment with Luke as the central figure. The plot was not all that different from the second screenplay (or the finished film, for that matter), but it featured Han Solo as Luke's older, battle-weary brother. He returns to Tatooine to enlist Luke in the rescue of their father, an old Jedi Knight. At one point Lucas even toyed with the idea of making Luke a young girl who falls in love with Solo, but the climactic assault by hundreds of Wookiees on the Death Star remained unchanged. Several revisions later, he knew he had enough material to make several motion pictures.

AUGUST 1975: The third screenplay demonstrates Lucas's command and final understanding of his great saga. The narrative is tighter and considerably more focused, and even though the dialogue is somewhat crude, the third screenplay captures the spirit and imagination that would become *Star Wars*. All that was left was for Lucas to polish some rough edges and rethink his notions about the Force. He would eventually jettison the Kiber Crystal, in the fourth script, and convey the Force in metaphysical terms.

MARCH 1976: The fourth screenplay was actually the one that Lucas chose to film. The narrative covers most of the action in the movie and became a final product that many consider to be one of the great motion pictures of all time, and a testament to the persistence and creative imagination of George Lucas.

THE CHARACTERS

The inspiration for many of the characters in the *Star Wars* saga comes from a variety of sources Lucas consulted while writing the first film. Whereas the characters themselves may have undergone various changes in gender and form, their basic personalities remain firmly rooted in mythic or literary traditions. Lucas studied dozens of ancient legends, including that of King Arthur, read a variety of fantasy and science fiction stories, including Tolkien's *Lord of the Rings* trilogy, and isolated the most common elements and archetypal characters in an effort to produce a story that is somewhat universal. It's fascinating to view these characters in hindsight, to see how certain premises and personalities were kept intact and how others were transformed or simply abandoned.

Luke, the hero of the space fantasy, was originally imagined as a swashbuckling adventurer like Flash Gordon or John Carter. Adept with both sabers and blasters, the character had risen to the ranks of general and Jedi Knight. In the thirteen-page summary, General Skywalker leads a rebel band of teenage boys against the Empire. By the first-draft screenplay, Luke was still a general in his early sixties, and the hero of the piece was now Anakin Starkiller, aged eighteen. Several revisions later, Luke was again the center of the story. He had become a teenager who must rescue his brother, Deak, from

the clutches of Darth Vader. Lucas felt there was much more room for character development if he introduced a young innocent who must grow to manhood and kept the story central to him. By the next-to-final draft, Luke had become a farm boy, son of a famous Jedi Knight, who must deliver R2-D2 to a rebel stronghold on a far-away planet. The evolution of his character was nearly complete; all he needed was a mentor.

Throughout the many rewrites, Luke's thoughtful old mentor, who appears as a "shabby old desert rat," was to have been the central role in the piece. Lucas saw the character as a combination of Gandalf the wizard in *Lord of the Rings,* Merlin the magician, and the samurai swordsmen often played by Toshiro Mifune. (In fact, Lucas first imagined Mifune in the role of Ben Kenobi but later went with Alec Guinness when he realized that the distinguished actor was available for the part.) He wanted Ben (Obi-Wan) Kenobi to be a kind and powerful wizard who had a certain dignity and could influence the weakminded. As first envisioned, Kenobi was probably the early General Skywalker, then, in later drafts, Kane Starkiller, an anonymous "seer," and finally the crazed desert hermit who was also a Jedi Master.

Leia was first conceived by Lucas as an amalgamation of Dejah Thoris (from *A Princess of Mars*), Lady Galadriel of Lothlorien (from *Lord of the Rings*), and Dorothy Gale (from *The Wizard of Oz*). Never really named in the original story treatment, she was an eleven-year-old princess with "goddesslike" powers who needed rescuing from Imperial troops. Subsequent drafts of the screenplay portrayed her as a sixteen-year-old princess who fell in love with Han Solo, the central male figure and, finally, as the twin sister of Luke Skywalker. At one point, in the third draft, Lucas even gave Leia the mind-control powers of a witch, but he later revised that when she became Luke's long-lost sibling.

Han Solo was introduced in the initial screenplay as a huge, green-skinned monster with gills and no nose and was only later developed into a human. Lucas probably saw Solo as an amalgamation of all the great sidekicks in literature and film, from Lancelot (in the Arthurian legends) to Tonto (in popular culture), but he eventually evolved into a fully realized leading player. By the second screenplay, Han had been transformed into a burly individual resembling Francis Ford Coppola. Though somewhat comic in appearance, with flamboyant clothes and a guinea pig girlfriend, he was clearly a person to be reckoned with. Lucas later made him a cynical smuggler and thought of him as a James Dean — "a cowboy in a starship: simple, sentimental, and cocksure." That persona stuck to Han Solo in the first film, but he gradually emerged as a "sexy Clark Gable" in the subsequent films, easily winning Leia from Luke (which was actually a good thing, as she was later revealed to be Luke's sister).

> In the movie, he [Alec Guinness] plays a teacher, Luke's mentor. It was a relationship that was echoed in the way Mark Hamill reacted to him. Guinness is the Jedi of the actors."
>
> — GEORGE LUCAS

R2-D2 and C-3PO began life, as noted previously, as a pair of bumbling bureaucrats in the original treatment, Lucas's initial concept for comic relief. Their characters are derivative of Samwise Gamgee and Pippin Took, in the works of Tolkien, and the famous comic duo of Laurel and Hardy. Much later, after Lucas had made them bumbling construction robots on the Death Star, they began to evolve into personalities all their own. C-3PO was the overbearing android who complained too much, and Artoo, as his much smaller counterpart, was the brunt of Threepio's angry jibes. While Artoo resembled one of the hapless drones in *Silent Running* and Threepio the Robotrix in *Metropolis,* they were both original creations of Ralph McQuarrie. Lucas had given him free reign to create whatever he thought was appropriate, and McQuarrie relied on his background as an illustrator for Boeing aircraft and NASA to visualize Lucas's ideas.

Lucas used Ming the Merciless, the evil ruler of Mongo (and later Mars) in the Flash Gordon comics, as the model for his emperor. Several early drafts described the Emperor as simply the evil sovereign who had taken control of the Alliance and proclaimed himself king. But Lucas was not satisfied with that back story and began thinking of the character in terms that a contemporary audience would recognize — Richard Nixon. The Emperor became a

corrupt politician who, with the help of his cohorts (General Darth Vader and Valorum, the Black Knight), destroyed all but one of the Jedi-Templar. Then, in a time of great chaos, he had himself declared ruler. By the final draft, the evil sovereign had evolved into a master of the dark side of the Force, as well as the tutor of Kenobi's young apprentice, Darth Vader.

The evolution of Darth Vader is also intriguing. He was conceived by George Lucas as the epitome of evil, the Black Knight of the Arthurian tales or Sauron from *Lord of the Rings*. Though he did not appear in any form in the original treatment, the character had two roles in the first-draft screenplay: General Darth Vader and Valorum. In that draft, Vader (under the name Captain Dodona) was an intergalactic bounty hunter who was hired to track down and murder Jedi Knights for the Emperor. Then Vader became a Dark Lord of the Sith, and Lucas created Boba Fett from that early concept of Vader as a bounty hunter.

However, in the novelization of *Star Wars* and the final screenplay, the reference to Vader as some sort of bounty hunter remains. According to Obi-Wan, Vader betrayed and murdered the pilot Skywalker, then "helped the Empire hunt down and destroy the Jedi Knights." Darth Vader was also given Kane Starkiller's exoskeleton to help him survive, and a background story was worked up by Lucas to explain his severe injuries. (Apparently, many years before, Ben Kenobi and Darth Vader fought a fierce lightsaber duel, and Vader was driven into the molten lava of an active volcano. He survived, but his body was ruined, and he was forced to wear an ominous black breathing mask that also hides his disfigurement, like the Man in the Iron Mask. Not much more is revealed about his character in the first film; but by the third, audiences learn that he was, in fact, Anakin Skywalker, a former Jedi Knight and father of Luke.)

George Lucas's vision for *Star Wars* began as a simple thirteen-page story treatment and evolved into its own galaxy of heroes and villains, droids and creatures of a thousand worlds. But getting there, of course, was the challenge.

INTERGALACTIC CASTING

Although *Star Wars* would ultimately be shot in England, Lucas was determined to fill the film with a mixture of American and English actors. Of his final choices for the film, Lucas explained, "They're good actors and they're more or less by nature like the characters in the story. The important thing about a movie like *Star Wars* is that it be believable to the audience and that they identify with the characters. And these actors, because of who they are, bring believability to the situation.

"Alec Guinness is the master of what he does," Lucas elaborated. "He has a strong pivotal personality that other actors look to. In the movie, he plays a teacher, Luke's mentor. It was a relationship that was echoed in the way Mark Hamill reacted to him. Guinness is the Jedi of the actors. I chose Carrie Fisher to play Princess Leia because I wanted someone who was able to stand up to the bad guys. Princess Leia is actually in charge of the rebellion. She's gotten caught, but she's fighting. Mark Hamill is young, fun-loving, slightly naive, and very enthusiastic. He's just like the character he plays."

MARK HAMILL

Although *Star Wars* was Hamill's first feature role, at the time he was becoming quite recognizable on television. He made his acting debut on an episode of *The Bill Cosby Show* in 1970, and he ultimately spent nine months on the soap opera *General Hospital,* appeared in numerous TV movies, and was one of the stars of *The Texas Wheelers* before being cast. As a youth, Hamill collected *Famous Monsters of Filmland* magazine, and he has always loved science fiction. "I thought if they were making a big space fantasy movie, I'd be satisfied just to watch part of it being shot. I even asked my agent if she could get me onto the set. I wanted to see some of the special effects being done. I wasn't even thinking of acting in it."

Of the casting procedure, Hamill related to journalist James Van Hise that he auditioned for the film in front of both Lucas and the director Brian De Palma, who was casting his horror film *Carrie.*

"I don't think George said a word through the whole interview; he's really shy, he let Brian do the talking," said Hamill. "He didn't tell me anything about *Star Wars*. Everybody from about 15 to 30 was out, and they were looking for Luke, yet I didn't know that; they didn't tell me anything about it. We knew it was called *Star Wars*, so it had to be something to do with outer space, and we knew it was George Lucas. Nobody saw a script until later when I did a screen test, then they sent me four, maybe five pages of scenes and no character description, really, so I just had to pretty much play it neutral; play it the way I would react to that situation, which worked out fine, because Luke is a simple farmboy, which is not to say that I am.

"It's funny," he added, "because when I finally tested for it, I tested with Harrison Ford. Harrison tested with a few other people and maybe George was leaning toward them, I didn't know, but Harrison had worked with George before in *American Graffiti*. I was really nervous. This was a screen test with George Lucas and I was all, 'Yes, sir,' and Harrison was all, 'Aw, shit, George, let's get this fuckin' thing over with and let's get the hell out of here!' I was really shocked that he was talking to George that way. I understand it now because George is one of the nicest men I've ever met, just an incredible man. I trusted him totally. Choices I never would have made as an actor, I did for him because I know he must be right. I never put up an argument, really. Usually if I can't do something the way the director tells me, something has to be worked out or I can't do it. We somehow have to reach a compromise before I'll be able to do what he wants me to. It would have to be at least shaded my way. But I was doing things that I felt were dead wrong in this movie, dead wrong, and I just trusted George that it would come out right."

> I was doing things that I felt were dead wrong in this movie, dead wrong, and I just trusted George that it would come out right."
>
> — MARK HAMILL

Interestingly, it was Lucas's personality that ultimately provided Hamill with the key to Luke's characterization. "I was doing the scene where I discover the robots," he said. "I said my lines very big, very dramatic. George came over and went over the lines with me. He didn't give me the line readings, but as he explained the intention of the scene, he was very low-key. I just watched him. I don't know why, but something in me told me to observe how he was speaking, to try to pick up his inflection. I even imitated a few of his gestures as he explained to me what he wanted me to do. At one point, I thought to myself that he was doing it so small. That can't be right. I thought I'd try it very small and he would see that it didn't work. He would tell me to go back to the way I was doing it before. So when I played the scene, I did it just like I thought George would react in the scene. When I did it like that, George called, 'Cut. Perfect.' I was flabbergasted. I thought, 'Oh, I see. Of course, that was right. Luke is George.' Even the names are similar, Luke — Lucas. From then on, I followed through on my feelings. I began to really feel like I was playing George. I guess if you sit down and write an adventure like this, you have to think of yourself as the main character. I actually think *Star Wars* is the adventure of George Lucas."

CARRIE FISHER

Cast in the role of Princess Leia was Carrie Fisher, daughter of Eddie Fisher and Debbie Reynolds, whose major claim to fame until that point was in the film *Shampoo*, where the nymphet looked at Warren Beatty and simply asked, "Wanna fuck?" Quite an auspicious beginning, to say the least, for an actress who would ultimately fight a dependency on drugs and emerge as a successful author and screenwriter. Of her screen test she told journalist Robert Greenberger, "The dialogue for our screen test was even more complicated than that in *Star Wars*. The sentences were sooo long. You didn't know what you were talking about, so finally you had to ask, 'George, in my motivation for this scene, you must tell me, *what* is a bantha? What am I actually saying?'"

Elsewhere she added, "I wanted to do the role of Princess Leia because I wanted to have real conversations with people with bubbles on their heads. I just wanted to be blasé about someone sitting across from me being a 'small person' or some strange looking person who was hired through the 'Ugly Agency.' I love that there's an agency in London called that. I can't tell you how thrilled I was to be casually sitting around with these people as if they didn't have

THE MAKING OF THE STAR WARS TRILOGY

hair-dryer heads and things like that. I wanted to sit next to Wookiees, which are tall, half-men, half-ape creatures with glowing eyes, and all kinds of robots."

Harrison Ford, most of whose sequences had been cut from the original print of *American Graffiti* but restored for a theatrical rerelease, was cast in the role of Han Solo. Ford, of course, has become the most successful of the *Star Wars* triumvirate, scoring as Indiana Jones, Dr. Richard Kimble, and Tom Clancy's Jack Ryan, among many others.

HARRISON FORD

English acting legend Sir Alec Guinness reluctantly signed on as Jedi Knight Obi-Wan Kenobi, fearing that somehow this little space opera would be deemed beneath him by his peers in England, although the exposure and financial return the role provided him quickly dispelled that fear. At the time of the film's release, though, Guinness offered, "I feel movies can be a positive influence in people's lives. Something really good should come from a motion picture. A good story can show people how they can overcome obstacles, rise to the occasion. When I read the script for *Star Wars*, it had something that made me high, held my attention. It was an adventure story about the passing of knowledge from one generation to the next. One of the difficulties of being in my sixties is that I can't pick and choose as much as I could in my thirties. But my role in *Star Wars* has been described as a blend of the wizard Merlin and a samurai warrior, and you can't beat that. Unlike most space fantasies, the characters George Lucas has created aren't cardboard. And the story is gripping. There's a quest, encounters with other forms of life, and conflict between good and evil. The good wins, which is a novelty these days."

Hammer Films veteran Peter Cushing took on the role of the evil Grand Moff Tarkin. "I don't mind being a horror film star," Cushing said back in 1977. "That would be like socking a gift horse in the mouth. And no one wants to see me do *Hamlet*, but millions want to see me as Dr. Frankenstein. Audiences are the most important thing to an actor. I have been awfully lucky in the amount of work I've been able to do. However, I don't think people should be called comedy actors or horror actors. They're just actors."

Well, one actor going through internal conflict in her scenes with Cushing was Carrie Fisher. "I like Peter Cushing so much," she said, "that it was almost impossible for me to feel the hatred I needed to act against him. I had to say lines like, 'I recognize your foul stench,' but the man smelled like linen and lavender. I couldn't say that to this nice English man, whom I adored. So I substituted in my mind the one person I hate. Although I never read SF before *Star Wars*, I had a kind of active space fantasy life of my own. Once, I saw a science fiction movie that scared the hell out of me. I do not know what it was, but it took place on the moon. And I used to be afraid of Martians. There was an invisible Martian in that movie who was surrounded by an electric field. If you got thrown into that electric field, it was good-bye forever. It was really scary, scarier than even burglars or snipers. You can't put Martians in jail."

> **W**hen I read the script for *Star Wars*, it had something that made me high, held my attention. It was an adventure story about the passing of knowledge from one generation to the next."
> **— SIR ALEC GUINNESS**

Of the casting of Guinness and Cushing, Lucas noted, "Peter Cushing, like Alec Guinness, is a very good actor. He got an image that is in a way quite beneath him, but he's also idolized and adored by young people and people who go to see a certain kind of movie. And so you say, is that worth anything? Maybe it's not Shakespeare, but certainly equally as important in the world. Good actors really bring you something, and that is especially true with Alec Guinness, who I thought was a good actor like everyone else, but after working with him I was staggered that he was such a creative and disciplined person."

In the original script, Ben Kenobi doesn't get killed in the fight with Vader. About halfway through production, Lucas took Guinness aside and told him the character was going to get killed halfway through the film. Lucas knew it would be shocking to the actor to learn that one of the film's intended heroes was going to suddenly die. Being a consummate professional, though, Guinness took the news in stride and used it to help him develop Obi-Wan Kenobi.

Guinness wasn't the only one surprised. Fox was not pleased

with Lucas pulling a Hitchcock by killing one of the leading players halfway through the film, but Lucas looked at the situation more pragmatically than anyone else. His problem, as he related it to

DARTH VADER

Rolling Stone, was that he had a climactic scene with no climax approximately two thirds of the way through the story. Added to this was the fact that there was no real threat on the Death Star, and as originally written Vader and Kenobi have a lightsaber duel that culminates in Kenobi hitting a door, the door slamming closed, and the heroes running away with Vader left behind, looking foolish. "This was dumb," he said. "They run into the Death Star and they sort of take over everything and they run back. It totally diminished any impact the Death Star had."

Lucas's wife at the time, Marcia, suggested that Kenobi be killed, after first suggesting that the victim be Threepio. Lucas resisted that particular idea because he was of the opinion that the droids were whom the films were really about, serving as the framework element of the film. Kenobi, however, was another matter. The appeal of the character's death for Lucas was that it made the threat of Vader greater and tied in with the whole concept of the Force and the fact that Vader could use the dark side. Both he and Guinness came up with the concept of Kenobi continuing on as a part of the Force, still a presence in the film and Luke's mind. "There was a thematic idea that was even stronger about the Force in one of the earliest scripts," Lucas said. "It was really all about the Force."

Peter Mayhew portrayed Han Solo's best friend, the Wookiee named Chewbacca. In describing just what a Wookiee is, Lucas explained, "I think a Wookiee is a kind of cross between a large bear, a dog, and a monkey. And he's very friendly until you get him riled. I'm very fond of Wookiees. I have a Wookiee at home. Well, she's not quite as big as the Wookiee in *Star Wars,* but she's a Wookiee just the same. Actually, she's a dog, but she looks just like a Wookiee. She's a very big, furry dog. She looks like a panda bear, but not as big. Her name is Indiana. And a Wookiee has certain dog characteristics — a Wookiee is protective, a friend, and kind of cuddly."

The term *Wookiee* was actually coined by California disc jockey Terry McGovern, who had done some voice-over roles in Lucas's *THX-1138* and had improvised a line about having just run over a Wookiee in the street. "I asked him if he knew what he meant when he said the word *Wookiee*," Lucas said, "and he just told me that he had made it up on the spot. But I liked it and used it in the film. I guess when I was trying to name this new creature, I thought it sounded like a good description of the creature I wanted."

Darth Vader actually had three real-life alter egos: English body-builder and actor David Prowse, who handled most of the character's physical scenes; sword master Bob Anderson, who portrayed the Dark Lord of the Sith during his lightsaber duels; and James Earl Jones as the character's menacing voice. In the pages of the *Star Wars Insider,* Jones noted, "After he put the film together, George Lucas decided he wanted a voice in the bass register." Jones was of the opinion that David Prowse wasn't a bass, and that he also had a Scottish accent, so Lucas began looking for someone to do a voice-over. He was contacted by the writer/director and asked if he wanted a "day's work," which he agreed to. But Jones has never been quick to grab credit for the character. "David Prowse worked very hard to create the character of Darth Vader," he explained. "I just considered myself to be the special effects."

JAMES EARL JONES
(the voice of Darth Vader)

As far as Lucas was concerned, the two most integral characters were the droids C-3PO and R2-D2. Although many of Artoo's scenes were actually played by barely functioning real-life robots, British actor Kenny Baker was occasionally inside the droid's shell. Playing his counterpart was Anthony Daniels, who has probably had the most sustained relationship of anyone in the *Star Wars* saga, having played the character in various television capacities and charity events, as well as providing Threepio's voice for the National Public Radio adaptations of each film, the Star Tours amusement ride at

THE MAKING OF THE STAR WARS TRILOGY

KENNY BAKER (R2-D2)

ANTHONY DANIELS (C-3PO)

Disneyland, and the short-lived animated *Droids* TV series. Indeed, Daniels and Baker are among the very few actors from the original trilogy to take part in the prequels.

"I love droids, they're my favorite people," Lucas told *Rolling Stone*. When making the film, he had no interest in the droids being traditionally cold robots. As he explained it, even the robots in *THX* were friendly and nonmalevolent. His hope was to give a little "equal time" to robots and their problems in life. At the same time, R2-D2 and C-3PO were designed to bring a Laurel and Hardy quality to the story, delivering a bit of comic relief in the process. "I didn't want the human characters to crack jokes all the time, so I let the robots do it, because I wanted to see if I could make robots be like humans."

THE PRODUCTION

While all the interiors of *Star Wars* were shot on soundstages in England, exterior sequences required a location that looked as if it might be found on another planet in another galaxy. To this end, all the deserts of America, North Africa, and the Middle East were researched and explored. A dry, arid landscape with limitless horizons — the perfect location to depict Tatooine — was found in Tunisia. In March 1976, the film's production unit and cast descended on Tozeur, a sleepy little oasis town in western Tunisia where the Sahara Desert begins. The construction crew worked for eight weeks to turn the desert and towns into another planet. In the town of Matmata, Lucas shot the interior of Luke Skywalker's homestead, in the depths of the Hotel Sidi Driss.

Following two and a half weeks' filming in Tunisia, the *Star Wars* cast and crew moved on to the EMI Elstree Studio, in London, for fifteen weeks of filming. Elstree was the only studio in England or America large enough to provide nine large soundstages and simultaneously allow the company freedom to handpick its own personnel. To accomplish *Star Wars*' complicated special effects, Lucas and producer Gary Kurtz set up their own in-house effects shop in a warehouse in the San Fernando Valley, appropriately called Industrial Light and Magic. Special photographic effects supervisor John Dykstra took full advantage of some new advances in computer-controlled stop-motion animation.

Additional second-unit Tatooine desert material was photographed in the Mayan ruins of Tikal National Park, Guatemala. Noted composer John Williams spent a year preparing his ideas for the movie's invigorating score. During March 1977 he conducted the eighty-seven-piece London Symphony Orchestra in a series of fourteen sessions to record the ninety minutes of original music.

C-3PO and R2-D2

When it came time to start work on the aliens for *Star Wars'* famous cantina sequence, makeup supervisor Stuart Freeborn contracted pneumonia and was laid up in a hospital. Freeborn had planned to create several detailed alien makeups. First, life-masks were to be constructed of the various actors portraying that scene's aliens. Over the life-masks, Freeborn and his assistants would then sculpt the various alien faces in clay, on which thin coats of plaster would be carefully brushed. The artists would build the plaster up in thickness until, after the entire thing had dried, it would be pulled off. The plaster cast would be used to make molds of the alien designs, into which would be poured a latex-rubber-type mixture. The filled mold would be placed in an oven until fully heated, after which the latex mask would easily come out of the mold. After additional trimming and decoration, made-to-fit alien masks would be ready for the actors to wear.

Instead, English makeup men replaced Freeborn and essentially designed vastly simplistic hairy animal–type heads. Upon returning to America, Lucas decided to refilm major portions of the sequence. He had wanted to shoot a second unit, but such a

THE MAKING OF THE STAR WARS TRILOGY

prospect was extremely expensive and Fox turned his request for additional money down flat. Lucas countered that the Cantina scene was a key sequence in the film and that it was absolutely necessary for him to have two more creatures. Ladd, who at that point was running the studio, agreed, but stipulated that the final tally for the additional creatures would have to be $20,000. "We ended up cutting out half of what we wanted," he told *Rolling Stone,* "but it was sufficient."

Lucas contacted young makeup man Rick Baker (the remake of *King Kong, The Autobiography of Miss Jane Pittman*) to design the supplementary masks. Lucas showed Baker and his associates photos and illustrations from past endeavors to emphasize the type of aliens he wanted.

Pressed for time, Baker's group utilized several masks that Baker had designed for unreleased films (including the werewolf and devil-head characters seen in the film). But Baker, who usually creates one creature in six weeks (and now had to design thirty creatures in that period), did get to design a few new makeups. Even so, the masks did not realize Freeborn's brilliant potential. After giving these masks to Lucas, Baker was told that the old designs would be used in background shots only, and that the new characters would be more prominently featured. Lucas did the exact opposite and spotlighted several "old designs," creating a somewhat embarrassing situation for Baker. When he viewed the final print, Lucas still did not like the effect. The aliens looked too plastic, but there was nothing he could do. *Star Wars* was already a million dollars over budget, and Lucas had depleted the extra money he had been allotted for the sequence to be reshot.

PETER MAYHEW (Chewbacca)

THE SPECIAL EFFECTS

While much of *Star Wars'* appeal is the fact that it recaptures the magic of early Hollywood, from the cliff-hanger movie serials to such fantasy classics as *The Wizard of Oz,* one of the most important elements of the film was its special effects, which had to somehow be a quantum leap beyond Kubrick's revolutionary *2001,* utilizing techniques that hadn't even been invented yet.

Producer Gary Kurtz felt that the biggest problem with the film was getting it produced at all, as Hollywood in general was extremely leery of any film that had the words "sci-fi" attached to it. Considering the time — the early 1970s — it wasn't such a ridiculous notion. "The only big budget science film was *2001,*" he told *Starlog,* "and most producers were worried that there wasn't a big enough audience." The truth is, Stanley Kubrick's epic did not make the kind of money MGM had expected it to, although it did show a profit some four or five years after its initial release. An additional Hollywood fear Kurtz related was that the best special effects technicians had retired. As a result, it would fall to the creators of *Star Wars* to develop their own approach to special effects. "Once we got into production," he said, "*Star Wars* was pretty straightforward as a picture, except that we had to work out a lot of bugs in the new special effects equipment."

At the time, Lucas noted that he was attempting to get the special effects up to a level that he had foreseen in his head and was happy with much of what the team had come up with toward the end of production. The beginning was much tougher, because the F/X team was learning how to fly models, move cameras, and provide a variety of other movements. "It is very difficult to plot out the way one of those planes moves in nonreal time, using tilting cameras and motors," he said. It was easy to say he wanted things to move a certain way, and something quite different for everyone to figure out how to accomplish it. "In *2001,*" he noted in the pages of *Rolling Stone,* "the ships run a straight line, they just go away from you or they cross the screen, they never turn or dive."

CHEWBACCA

THE MAKING OF THE STAR WARS TRILOGY

While the name ILM (or Industrial Light and Magic) is a pretty common one in 1998, as Lucas's F/X outfit handles the majority of effects in today's motion pictures, back in the mid-seventies it was a fledgling operation desperately trying to accomplish the impossible while handling the effects for *Star Wars* out of a California warehouse. The operation was headed up by John Dykstra, who sat down with journalist James H. Burns in 1978 to reflect on the creation of the film's effects.

"*Star Wars* is going to produce a whole lot of effects-oriented, escapist films," said Dykstra. "I think that *Star Wars* reflects the public's want for entertaining, fantasy-type movies. Whenever you have a show like *Star Wars* or *Close Encounters of the Third Kind* or *Silent Running,* where the special effects contributed a major amount to the success of the film, then the effects people become very much like talent, very much like actors. It is their creativity that is providing something that didn't exist before. I think *Star Wars* has provided an opportunity for the production of fantasy movies that the public wants. Special effects seem to play an important role in those kind of movies."

Dykstra was hired to head *Star Wars'* special effects department in June 1975 by Lucas and Kurtz, and he immediately realized that the film would not be easy to accomplish. Each special effects shot in *Star Wars* combined several elements — spaceships, animated overlays, miniatures — photographed separately and then printed together. *Star Wars* finally utilized 3,838 individual elements in its 365 miniature and photographic effects shots.

"My first meetings," Dykstra told Burns, "with Gary and George to discuss *Star Wars'* special effects were very loose and general. With the quantity of material that was in the film, it would be difficult to go through it specifically. We just talked about some very general ideas — about the way things should look and how things should be done."

Dykstra assembled a team to pull off the film's effects. "This group of people got together and walked into this building in Van Nuys, California — 14,000 square feet of empty building," he told

Burns, "and began constructing a special effects studio. The first thing we did was get two groups of people working together concurrently — one on the construction and development of miniatures and the other on the construction and development of the miniature photographic equipment."

With sometimes more than a hundred people working under him, Dykstra's biggest problem became organization. "What made these people work was that they talked to each other. Everybody knows enough about the other person's field to be able to talk articulately with the next guy."

Lucas's script required that *Star Wars* present space sequences in which the camera pans, tilts, and offers multiple angles. Since traditional special effects procedures couldn't do this, new cameras and systems had to be created.

One of the film's pioneers, along with John Dykstra, was Dennis Muren, who told journalist Ron Magid that in the beginning the ILM team looked back at what had been done previously in terms of special effects.

"There were two LA effects groups during the late '60s and early '70s," Muren explained. "The group I was in came from the *King Kong* school, literally. We had no money for tools, so we had to make our shots by adding camera moves or artistic lighting or something to make them look special. The other school was the one that came out of the success of *2001*. They used mechanical technologies. I think that *Star Wars* was a mixture of those two groups. Ken Ralston and I weren't particularly interested in the mechanical stuff. I was always watching the dynamics of motion in movies, where they used camera pans to add some style and stuff like that, but it didn't have anything to do with technology. I can't remember exactly what my influences were, but they would've been literally as screwy as *The Flying Tigers* and *The Bridges of Toko-Ri*."

Dykstra told James H. Burns, "We took effects methods that have been used for years as individual jobs and combined them into

> **W**here the special effects contribute a major amount to the success of the film, then the effects people become very much like talent, very much like actors. It is their creativity that is providing something that didn't exist before."
>
> **— JOHN DYKSTRA,**
> special effects, *Star Wars*

one system, so that we have the ability to make accelerations and decelerations in motion, without having to set one move up and another on separate passes. We've taken the best of the techniques that existed when I started *Star Wars,* sophisticated those as much as we could, and then developed a work horse system to do those."

More important was the development of motion control, which allowed ILM to computer-program the movement of the spaceship models as well as the camera itself. The "control" aspect is a function of computerization and precisely machined mechanical dollies, pan and tilt heads, and model movers — allowing for frame-by-frame repeatability, which is the key to modern effects shots. This means that the computerized motions of the camera can be translated and scaled to live-action backgrounds, so that the models and the background can be locked together in the same frame with the same camera move. It also means that the models themselves can be photographed in several passes for optimum aesthetic beauty: separate passes can be shot for each color separation, for miniature lights, and by backlighting the model, to create perfect mattes. And because each pass is filmed with the same computerized camera movements, all of the shots lock together perfectly. The end result was more fluid movement than anyone had ever been able to achieve in special effects prior to that.

"I thought *Star Wars* was the first big application of motion control," said Muren. "But someone mentioned that Doug Trumbull may have done something like it for *Silent Running.* I know for *2001* they turned motors on and kept their fingers crossed. *Silent Running* was probably a little more sophisticated than that, but not a whole lot. We could program and vary the speeds of the three motors on the camera, the two motors on the track, and the five motors on the model and run them forward or backward and get them to repeat. The operator programmed all the dynamics of the shot, so the vision of the shot was lifted off a flat 2-D storyboard and came alive in 3-D space and time. That meant we no longer had to worry about the 'strobines' of stop-motion or rely on gravity and accidents when we used things like wires."

JOHN DYKSTRA

This camera system was initially dubbed the Dykstraflex.

"The basic concept for the Dykstraflex was designed over a bottle of wine on the floor of my house in Marina del Rey," Dykstra reflected to James H. Burns. "A lot of our innovations came together that way, because the people at ILM are a very personable group. We talked instead of sending memos. Initially, we got a lot of flack from people about the way we worked, because I didn't want all of the things that to me smack of organization for organization's sake, and *not* organization for *efficiency's* sake. I got into some trouble there."

The Dykstraflex enabled the effects artists to limit moving miniatures, an important advantage. "When you begin to move miniatures," Dykstra told Burns, "you end up with shakes and lighting problems. Remember, we don't have a sun to work with. We put a single spot lamp on the model and it's got to be spotted down to give us a parallel shadow effect. If you move the model out of your key lights, you end up going into multiple shadows."

Dykstra also utilized motors to manipulate *Star Wars*' miniatures. "When we wanted the ship to roll over, while it's flying over the camera," he explained, "then you have to make the ship roll to do that. When you have ships that you are shooting concurrently with one another in order to cut down the number of composites, often we put one of the ships on a track that moved laterally, or sideways, perpendicular to the axis of camera motion between the two ships. In the scene where the *[Millennium Falcon]* is backing out of the door of the docking bay, where it did the flip-over, the *[Falcon]* actually made that movement."

To combine miniature footage with coordinating backgrounds (additional spaceships, stars, planets, and so on), ILM's Robert Bialack and Richard Edlund developed a vastly improved blue-screen system. The standard blue-screen system involves shooting one object against a blue background. Your *desired* background is filmed and printed through a red filter. After several negative reversals of each piece of film, the final negative and prints are run through an optical printer and you finally have your completed effect.

DEATH STAR = DEATH TRAP

by DAN VEBBER

For all the yipping that Admiral Motti does about his station being the "ultimate power in the universe," certain aspects of the Death Star's construction leave a lot to be desired. Indeed, on several occasions the Death Star's sinister engineers seemingly designed things to be as dangerous as possible. Consider these examples:

1 • THE SUPERLASER

Each of the superlaser's seven constituent beams shoots down a manned accelerator tunnel, causing anyone who might be standing next to these beams to shrink up against the wall and hope not to be disintegrated by a stray static charge. Each beam has at least enough power to destroy a planet one-seventh the size of Alderaan, so we can assume close-up exposure to any of them could lead to massive epidermal ionization, incurable melanoma, or at the very least, unwanted freckles. The superlaser accelerator tunnels probably have to be worker accessible — and I'm not calling for a removal of the catwalks alongside the beams' paths — but couldn't they sufficiently warn the technicians before the thing was going to be fired so they could move out ➤

of harm's way? Would the installation of a few lousy warning lights really have cost that much more in the Emperor's grand scheme of things?

2 · DANGEROUS ALLOCATION OF ARTIFICIAL GRAVITY

Any spherical battle station the size of a small moon would have its own gravity, wherein "down" would be directed toward the station's center. But we can tell the Death Star uses artificial gravity generators, because "down" is always in the direction of the station's "south pole." (Those Imperial boobs actually expend energy to defeat a core-oriented gravity situation that would have made more sense to begin with! Suckers!) Given that the station utilizes artificial gravity generators, why aren't they turned off or just plain not installed beneath the station's slew of virtually bottomless chasms? Countless stormtroopers (stormtroopers with families, I would remind you) would have lived to fight another day were their minor blaster wounds not followed by a plunge into oblivion.

3 · COMPLETE LACK OF SAFETY RAILS AROUND DEADLY CHASMS

Take docking bay 327, for example. There's a huge elevator shaft in the floor, in the middle of which is obviously a high-traffic area. And there's not so much as a Watch Your Step

ILM innovated daylight corrected, fluorescent tubes to "facilitate movement of the screen and to optimize the screen's efficiency." The procedure was adapted from AC to DC to eliminate potential flicker problems with "real-time or high-speed photography."

Star Wars also improved Rotoscoping processes. Rotoscoping is when "a film is projected under a light box. Artists trace over this frame by frame, sometimes adding in new material." The final effect is startlingly realistic.

To help choreograph the film's gun-port battle and climactic dogfight sequences on the Death Star, Lucas and Kurtz compiled a 16mm dupe featuring battle scenes from various war films. It was for this sequence that Dennis Muren's fascination with war films came into play.

Lucas pointed out that the dogfight was extremely hard to cut and edit. Storyboards the company had taken from old movies and black-and-white footage of old World War II movies were intercut with pilots talking so that the sequence could be cut in real time. Normally his wife, Marcia, could edit a ten-minute sequence of film within a week, but this sequence took her eight weeks to cut together. There were 40,000 feet of dialogue footage of pilots saying their technical jargon and that had to be intercut with the battle itself. "Nobody really has ever tried to interweave an actual pilot story into a dogfight, and we were trying to do that," he told *Rolling Stone*, "however successful or unsuccessful we were."

Dykstra, however, wasn't so enthusiastic about Lucas's compilation of footage, and felt that the ideas presented to ILM were going to have to be revised.

"We departed from that black and white film storyboard sequence in many, many areas," he explained to James H. Burns. "As innovative and intelligent a way to approach the scenes as the dupe was, one problem was that the ships on the storyboard were black against a white background. In many cases, George wanted the size of the ship different than what he had in his storyboard. That made it impossible to make the shot the length that you saw on the dupe."

Lucas wanted to be heavily involved with *Star Wars*' special effects, but communicating with Dykstra (who was in Los Angeles doing effects) while George himself was in Europe shooting live-action footage proved nearly impossible.

"I think George was so involved with what he was doing in Europe that it was very difficult for him to communicate effects information," Burns was told by Dykstra. "In fact, we basically ran on my concept of what we were going to do for an awful long time, before George had any hand in it at all. We were in contact via the telephone. But I didn't talk to George as much as I talked with Gary Kurtz, and then it was usually just progress reports."

Lucas's forced silence helped heighten the growing tension between him and Dykstra. "George and I are not what you call the best of friends," said Dykstra. "We are two different kinds of people. I like George Lucas. I don't know whether he likes me or not. I assume he can tolerate me. He did for two years. I don't think that our conflict was based on anything other than the fact that we have different interests as people. We had a common interest in the movie.

"George feels that he is capable of doing the technical end of the special effects more effectively than I," he added. "Perhaps that's why we didn't see eye to eye on so much of the stuff, because he wasn't in a position to come and be there, to actively have a hand in it and say, 'Let's use this camera to shoot this shot.' I think that if he had come and done that, perhaps he would have had a little more respect for what I did. If he had come and done that, he would have known a lot more about special effects. Therefore, I probably would have paid a lot more attention to his suggestions.

"Special effects people are *not* technicians, they are *artists,* and deserving of the same kind of deference that is given to the people in 'star' roles — actors. They don't work actors too hard; they get their trailers and stuff — they're creative people. I'm not talking about me and my people, I'm not asking for the velvet glove or a fancy doo-dah situation. I'm just talking about some respect and some fair treatment."

Of the strained relationship, Lucas explained that he was

sign! Even more preposterous is the placement of controls for the tractor beam hundreds of feet up and surrounded only by a precarious six-inch circular ledge. Sure, this setup worked to the Empire's advantage at least once, significantly slowing down Obi-Wan's attempts to sabotage the controls, but I'll bet the ratio of Rebel sabotage incidents to legitimate tractor beam maintenance by certified Imperial workers wasn't low enough to justify the risky panel placement.

4 · UNPREDICTABLE, GUILLOTINE-SPEED PRESSURE DOORS
Sure, they look cool, but how many stormtroopers have to whack their heads running into rooms before the Emperor takes notice? We saw it happen once, and we were privy to only an hour or so of Death Star footage. Imagine what goes on during those thousands of hours we didn't see! How many concussions have occurred? How many slow-moving saps have been cut in half by the doors as they sliced down into the floor with the efficiency of a galactic-scale French Revolution? It is my hope and dream that one day the Emperor's dark servants will form a union and work to correct these flagrant safety violations.

Oh, wait, I guess it's only a movie. ✦

merely determined that the composition of the effects and their lighting would be effective, plus he wanted everything done on time. His feeling was that special effects could be produced with the same intensity and on the same schedule as any other aspect of a film, and he was frustrated that that wasn't happening the way he felt it should. "It was purely a working problem and being at odds with John was no greater than being at odds with everybody else," he related to *Rolling Stone*. "I had just as many problems with the robots and the special effects people in England as with the special effects people in California."

In perfect honesty Muren admitted that throughout production he wasn't sure — really — what the end result of this film would be. "You know, I thought the script was terrific but impossible to do," he explained. "It reminded me of *The Wizard of Oz* with all these crazy creatures running around a Death Star, and I thought, 'This movie is just wild,' but I didn't know if there'd be any audience for it. And the visuals — it was too hard for me to see what was unique about it because all I could see then were the problems we had getting the motion-control work to look fluid. I still look at the problems. But I think the dynamics of the movement were so staggering to people that they didn't see those things."

> **G**eorge feels that he is capable of doing the technical end of the special effects more effectively than I. . . . Perhaps that's why we didn't see eye to eye on so much of the stuff."
>
> **— JOHN DYKSTRA,**
> special effects, *Star Wars*

THE SELLING OF STAR WARS

A long time ago, in a galaxy far, far away . . . no one would touch *Star Wars* with a ten-foot pole.

As unfathomable as it may seem, in the mid-seventies George Lucas had an incredibly difficult time selling his concept to both production companies and movie theaters. Helping him break through the barrier of debilitating indifference from the world was Charles Lippincott, the vice president of advertising, publicity, promotion, and merchandising for the Star Wars Corporation, whose task it was to build an awareness for the film prior to its release.

"The reason I had this long title at the time is that nobody in the movie business really used marketing as a term to incorporate advertising. They still talked about departments with all three titles," reflects Lippincott. "I really conceived marketing as a different way of handling science fiction. In a sense, it was like preadvertising."

In the early seventies, Lippincott noted with fascination the growing interest in science fiction and comic book conventions, and the proliferation of stores like A Change of Hobbit, all of which indicated that *something* was happening within the genre.

"My thinking," he says, "was that we should sell to the science fiction and comic book crowd early on. Why not tailor a campaign and build off that? Do a novelization and comic book adaptation early. The only science fiction film that we had to go on, really, was *2001,* which had been sold quite differently."

To begin his efforts in bringing awareness of *Star Wars* to America, in November 1975 Lippincott sold the novelization of the screenplay. "The lawyer for Lucasfilm wanted to put it up for auction, and I wanted to go to the best science fiction publisher, and I won out. So we went with Ballantine Books."

Interestingly, this process began a month before Twentieth Century Fox's board of directors gave the green light to *Star Wars.* "Their decision," Lippincott explains, "was based on the fact that *2001* had finally broken even in November of 1975 and we were to do the film for around the same budget *2001* was done."

In January 1976, Fox held the last of their sales conventions, which until that point had been an industry mainstay wherein studios invited exhibitors out to Los Angeles to discuss and preview future products.

"The presentation was called 'Twenty-Six in '76' and we were one of them, though far down the line," Lippincott says, smiling. "The exhibitors weren't interested in *Star Wars* at all. I did a presentation, similar to what I would do at conventions, based on the Ralph McQuarrie paintings. I did a slide presentation and they were bored out of their skulls. However, the younger people in the

My thinking was that we should sell to the science fiction and comic book crowd early on."
— **CHARLES LIPPINCOTT**

audience who worked for exhibitors really loved it. Those few thought it was great, but the older exhibitors thought it was terrible."

Shortly after the presentation, Lippincott proceeded to New York, where he hoped to meet Stan Lee of Marvel Comics to work out a deal for a comic book adaptation of the film.

"Stan kept turning me down," he says. "He said, 'Once you shoot the film, come in and see me.'"

Refusing to give up, Lippincott had a friend introduce him to former Marvel editor Roy Thomas and discussed the idea with him. Thomas was intrigued, knowing he could get a meeting with Lee, and asked Lippincott if he could edit and write the comic book if Marvel went ahead with it. Lippincott agreed and the two of them then approached Howard Chaykin about doing the artwork. Next up was the meeting with Stan Lee.

"Finally," remembers Lippincott, "Stan Lee said, 'All right, if you want to do it, fine, but the deal is you don't get any money for the comic book for the first 100,000 copies sold.' I said, 'Fine, but I want a miniseries of comic books.' Nobody had done a miniseries at that time. I said it had to be at least five comic books because I wanted to present three of them before the film came out and two of them after the film came out. Stan Lee agreed to that. I got the deal through and went back to Twentieth and they said I was stupid. They didn't care about the money issue. They just thought I was wasting my time on a comic book deal."

Shooting of *Star Wars* began in March of 1976 and Lippincott almost immediately began doing presentations at conventions. The first was Los Con in late June.

"That's where I was heckled off the stage by Jerry Pournelle," he says, laughing. "He really gave me a tough time, saying things like, 'This is space opera. It's not science fiction.'"

Next up was the annual San Diego Comic Con, where Lippincott, Thomas, and Chaykin did a presentation on the idea of adapting a movie to comic book form. "Marvel didn't do anything to push

> I did a slide presentation and they were bored out of their skulls. However, the younger people in the audience who worked for exhibitors really loved it. Those few thought it was great, but the older exhibitors thought it was terrible."
>
> — CHARLES LIPPINCOTT

the comic book and the movie had just finished shooting, so nobody knew much about it. But Howard drew a poster that we printed up a thousand of, and we went there with the poster and a little information about the film and we did our presentation. We had a fairly good crowd show up for it. I talked to a lot of kids, particularly younger kids, about what toys they liked, what models they liked, to figure out what companies we should go with."

World Con in Kansas City followed, and although the convention was weary of the whole *Star Wars* "thing," they gave the film a room where material and displays were brought in. Also joining Lippincott at World Con were star Mark Hamill and producer Gary Kurtz.

"There were the Darth Vader and Threepio outfits and a number of models, all under a great deal of security," Lippincott notes. "There were science fiction fans who said, 'It's just a movie, it's not serious. This is not speculative.' On the other hand, we had a lot of people who were very enthused. I would say San Diego and World Con were two big moments for the film."

After that, fandom began to pick up on the film, fueled in no small way by Don and Maggie Thompson's support through *The Comic Buyer's Guide* and James Van Hise's *RBCC*. The theatrical trailer from Lucasfilm began to develop a following, with word leaking back to the company that there were kids actually buying tickets to other movies so that they could see the trailer. The novelization was published in November of 1976 and sold extremely well.

"Normally, for a first novel — George had his name on it — there was a print run of 100,000," said Lippincott. "They had actually done a print run of 125,000 around Thanksgiving. By February they had shipped all of them out of the warehouse, which was considered unbelievable for a first novel. They were very enthusiastic, but they wouldn't go back and reprint it until the movie came out. That had been a painted cover, not a movie cover."

> **W**hat all of this indicated was that there was already a big buildup among fans — both comic book and science fiction — and that we had a fan following before the movie even came out."
>
> **— CHARLES LIPPINCOTT**

The first issue of the Marvel comic came out in March 1977 and did very well in major cities, though it was not an immediate sellout. "What all of this indicated," explains Lippincott, "was that there was already a big buildup among fans — both comic book and science fiction — and that we had a fan following before the movie even came out."

The impression, of course, is that when *Star Wars* was finally released in May 1977, it was an immediate hit. Lippincott emphasizes that this was definitely not the case.

"If the film was redone today, on the basis of the way movies are released with a couple of thousand prints, it probably would have been unsuccessful. Theaters didn't want the movie. The exhibitors were still put off by the movie. We were lucky to get thirty theaters to open it. At that time, Hollywood Boulevard was still very important for opening films. We only got on Hollywood Boulevard because the new Billy Friedkin film *(Sorcerer)* wasn't ready yet. It was supposed to be ready by May 25 but wasn't, and we were given a month in the Chinese. It was the only way we got into Grauman's."

Once *Star Wars* came out, because there wasn't much prior to the film coming out, the merchandising just took off. It was astounding. We were making deals right and left."
— **CHARLES LIPPINCOTT**

Probably the greatest contributor to the earliest stages of the *Star Wars* phenomenon was *Time*. Originally the film was supposed to be the main cover story, but it was bumped by the Israeli election.

"Instead, we got a snipe at the top of the cover," says Lippincott. "This was in May and it said, 'Best Film of the Year.' I was stunned. Needless to say, you can never judge the public. They bought the magazine to see what the best film of the year was. The initial genre crowd going in to see it and the people buying *Time* to read about the snipe are what got the whole groundswell started."

With that groundswell under way, the merchandising machine kicked in, providing an unprecedented number of products inspired by the film — the benefit of which Lucas, and not Fox, was the recipient. Until that time, *Star Trek* was the only true phenomenon in merchandising, much of that coming from the fans themselves, as Paramount had been essentially ignoring the franchise at the time, though they eventually did jump aboard that runaway locomotive. Lippincott also looked to what had been done with Buck Rogers in the thirties.

"They did a remarkable job, considering the time," he comments. "So *Star Trek* and Buck Rogers had a lot to do with what I used as a jumping-off point. Once *Star Wars* came out, because there wasn't much prior to the film coming out, the merchandising just took off. It was astounding. We were making deals right and left, and then the people we already had deals with were concerned about how they were going to get merchandising out because they just saw this thing growing."

Another challenge he faced was keeping the film alive at the box office. Crediting *Star Wars* for teaching him a lot, Lippincott notes that there were times when the box office would start to go down and he would go out and do a promotion that revived it.

"Most summer films, even if they do go through the summer, start to wind down — or they did at the time — around Labor Day," he explains. "I got some offers to go on TV and took advantage of them. In those days there were a lot of variety shows. I went on a one-hour variety show and a half-hour comedy variety show, and we did a 'making of' TV special — all three within the first few weeks of the new season. Basically we did skits on *Star Wars,* which was what everybody wanted. Then the box office went back up and we hung on through Christmas, though that created problems as well. There were theaters that were supposed to get *Close Encounters of the Third Kind* that had to bump out *Star Wars* because of contracts."

In trying to figure it all out, he adds, "People were so excited because they were actually seeing a film that had stuff in it they'd always wanted to see but had never seen before, which was that sense of wonder. Needless to say, the word of mouth started and spread like wildfire."

THE IMPACT

Despite the fact that Twentieth Century Fox had virtually no faith in *Star Wars* and did little to help promote the film when it was time to be released, it nonetheless went on to become the highest-grossing film of all time — an amazing feat, considering that, initially, it had been playing in only a handful of theaters. But the truth is that the audience, which was, as Lippincott noted, seeing something never seen before, was going to see the film literally dozens of times. Eventually the number of theaters playing the film expanded and Lucas's space epic eclipsed his pal Steven Spielberg's *Jaws*.

In many ways, the phenomenal success of *Star Wars* also changed Hollywood forever. From that moment on, a quantum shift in the perception of what makes a successful film took place. While box office had always been an important factor, it suddenly became *the* most important aspect of a film. Eventually this would change even more, to the point where your opening weekend at the box office determined whether or not you were a hit. And as films that would have been "B" pictures in the past (for example, *Independence Day*) are suddenly elevated to "A" status in terms of importance, many critics have felt the decline in more serious-minded films with multifaceted characters and human drama. One person who *does not* agree with this perception is Lucas himself.

"I think that's unfair, and I also think it's extremely naive," he said. "They've been making blockbusters ever since *Birth of a Nation;* this whole industry has been built on making blockbusters. There's a creative side of it and then there's the business. There have always been periodic changes. Again, that's simply a reality of life; everything changes all the time. The film industry is not going to stay the same. We're not going to make Humphrey Bogart movies. The film industry is a living organism, and if it's not nurtured in a particular way, it will be destroyed.

"But at the same time," he added, "it's an economic animal, and

> The film industry is a living organism, and if it's not nurtured in a particular way, it will be destroyed."
> — GEORGE LUCAS

it will not survive if it is not economical. The film industries in many other countries are having a very difficult time, because they're making, in some cases, one kind of movie. Hit movies are the things that allow more avant-garde and artistic movies to be made. *American Graffiti* was a very avant-garde movie that nobody wanted to do, and it was the success of *Easy Rider* that made it happen. *Easy Rider* was the hit that allowed *Graffiti* to be a hit. Every time a movie makes a lot of money, it spawns many little movies that they can take a chance on. The other assumption, that we live in a land of blockbusters, mindless, amusement park–ride movies, is really a crock. There are actually more art films made in the United States today than there were twenty years ago when *Star Wars* came out. The number of nonpopcorn pictures has actually grown more rapidly than popcorn pictures."

While there are undoubtedly many critics and Hollywood executives who would argue Lucas's point (not to his face, of course), the success of *Star Wars* had one undeniable effect on Hollywood: it required a sequel.

THE EMPIRE STRIKES BACK

When George Lucas reached the point where he was ready to shoot his first sequel to *Star Wars,* two things were pretty much set in stone (well, sort of): one, he would finance the film himself with the profits of the original (though production problems caused him to negotiate a bit with Fox), and two, there was absolutely no way that he was going to direct the film.

Naturally, the film had to begin with the story, which Lucas had, in rough form, mapped out. To turn that story into a screenplay, he hired veteran writer Leigh Brackett, who had written many films for Howard Hawks and penned a series of science fiction novels. Ms. Brackett wrote one draft before she died of cancer. Out of desperation — and unable to miss *Empire*'s summer 1980 release date —

THE MAKING OF THE STAR WARS TRILOGY

Lucas began writing a first draft he hoped could then be handed to a new writer to refine. That writer turned out to be Lawrence Kasdan, who had also written Lucas's *Raiders of the Lost Ark* before carving out his own directorial career in the form of *The Big Chill, Body Heat,* and *Silverado,* among others. As Kasdan explains it, he finished the script for *Raiders* and brought it to Lucas on a Saturday, and the two of them shared a lunch.

"When we sat down at the restaurant," Kasdan told journalist James H. Burns, "George said, 'You know, Leigh Brackett was writing *The Empire Strikes Back*. She finished a draft, but when I called her up to talk about it, I found out that she was in the hospital. Unfortunately, she just passed away. I wonder if you would like to continue writing the screenplay.' I replied, 'Don't you think you ought to read *Raiders* first?' He answered, 'Well, I just get a feeling about people. Of course, if I hate *Raiders,* I'll take back this offer.' The next day, Sunday, George called me up to tell me that he was ecstatic about my *Raiders* script and that he was now very anxious for me to do *The Empire Strikes Back*. I was *shocked* by the previous day's offer and by that confirmation. I had had absolutely no indication before our lunch that my writing *Empire* was even being considered. Once I got the job I was excited because I liked *Star Wars* very much. I thought it was great art, in that *Star Wars* hooked into the archetypical images registered in our subconscious of how children perceive the world."

Before he began, Kasdan was given Lucas's draft and only skimmed through Brackett's. "It was sort of old fashioned and didn't relate to *Star Wars*," he told Burns of Brackett's take on the material. "The characters all had the right names, but her story's spirit was different. I'm a little wary about talking about Leigh's script, because I'm not sure if people realize how much a first draft is always changed in the development of a screenplay. I'm sure that had Leigh lived, she could have made the changes that George wanted in an excellent way. George's draft was something that he wrote very quickly when Leigh passed away. George had the story very well outlined, but there were sections in the script which, when I read them, made me say to myself, 'I can't believe that George wrote this scene. It's terrible.' I later learned that George wrote stuff like that simply so that whoever did the next draft would know that a scene covering approximately the same kind of material that his sequence dealt with belonged at that point in the script. My job was basically to take George's story and make it work through altering dialogue and structure. Naturally, a movie is not a screenplay, but you can't make a good movie without a good script."

The writer didn't feel that he needed to steep himself in all sorts of science fiction to write the script. All that he really had to do was watch *Star Wars* again — repeatedly.

"I felt that my responsibility was to understand the *Star Wars* galaxy, not the basic concepts of science fiction," he offered Burns. "*Star Wars* doesn't have all that much to do with SF or what its fans are interested in. Now, I might have misconceptions about what concerns science-fiction enthusiasts, because although I've read some SF, I'm generally ill-informed about the field. From what I have read, though, a lot of science fiction seems to be based on extensions of real life in a way that the *Star Wars* series doesn't really care about."

Interestingly, despite the fact that *Empire* ended with a variety of cliff-hanger solutions, Kasdan had absolutely no clue while he was writing what the third film, *Return of the Jedi,* would ultimately offer in terms of resolution.

"On *Empire* we were all working within George's grand scheme. Working within it, I was not seeing the story's beginning or conclusion. I felt that I had to develop *Empire*'s screenplay based on my perception of the characters in *Star Wars* and what George wanted them to do in its sequel. I had to write it much the same way I have to live my life — I don't know how it will end, but I have some way of feeling with my personality the way that it exists right now."

> There are no real winners in *Empire* as there were in the first film, and for the characters, it's an emotional tragedy. I think it's a better film than the first one."
>
> — GEORGE LUCAS

Ultimately, the refining of the screenplay came after close consultation with Lucas and Irvin Kershner — who will be discussed shortly — the film's director.

"We had very intense sessions on how the story would be done," Kasdan reflected in the same interview. "I had much less of a free hand on *Empire* than on anything else I've ever written. When I took the script on, there was very little time left to do it in. Preproduction was already well under way, which usually doesn't happen until a script is essentially completed. Because of that time factor, I felt that the best thing for me to do was to be an instrument for George and Kersh. That suggests a very mechanical form of writing, but it really wasn't. I mean, I had a big influence on *Empire,* but probably the smallest influence that I've ever had on a film that I've written."

> *F*ortunately, George didn't want a typical sequel, and that made it a bit frightening because it was a much bigger picture than *Star Wars*."
>
> — IRVIN KERSHNER, director, *Empire*

The Empire Strikes Back, while continuing its exploration of the Rebel Alliance's struggle, focuses more on character, though it's the relationships between Leia and Han and between Luke and Darth Vader that become most pertinent. It's Vader who arranges the capture — with the help of Billy Dee Williams's Lando Calrissian, who turns out to be a good guy — of Leia, Han, Chewie, and C-3PO to lure Skywalker — who has been training with Jedi Master Yoda — into his trap. It is also a struggle in which Luke is told that Vader is actually his father. As the film ends, Luke's mind is struggling with both sides of the Force, while Han is carbon-frozen and taken to the powerful Jabba the Hutt by bounty hunter Boba Fett. Like the serials that inspired it, *The Empire Strikes Back* ends on a cliff-hanger.

"I've taken a lot more chances in this story," Lucas told *Time* magazine. "It's a tragedy, a traditional second act. In the second act you always give your characters a problem. Luke's problems are resolved in the third act, *Return of the Jedi.* There are no real winners in *Empire* as there were in the first film, and for the characters, it's an emotional tragedy. I think it's a better film than the first one."

Much of that is probably owed to the choice of Irvin Kershner as director. Cutting his teeth on such quirky character pieces as *A Face in the Rain* and *The Flim Flam Man,* and on action pieces like *The Raid on Entebbe,* Kershner managed to hit the right note with Lucas. Whereas the late Richard Marquand, director of *Return of the Jedi,* said directing a *Star Wars* picture with George Lucas as executive producer was like directing *King Lear* with Shakespeare standing in the wings, Kershner says he insisted on maintaining his creative independence.

"George chose me because he wanted a film in which the people really came alive," he explains. "I was afraid of the challenge at first, because *Star Wars* was such a unique film and I didn't want to try to follow it. *Empire* has many more special effects, tons more sets, and much more complexity in the characters. I had my hands so full that I stopped worrying about trying to make it better than *Star Wars* and just tried to make it right. It was daunting, which is why I turned it down at first. When George first came to me I said, 'Wow, what the hell can you do with the second one that you didn't do with the first one?' And I worried that maybe the audience had already had enough and they'd view a sequel as something just to make a few bucks. I'm not especially interested in sequels. I had made one before, *Return of a Man Called Horse,* but I did that because I really loved the subject and felt they failed in the first film. Fortunately, George didn't want a typical sequel, and that made it a bit frightening because it was a much bigger picture than *Star Wars.* We had sixty-four sets — which is unheard of — and they were big. I would work on a giant set for two days and they would rip it down overnight and start building another one because we had to put sixty-four sets on seven stages. The film was all shot inside with the exception of the first ten days in Norway [where we shot the Hoth sequences]."

When he was hired, Kershner was told by Lucas to make a sequel that was better than the original. "Actually," says the director, smiling, "that was a nice way of saying, 'Hey, this is important to me.' You see, if *Empire* didn't work, then there is no third one and it's all over. We didn't know if the audience was still there for a second

BILLY DEE WILLIAMS

THE MAKING OF THE STAR WARS TRILOGY

FRANK OZ

one. We had no idea. We assumed it was, but we didn't know for sure, and George was putting up his own money. Fox didn't put up the money. When I went up to seek approval for something, George said to me, 'Do you know why you're making this picture?' And he showed me all these detailed plans for [Skywalker Ranch], and he said if the picture is successful, this is what he was going to build. The fantastic thing about George is that he invests all the money he makes into moviemaking, and no one else does that. No one else who makes a lot of money in movies puts it back into the medium. Look at ILM and the other stuff he has developed. It is incredible. I really have tremendous respect for him. But that's getting away from the point at hand. I analyzed *Empire* before production and came to the obvious conclusion that it was not just a sequel but the second act of a three-act space opera. Now, the second act does not have the same climax as the third act or even the first act. The second act is usually more ambiguous. It is quieter, but the problems are accentuated; you get into depth. It is not fast, like the end [of a three-part drama]. So, therefore, I knew that I would never have the climax because if it comes to a complete climax, where do you go with the third one? It is about revealing character.

"George gave me tremendous freedom," elaborates Kershner. "George and I worked closely with Larry [Kasdan] for three months getting the script right. Then when the script was right, I went off to London alone, where the production was set up. I spent about a year locked away doing storyboards for the script so that every single effect, every scene that had anything unusual in it, was storyboarded. I insisted on being locked away to do the storyboards because by the time I went to shoot, I wanted to know every single scene. In fact, I knew every word in the script by that time so I didn't have to even think, 'Now what am I going to do next?' Not that I followed the storyboards *that* religiously. I did follow them, but where things didn't work I could change it because I knew where to go. So I could concentrate on the characters.

"You see," he continues, "the biggest problem with epic productions like this is that the special effects take so much attention that you tend to let the acting slip by. I didn't want that to happen, and Harrison [Ford] was constantly calling me on it. If we did just two takes and I'd say, 'That's great,' he would say, 'Wait a minute, wait a minute. What's great? Was it great for the special effects or for me?' And I'd say, 'Harrison, I wouldn't say "great" unless it was for you. It really was great.' And he would give me that wonderful look of his, you know, that wry look, and we would move on. We had a great relationship. I had good relationships with all the actors. I got Mark Hamill and Carrie Fisher and Harrison together, and we talked and talked. I explained things, told them what the characters were doing, what they could try and how they could try to feel out their scenes and physicalize whenever possible. This was their language, they responded to that approach. If I hadn't done that, I think I would have been in trouble. The way we worked made it fun; we really had fun doing the takes."

The approach apparently worked, as evidenced by sequences between Mark Hamill's Luke and Yoda — the Jedi Master that is essentially a Muppet. Those scenes, featuring Luke in training as a Jedi, are completely believable.

"Let me tell you how that was done," says Kershner. "The floor [of the Dagobah set] was about five feet above the actual floor of the stage. We built it up and put Yoda there, and there were splits in the floor so that they could manipulate him. Below the floor were about five TV sets and Frank Oz [voice of Yoda] and his crew. One person would control the ears, one person would blink the eyes, another person would move the mouth, one person moved one arm, another moved another arm. It was all scrutinized carefully, and all they could see were the television sets around them. Because we were getting sick from all the smoke [from the fog machines] on the set, I was wearing a gas mask with a microphone in it and I had a speaker through which I would talk to Frank and Mark and the crew. And Frank would use a speaker for rehearsal, so that when Mark would say to Yoda, 'Can you tell me where I can find the Jedi Master?'

> The biggest problem with epic productions like this is that the special effects take so much attention that you tend to let the acting slip by. I didn't want that to happen."
>
> — **IRVIN KERSHNER,**
> director, *Empire*

he would hear, 'Why do you want to know?' — which was Frank answering him — through a speaker somewhere. But when we actually did the take, Mark didn't hear anything. [Yoda's dialogue] was put in later. We rehearsed, rehearsed, rehearsed until we got the rhythm, and then we'd do the take and he'd say, 'Can you tell me where I can find the Jedi Master?'; there would be a pause, then he'd say, 'Well, I want to know' — pause — 'It's my business. . . .' And so on. See what I mean? Mark would know exactly how long to pause. He did a wonderful job of reacting to nothing but memory. Though Mark couldn't hear him, he could see him. I wanted Yoda to look like he was Luke's equal. I wanted Yoda to look like he could climb around. I wanted to give the illusion that he had emotions. It was not something that was put into stop-motion, you know, like King Kong, which is a miniature put in later. This was actual time. Anyway, these challenges are what make films so exciting — when you have interesting, believable characters and you see how they react to each other and their surroundings. The characters have to be real, no matter how fantastic the situation."

Also having to be just as real were the film's special effects — a quantum leap beyond those of the original — as well as the action sequences, which were considerably larger in scope. This was particularly true in the opening sequence taking place on the ice planet Hoth, in which the Rebel Alliance wages an all-out battle with Imperial forces and the mechanical dinosaur-like walkers.

"Only if you wanted to die would you go out at night."

So remembers Peter MacDonald, who directed the Hoth sequences on location in Norway. If the cast and crew of the most anticipated movie in Hollywood history were expecting an exotic location shoot where they could get some sun between takes and have every whim catered to, they were quickly disabused of that notion by the harsh Nordic winter. On location, where the subzero

> The weather was our enemy. But the great thing about a George Lucas production is that everything is very well organized and you have the money and facilities to do it properly. So we had a fighting chance because we were very well prepared."
>
> — **PETER MACDONALD,**
> second-unit director, *Empire*

temperatures were indeed life-threatening, it was every actor for him- or herself.

"The weather was our enemy," says MacDonald, a second-unit director of *Empire*. "But the great thing about a George Lucas production is that everything is very well organized and you have the money and facilities to do it properly. So we had a fighting chance because we were very well prepared."

Aiding MacDonald were the local "actors" he used in these action-oriented sequences, in which the Rebels battle Imperial walkers. Most of the locals playing soldiers on both sides were members of the Norwegian Red Cross Mountain Rescue team, an elite group of athletes trained to handle extreme weather and complicated situations. While the detailed storyboards provided by director Irvin Kershner would have been difficult for most extras to grasp, the Mountain Rescue team understood that teamwork, planning, and choreography were necessary to pull off such an undertaking. "They all understood it and actually were very into it," MacDonald says.

Besides directing the on-set battle between the soldiers and nonexistent mechanical creatures, MacDonald had to shoot background plates — perspective and landscape shots to which special effects would later be added.

BOBA FETT

"At the time, shooting aerial plates was fairly new," MacDonald explains. "They actually turned out to be so steady that [the technicians] were able to matte on the walkers. Usually when you did a matte shot it was a still image that didn't move, but this time we were flying, and it was close enough that they were able to put the walkers right in there. Definitely a first."

He admits to being as amazed with the final version of the

sequence as anyone. "I was really shocked by how well it worked," he says with a laugh.

According to journalist Ron Magid, ILM's Dennis Muren looked upon this sequence as his F/X Waterloo. There were many shots that had to be done with so very little time to do it. For a time there was talk that the walkers should be animated using motion control, which was a worrisome idea to Muren.

"It would have been neat, but I don't know if they ever would have worked," he said. "It would've taken forever just to [film it]. So I introduced stop-motion animation back into the *Star Wars* series with the walkers. That was something the technical group didn't want to do. But stop-motion was tried-and-true and George thought it was a good idea because it made everything look more mechanical, it helped us get the movie done."

The biggest hurdle was the fact that the original *Star Wars* gave the F/X crew a break in that most of their sequences were composited against the blackness of space, which hid any dark matte lines around the blue-screened spacecraft. Conversely, the pristine white ice planet Hoth, at high noon, would give no quarter. Having overcome the new-technology folks on the motion-control issue, Muren now had to fight to shoot the walkers in a miniature snowy landscape rather than compositing blue-screen walkers into live-action snow background plates. "The technological guys wanted to do it all blue screen," he said. "I thought the technology we'd developed for *Star Wars* should not be applied to those scenes because blue screen doesn't work well in daytime. So I managed to wrangle it in the other direction, the idea being that looking through the camera we could see what was wrong with the shot, and once it was shot, it was virtually finished."

"Everything that C-3PO said made him sound like a cranky nag, simply because he wasn't integral to the story."
— **LAWRENCE KASDAN,** screenwriter, *Empire*

Although darker in tone than either its predecessor or *Return of the Jedi, The Empire Strikes Back* is generally considered the strongest entry in the trilogy, exploring the characters in ways that neither of the other films was able to do, and conveying a sense of reality that was far removed from the fantasy of the others. Surprisingly, one person not as enamored of the film as others is writer Lawrence Kasdan.

To begin with, Kasdan felt that C-3PO went from being an intelligent sidekick to a whining buffoon. "It was almost a built-in problem with George's design for *Empire* that C-3PO wouldn't be able to come off well," he explained to James H. Burns. "C-3PO didn't really have anything to do, so I tried to keep his lines in my script to a minimum. I also had C-3PO being a little more intelligent. Yet, due to *Empire*'s structure, I'm afraid that even in *my* script, C-3PO was superfluous. Then, to make matters worse, we had to give C-3PO more dialogue during looping. That wasn't a good idea, because *everything* that C-3PO said made him sound like a cranky nag, simply because he wasn't integral to the story. Of course, giving C-3PO more lines during looping to help add something to a scene is always an easy solution, because his mouth doesn't move. You can have him say *anything*.

"What disappointed me even more than C-3PO was what happened with Chewbacca," he elaborated. "I had had the idea that Chewy would have a real emotional response to Han's courtship of Leia; that it meant something to his relationship with Han. Some of that good stuff was filmed, but it got eliminated when editing choices had to be made. At least Chewy's character development originally had some dynamics, but C-3PO's never did."

As with *Raiders of the Lost Ark,* Kasdan's biggest frustration with his filmed script for *Empire* was its depiction of the film's love story.

"Han and Leia's relationship is not all what I envisioned," he says. "I could be the only person who feels this way, but I thought that their romance had a touch of falseness about it. Han and Leia's scenes were among what I was proudest of in my script, but they barely remained. Their being changed had a lot to do with the circumstances of filming, Kershner's and the actors' feelings about

> I also like *Empire* in the sense that it succeeds as an extension of *Star Wars*, even if it was hard to make every character have his place."
>
> — **LAWRENCE KASDAN,** screenwriter, *Empire*

doing their roles again. I'm thrilled with Harrison Ford in *Raiders,* because I was one of the people who wasn't crazy about him in *Empire.* In *Raiders* he's shockingly good."

At the time of the film's release, quite a bit was made of the sequence in which Luke is unable to lift his X-Wing fighter out of the swamp but is stunned to see Yoda do so. Science fiction author David Gerrold, in the pages of *Starlog* magazine, suggested that perhaps it meant that Luke could not ultimately become a Jedi, and that a stronger lesson from Yoda might have been given if the Jedi Master had left the vessel in the swamp until Luke was able to lift it himself.

"I think that too much has been made out of that scene," mused Kasdan to Burns, "but it's a very popular moment with audiences. What Gerrold was getting at is a very valid question: to what extent is Yoda a pure Zen teacher and to what degree is he just a movie invention designed to be popular? I think that we very often got away from Yoda's being a 'Master of the Force' and made him more of a satisfying little creature. I don't know if Yoda's lifting the fighter was to show that Luke can't master the Force, because I wasn't told what would happen in *Return of the Jedi.* Luke *is* shown to be a screw-up, which I think is one of the most interesting things about *Empire.* Luke gets beaten because he is impatient. Carrying out the concept of the hero never succeeding throughout *Empire* was very daring on George Lucas' part."

Kasdan does point out that the scenes between Luke and Yoda are among his favorite from the film. "That could be because those sequences remained relatively unchanged," he reflected. "Perhaps they weren't altered because Yoda isn't an actor who can change his lines. The other stuff that I loved about *Empire* were the things that I had the least to do with: movement, sound and special effects. Liking best what you didn't work on in a film is a very disconcerting feeling when you've spent a lot of time on its script. Obviously, though, I could enjoy those things because they weren't components that had been changed from my screenplay that could disappoint me. I also like *Empire* in the sense that it succeeds as an extension of *Star Wars,* even if it was hard to make every character have his place."

RETURN OF THE JEDI

While nothing but uncertainty seemed to surround the original *Star Wars,* its unprecedented worldwide success guaranteed a sequel. When *The Empire Strikes Back,* like its predecessor, surpassed *Jaws* on the box office charts, there was no doubt that George Lucas would be given the opportunity to conclude this particular trilogy in the overall *Star Wars* saga.

Yet after the decidedly dark tone of *Empire,* Lucas was determined to lighten things up considerably. Actor Mark Hamill seemed to represent the audience's point of view at the time of *Jedi*'s release, when he betrayed the frustration he felt as he saw that the film's direction did not meet his expectations following the story line of entry number two.

"Let's face it," Hamill proclaimed to *Time,* "we made a film for children." In the pages of *Starlog* he added, "I was under the impression that the third film would have the conflict of Luke turning to the dark side of the Force and reaching a point where he could dispose of the antagonist. I had preconceived notions going in of what the third film would be."

At the time of *Jedi*'s release, Hamill spoke to journalist Steve Swires, who has given permission for quotes from that interview to be reprinted here.

"I know there will be people who'll be disappointed," Hamill said. "With everything that's been set up, you can't bring the trilogy to a conclusion *without* disappointing some people. However, I'm sure many others will be surprised and pleased. I don't think this chapter will confound and confuse them. It's the logical resolution to what has gone before. It's very traditional storytelling. It's *not*

meant to have an O. Henry type of twist. The trilogy is structured as a fairy tale set to a classical three-act play. *Star Wars* was act one. It introduced the characters. *The Empire Strikes Back* was act two. It developed the characters and gave them problems, with tragic overtones. *Jedi* is act three. It's the big finish, and *everything* is brought to an end."

As had become his wont, Lucas was playing everything about *Return of the Jedi* close to the vest, refusing even to allow primary cast members to know where the script — again written by Lawrence Kasdan — was going until it was absolutely necessary. Indeed, when the cast finally did get to see the script, they realized that there were several false scenes to throw everyone off.

"It told the story from start to finish," Hamill explained, "but as with the *Empire* script, it contained several 'false scenes.' They were substituted for key scenes which we weren't given until much later in the production. This plan was organized to prevent crucial information from leaking to the press and public, as happened with *Empire*. During *Empire*'s shooting in England, for example, it was rumored that Obi-Wan killed Luke's father, and that Luke cut off Darth Vader's head. What happened was that someone in the cast or crew read those scenes, didn't know they were deliberately false, and spilled the beans. I imagine some British reporter took this person into a pub, bought him a few drinks and slipped him some money.

"As soon as I was given the *Jedi* script, I was told which scenes were false," he continued. "There were more of them in *Empire*. And they were only willing to tell me that in person, rather than over the phone or in a letter. I felt like Boris Badenov in *Rocky and Bullwinkle,* but it was all part of the fun. It set me thinking about what the *real* scenes could be. There were three major false scenes. The way they were written and whom they involved indicated where they were going. I got two of them right, and one of them was a surprise to me. The *biggest* surprise was that all the pieces to the puzzle were

> **B**ecause of the mechanical problems with Yoda, I was the only human being listed on the call sheet for months. Everything was the puppets, props, and special effects. ➤

present. Like many people, I was looking for something out of left field, but *everything* was really set up in the first two pictures. It all had a purpose, so nothing was arbitrary."

Neither was the choice of director. Lucas wanted someone he could more easily control than Irvin Kershner, who brought *Empire* in $6 million over budget and ten weeks behind schedule. While the end results speak for themselves as to whether Kershner was the right director for the second chapter of the trilogy, he was a film-maker who had very definite opinions on how the film should be made. This time, Lucas needed someone who saw the *Star Wars* universe much the way he did — whom he found in Richard Marquand, who had just come off the psychological thriller *Eye of the Needle*.

The late Marquand related to journalist Lee Gold-berg, "I knew then what George was looking for was *not* the old school movie director who would wait for the weather to get the shot he wanted. He wanted someone who could improvise, think on his feet."

> So much of the acting in these movies has been technical. To the average viewer, it looks like all we do is show up and react. Still, the idea that people don't think we're doing anything is actually a compliment."
>
> **— MARK HAMILL**

In comparing and contrasting Marquand and Kershner, Hamill told Swires, "Overall, I probably had more differences of opinion with Kersh. I liked his work, but he was an eccentric guy. I didn't find that to be a problem, but sometimes it was more diffi-cult to get across what I was trying to say. He was very pre-occupied, so I had to grab him by the collar and look him in the eye to get his attention. Kersh also changed his mind frequently, particularly with camera set-ups. For example, we would rehearse a set-up for the next morning, but the odds were by that time, the shot would change. Usually, it would be a better shot, but if they had let him, he would have changed it *again*. By contrast, *Jedi* was more of a return to the 'smash-and-grab' technique, which I think worked very well in *Star Wars* and *Raiders*. You make do with what you have, and a certain kinetic energy emerges which sets up a rhythm that works."

The real rumor surrounding the film, of course, was that Lucas was actually directing Marquand's direction.

According to actor Sebastian Shaw, who portrayed Darth Vader in the film's climactic moments as the Dark Lord's helmet was removed for the first time in the films, Lucas's presence was most definitely felt. "Richard Marquand directed the scene," Shaw told *Starlog*, "but George Lucas was around all the time keeping an eye on things, because, after all, *Star Wars* is his baby. And they were very careful, clearly."

Actor Ian McDiarmid, who portrayed the Emperor (and reprises the role in the prequel trilogy), supports the notion that Lucas certainly helmed the final sequences of the film. In issue 37 of the *Star Wars Insider*, McDiarmid discussed the moment in which Darth Vader saves Luke by hoisting the Emperor in the air and throwing him down a shaft, apparently to his demise. "He [Lucas] did the final sequence, when the Emperor is being sent down that chute, and Richard [Marquand] was off doing other scenes with the second unit."

Mark Hamill said that Lucas's presence on the set was felt considerably more on *Jedi* than it had been on *Empire*. "George came over to England and was involved with production meetings and seeing rushes every day. On the set, he was much more vocal regarding technical matters, such as the choice of lenses. Occasionally, he would come up with a more economical way to shoot something. All of his input came within the bounds of good taste. He avoided making Richard feel like he wasn't the captain of the ship — which he was. Actually, George was almost a second-unit director. I shot second unit with him quite often, whereas he didn't do that even once on *Empire*."

For Hamill, one similarity between *Empire* and *Jedi* was the physical toll both films took on him. "*Empire* seemed like nine months of torture to me," the actor noted. "I really got the stuffing kicked out of me on that movie. I'm supposed to be an actor, not a stuntman. And, because of the mechanical problems with Yoda, I was the only human being listed on the call sheet for months. Everything was the puppets, props, and special effects. So much of the acting in these movies has been technical. To the average viewer, it looks like all we do is show up and react. Still, the idea that people don't think we're doing anything is actually a compliment. As with a magician performing his tricks, it's all a matter of diversion. But, in many ways, these three motion pictures have been harder than anything I've ever done."

Including, he noted, a moment when he was actually required to act *backward*. "You must think out the shot in advance and perform it in reverse, so that when it's projected, you get the opposite effect. For instance, there were scenes in which my lightsaber had to jump into my hand. To accomplish that action, I had to enter the shot as though I were exiting it, with my final mood intact. Then I had to make an abrupt move into calmness, put my hand up, and throw my sword away. It was very difficult to coordinate. I had to go over to a corner, close my eyes and think for a moment, because it didn't come naturally. It was very much like mime."

No matter what went into its physical production, the bottom line is that *Return of the Jedi* is considerably more "viewer friendly" than its predecessor, dissipating most of the darkness of *Empire* and returning to the cartoon-adventure basics of the original, with plenty of comic moments and those damned, supposedly cuddly Ewoks.

The film begins excitingly enough with Luke, Leia, Chewbacca, and Lando rescuing Han from his carbon-frozen prison in the lair of Jabba the Hutt. From there the action switches to Luke completing his training with Yoda (who dies shortly thereafter) and the Rebel Alliance's struggle — alongside the annoyingly cuddly and furry Ewoks — against the Empire's new and improved Death Star, and culminates in a battle to the death between Luke and Darth Vader, both of whom are pawns of the dark Jedi Master, the Emperor. By *Jedi*'s conclusion, all of the loose ends are tied up, Luke is a full Jedi,

> **T**he actual *Star Wars* saga from chapters one through nine is a total symphony, if you like. I'm not making a sequel. I'm doing the third movement of a piece of music. The themes are being developed and ended here."
>
> — **RICHARD MARQUAND,**
> director, *Jedi*

Leia and Han have declared their love for each other, and Darth Vader, before his death, is retrieved by Luke from the dark side of the Force, destroying the Emperor in the process.

While many fans felt that much of this last entry in the trilogy was a bit lackluster in comparison with its predecessors, the one undeniably exciting sequence took place on the planet Endor and involved Imperial troopers in pursuit of our heroes while on speeder bikes, antigravity vehicles that drove at incredible speeds. In many ways, this was a refined expression of Lucas's space-battle concept in which the spaceships were in sharp focus against an incredibly blurred background. ILM's Dennis Muren insisted that the animatics he created enabled him and his team to visualize and "adrenalize" the sequence. "They sure did," he said, "just like in *Star Wars*. By doing the animatics first, we were able to break the sequence apart, then shoot the footage, and it came out just about the same. I tried not to think about it too much, because then you start shooting custom speeds for side views and back views and you end up hurting it. Taking it an element at a time like that, everyone likes to tweak it, make each shot a little faster or slower, and then it wouldn't have been as effective when it was all cut together. I approached that sequence like a documentary and shot it the way it would've really been — and when we put it together, it was right."

In approaching the film, Richard Marquand didn't feel that he was asked to direct a sequel but rather a part of a complex story. "The actual *Star Wars* saga from chapters one through nine is a total symphony, if you like," he told *Time* magazine. "I'm *not* making a sequel. I'm doing the third movement of a piece of music. The themes are being developed and ended here."

But the audience wouldn't allow it to end there. *Return of the Jedi*, released in 1983, actually surpassed *Empire* in the box office charts, settling in nicely behind *Star Wars*. Beyond that fact, ever since, the fans have clamored for Lucas's prequel trilogy, which is finally nearing release after a seemingly interminable delay.

Unwilling to exploit either his creation or the fans, Lucas has waited for special effects technology to catch up to his imagination. Given the computer-generated success of his *Young Indiana Jones* television series and the strides achieved by ILM in Steven Spielberg's *Jurassic Park* films, he deemed the time right to continue the saga.

Insofar as the trilogy already captured on film is concerned, Lucas noted in the same *Time* article, "I look upon the three *Star Wars* films as chapters in one book. Now the book is finished and I have put it on the shelf."

THE STAR WARS TRILOGY RADIO DRAMAS

UNLIKE THE AUDIO NOVELS that a generation of "too-busy-to-read" readers have consumed, the audio dramatizations of the *Star Wars* trilogy actually offer a bit more.

Somehow it seems a natural and logical progression. If the *Star Wars* films could serve as a throwback to the movie serials of yesteryear, why shouldn't they revive the basic concept of the radio drama as well?

These dramas began when George Lucas donated the rights to them to National Public Radio station KUSC-FM, a station connected with his alma mater, the University of Southern California. With rights to the scripts, the trilogy's myriad sound effects, and John Williams's score, NPR turned to science fiction author Brian Daley — writer of, among other things, a trilogy of novels focusing on Han Solo — to handle the adaptation itself.

According to the late Daley, the powers that be had apparently read his novels and felt that he had a good grasp of the *Star Wars* universe. As he noted, the Han Solo novels he wrote were under a great deal of thematic limitation because no one really knew at that point where the *Star Wars* saga would go from there. "With the radio play," he explained, "I was a little freer to go into the story."

Indeed. His adaptation took a two-hour film and turned it into a six-hour drama, a feat he repeated for *The Empire Strikes Back* and, many years later, *Return of the Jedi.* Daley noted on the liner notes for *Empire* that the situation reminded him of a joke about a pair of boxers, with the referee saying, "I don't want to see any gouging, biting, or kicking," with one of the boxers responding, "There go *all* my best punches."

"When you're writing a novel," he wrote, "you have all sorts of time for expository prose. [But not] with this medium. Actually, scripting *Empire* involved fewer limitations than one might suppose. You must remember that *Star Wars* and *The Empire Strikes Back* aren't just *films* — they're also a story, in the finest traditional sense of the word. They're about a universe in which human beings, aliens, and machines experience things common to all of us: love, vengeance, fear and wonder."

The films, he pointed out, were rich with dramatic possibilities for radio, particularly in terms of story-line origins, events taking place off screen, and facets of the characters that he felt deserved exploration.

Helping to provide that exploration was the show's cast, which featured Mark Hamill reprising his role of Luke Skywalker (with the exception of *Jedi*, as the actor has spent years trying to distance himself from Luke; he was replaced by Joshua Fardon); Anthony Daniels as C-3PO, Brock Peters (Captain Sisko's father on *Star Trek: Deep Space Nine*) as Darth Vader, and Ann Sachs as Princess Leia.

In the pages of *Starlog,* Hamill enthused, "It appealed to me because it wasn't money-oriented. It sprang purely from the desire to help revitalize interest in radio."

In the same interview, Hamill noted that he felt bad that toys are so expensive that many kids could not afford to buy a "glow-in-the-dark Yoda." He also pointed out that Lucas himself felt bad about the perception in many quarters that the films had been too commercial and overmerchandised. This, because it was being produced for public radio, was a way of giving something back to the fans. The situation, he felt, was great not only for kids who couldn't afford the price of a movie ticket, but for those people who were shut-ins as well.

"The radio shows are great because you can take them into your mind," he explained. "For visual effects, you need a budget of millions of dollars. There is no budget on imagination."

Naturally, in the expanding of the drama there were numerous additions to the adventure as seen by movie audiences. What follows is an exploration of those differences.

STAR WARS

The first *Star Wars* radio drama (all thirteen parts, totaling some six hours of airtime) was produced by the University of Southern California (in Los Angeles), the alma mater of George Lucas. As already noted, the only actors from the film appearing in this radio drama were Mark Hamill and Anthony Daniels. Although Harrison Ford had been intrigued with the idea of portraying Han Solo on radio, his commitment to the film *Raiders of the Lost Ark* superseded this.

While the *Star Wars* radio drama proved to be very popular, the vocal casting replacements did seem somewhat odd. Truth be told, the sequences without the character of Luke were fairly distracting, as the audience was hearing familiar dialogue coming out of completely unfamiliar mouths. Considering that this was an adaptation of one of the most well known films of all time, the audio conflict was ever present.

Additionally, although it seems that Lucas recognized — on film at least — that a little bit of C-3PO and R2-D2 goes a long way and padded sequences featuring inconsequential scenes of the droids bickering didn't exactly move things along, the radio adaptation, while building on and expanding the great scenes in *Star Wars,* also seemed to feel the need to expand even the most inconsequential sequences.

The film itself had its own legends surrounding it both at the time of its release and two years later when it was rereleased after

some scenes were cut. For those who aren't aware of the situation, when *Star Wars* was released in 1977, Luke encounters his friend Biggs at the base and then reacts strongly when Biggs is killed during the assault on the Death Star. In spite of the fact that millions of people had seen those scenes numerous times, Lucas decided they were "confusing" because none of the sequences of Biggs and Luke back on Tatooine were left in the film. Luke does refer to Biggs early in the film, so there was a connection, especially for those fans (of which there were many) who'd seen the film in theaters numerous times and began noticing the secondary and background details during their repeat viewings. But Biggs died a second time when the character's scenes were cut in 1979, and they weren't completely restored even in the special edition.

While the film opens with a now-famous space battle, the radio drama commences with Luke and his friends, who are teasing him about his dream to go to the Academy. While such a scene was reportedly filmed, one has to wonder if the dialogue was as trite as this. It's pure nonsense, with Luke hanging around with people who are supposed to be his friends, but they're such dimwits one has to wonder why he would even bother. Unfortunately, all of these scenes seem like so much filler. They don't tell us anything new about Luke and his situation on Tatooine; they just show us, instead, more of what we'd already seen in the film. There's no understanding provided about why these people live on this desert world if life is so difficult here that moisture evaporators are needed to secure water. Luke's having additional arguments with his Uncle Owen doesn't provide much in the way of expanding the mythos.

Unlike the serials, which *Star Wars* is the modern day descendent of, the episode ends flatly, with no cliff-hanger to speak of. While the old serials certainly stretched to create the not always effective artifice of a cliff-hanger, episode one of *Star Wars* just stops, like the chapter in a book.

Episode two reveals that Leia came into contact with the plans for the Death Star by an encounter with a new character named Lord Tion. There's also a previously unseen — albeit brief — encounter with Darth Vader, which doesn't add anything particularly dramatic to the proceedings. In general, this seemed like unnecessary padding. If they wanted to do an episode concentrating on Princess Leia, why not an explanation of how a member of planetary royalty came to sympathize with the Rebellion? Since the structure of an empire would support the status quo, wouldn't planetary leaders support the Empire unless it threatened them personally? Alderaan is not portrayed as being threatened in any way and yet Princess Leia and her father are clearly active members of the Rebellion. Even if it is for social and humanitarian reasons, why not portray that a bit more eloquently than it is here?

As episode three opens, we discover that being told Leia is going to intercept the Death Star plans from a Rebel ship and take them to Tatooine to look for Obi-Wan Kenobi wasn't enough; now they have to "show" us how she intercepted the plans. And while we listen to the attack that opens the actual film, there's an interesting alteration in terms of Threepio and Artoo. In the film, Threepio says, "There'll be no escape for the princess this time," implying that he's been with her for a long time and is a part of her Rebel activities. In the radio show, conversely, Threepio is chosen at random from a droid pool and is introduced to her for the first time by Captain Antilles. It is a significant difference and an intriguing element offered by Daley.

Episode four takes us from the droids being captured and sold by the Jawas to Luke discovering Leia's message hidden within Artoo. While there are certainly additions to what we saw in the film, nothing of much consequence is added. One real missed opportunity was expanding the characters of Luke's Uncle Owen and Aunt Beru. We really don't learn much about them in the film and this would have been an interesting way of providing some depth to their relationship with Luke.

At this point the radio drama is concentrating more on dealing

with scenes portrayed in the movie, all of which is a preamble to the real story everyone has tuned in for.

Once Ben and Luke are united as a team, it's off to Mos Eisley where, in episode six, they enter the cantina and familiar events transpire. One "exterior" addition has Threepio and Artoo attempting to hide from a team of stormtroopers, who have been dispatched to Tatooine by Vader to capture them. What's effective about this is that it keeps alive the threat of Vader without his having to be in the scene itself.

Star Wars and *The Empire Strikes Back* aren't just *films* — they're also a story, in the finest traditional sense of the word. ➤

One correction made: in the film Han notes that the *Millennium Falcon* made the "Kessel run in 12 parsecs," referring to parsecs as a measure of time rather than distance. As this scene has often been criticized, Daley changed the line to "twelve time parts." The scene within the Cantina between Han and the bounty hunter named Greedo is as it originally was, avoiding the annoying alteration George Lucas added in the 1997 version, where Greedo shoots first and Solo fires in self-defense, thereby softening Han's character (which was pretty homogenized in *Return of the Jedi*).

With episode seven Ben, Luke, and the droids prepare to leave Tatooine. The unnecessary scene showing them sell Luke's landspeeder is just a repeat of events that occurred when Obi-Wan used the Force to get the stormtrooper to let them pass. Too often the dialogue in these new scenes is pretty flat, and throwing in "I've got a bad feeling about this" doesn't make it any more interesting. That was a throwaway line in the film that fans picked up and turned into something more than it was. It was never there to draw attention to itself the way it is in the radio drama.

At this point it seems the serial has pretty much settled into adapting the movie with only minor variations and scene additions — at least for the time being.

With episode eight we get some new scenes as Darth Vader arrives at the Death Star with Princess Leia. The episode really kicks into gear with Vader's interrogation of Leia. In the film version, this was literally done behind closed doors (heck, we even saw the doors close). Now we're a fly on the wall for the session, as Vader uses the Force to inflict pain on the princess in a pretty powerful sequence. Another improvement to the film is a real visceral response on Leia's part to the threat and destruction of her home world. In the film, her response is fairly low-key.

Episodes nine, ten, and eleven follow the film pretty closely, with bits and pieces of new dialogue offered to pad out the proceedings. Events start closing toward resolution in episode twelve. There's lots of new dialogue, but primarily it just extends conversations as characters say the same thing in different ways. Han Solo makes a guarded reference to his past and his reluctance to get involved in causes, but he won't explain what he means. There's even a sequence in which Luke practices in a simulator minutes before he has to pilot a real X-Wing in combat. The episode closes as the Death Star is closing in on the Rebel base on the fourth moon of the planet Yavin.

The climax, which is episode thirteen, is what the radio drama has been building up to as radio audiences wondered how the final battle — fifteen minutes on film — would fill a half-hour adventure.

> They're about a universe in which human beings, aliens, and machines experience things common to all of us: love, vengeance, fear, and wonder."

— BRIAN DALEY

While the climax certainly challenges the imagination with audio imagery, it is difficult for the battle to live up to expectations, particularly when one considers that that particular sequence in the film represented one of the most innovative uses of special effects in the history of motion pictures up until that point.

There is, however, an interesting piece of side dialogue in which Motti, Grand Moff Tarkin's right-hand man, talks him out of considering escape from the Death Star because it could weaken his position politically. As in many classic stories, the man's hubris — in this case his vanity and pride — is his undoing.

After the Death Star is destroyed, the awards ceremony, told with visuals and music in the film, is filled with chatter in the radio play as the characters have to explain what they think about all

this and what's happening. It all ends well, and while the radio drama is well done, it's next to impossible for it to compete with the sheer magic of the feature.

THE EMPIRE STRIKES BACK

The radio adaptation of the second *Star Wars* movie was written and produced in 1982 and aired on National Public Radio in 1983, shortly before the original theatrical release of *Return of the Jedi*. The cast was pretty much the same, with the addition of Billy Dee Williams reprising his role of Lando Calrissian.

Because of budget constraints, *Empire's* radio play was only ten episodes instead of the rather windy thirteen done to adapt the first *Star Wars* film. Written by Brian Daley, the script for the radio sequel was more effective, the dialogue proving itself to be more interesting than that of its predecessor.

The first episode of *The Empire Strikes Back* begins much closer to the point where the actual film begins, unlike the *Star Wars* radio play, which took three episodes to get to the film's opening moments. In keeping with the theme of the Empire's forces closing in on the Rebels, a Rebel supply convoy is surrounded and destroyed in the opening scene of the radio drama. It's a significant sequence that plays right into the heart of the story in terms of its connection to the Rebel base established on the planet Hoth — an installation in desperate need of those supplies. When Leia and the others learn about the destruction of the convoy, it comes as grave news indeed.

The sequence in which Luke is attacked by a Wampa is only very slightly expanded, and this is because Luke has to describe everything that's happening to him. The explanation for this chatter comes from Luke's effort to contact Han over his comlink. The first episode actually ends on a cliff-hanger, as Luke has crawled out from the Wampa's lair in his attempt to find help.

While the cliff-hanger to episode one was Luke trapped out in a blizzard, the cliff-hanger to episode two is Luke and Han out in the blizzard after Captain Solo has found him. There's some extended dialogue between the duo, but it doesn't add anything to the scene. There's also a silly scene added to give the robots something more to do and it's pretty pointless, as it involves their having raised the temperature in Princess Leia's quarters and caused the walls to melt. Not exactly an effective means of adding dimension to their characters.

The third episode just links things up. Overall, this chapter is well done, the additional lines of dialogue proving quite interesting, despite the fact that neither the plot nor the characters are really expanded.

The rout of the Rebel base composes most of episode four, including the snowspeeders' attack on the Imperial walkers. This points up a problem with radio drama in that *everything* that was portrayed with special effects in the film has to be described. While the sound effects are top-notch, the action scenes are overly talky owing to the restrictions of the medium. Action scenes were never radio's strong suit and have tended to be handled judiciously. Even with excellent sound effects, several minutes of characters talking about what they're doing is effective only to a degree, and, again, it depends largely on the fact that we've *already seen* all of this in the movie. So, essentially, this is a slightly expanded version that doesn't really expand on the action because of the difficulty of conveying such a sequence with words. It's probably the same reason that gunfights in the old days of radio drama were brief and to the point, because hearing a sound effect accompanied by a character describing who he's shooting rapidly causes the scene to lose any sense of reality.

One interesting bit in this is that an explanation is provided for why the ion cannon, which is used to open an escape route for the Rebel shuttles, isn't turned on the Imperial walkers: it wasn't constructed to fire at that low an angle. It may seem like a minor point,

but it really does address a logistical question that the film itself raised.

Luke Skywalker's visit to Dagobah and his meeting with Yoda occupy episode six, as do the early stages of his training. Nothing new or intriguing in the dialogue, as it just adapts events from the film with some additional lines here and there (though John Lithgow handles Yoda's vocals well). Been there. Done that.

One interesting addition to episode eight: we gain some insight into Lando's assistant, Lobot, who is described as a human who's had computer ancillaries attached to him. Lobot is the character seen in the film who communicates with other parts of the city without speaking. A nice touch.

When Vader makes his move, there is an interesting extended scene wherein Han Solo wants to fight Vader man-to-man, but Vader reveals that the price of such an attack will be Chewbacca's life. Solo relents, particularly after the room fills up with Imperial stormtroopers. Definitely a good scene.

The episode climaxes with the carbon-freeze scene. Unlike in the film, Chewbacca puts up a struggle, which Han Solo forces him to stop after Vader threatens to kill the Wookiee (again). Ending the episode with the carbon-freeze scene makes for a compelling cliffhanger.

Episode nine features the confrontation between Luke and Vader. Unfortunately, things become awfully talky, as such things must in the theater of the mind. While part of this is believable, since this is, after all, the first time that Luke and Vader have met face-to-face, it's not believable to have them talking when they're fighting because fighting requires 100 percent of a person's concentration; talking is distracting not just to one's opponent but to oneself, as concentration is divided between the fight and what you're saying. But Brian Daley did his best to keep the dialogue interesting and dramatic.

The finale arrives in episode ten as Luke and Vader complete their confrontation. Thankfully, when Luke drops down the shaft he *doesn't scream* the way he does now in the 1997 revised version of

The Empire Strikes Back. As was the case in the original film, Luke dropped down the shaft on purpose in the radio script. In the revised film, the scream implies that Luke fell accidentally, when, in actuality, he dropped away to escape from Darth Vader and the horror that was just revealed to him. Screaming all the way down may sound dramatic to George Lucas, but it sounds silly to us. Why change it now, after seventeen years?

The story ends as the movie did, with just some extra chatter, although telling us that they're going to the viewport to watch the *Millennium Falcon* take off isn't quite the same as seeing that amazing final shot in *The Empire Strikes Back.*

The adaptation of *Empire* is actually stronger than its predecessor, largely because few of the extra scenes in *Star Wars* added much depth. This adaptation follows the source material quite faithfully, largely adding dialogue only to convey imagery. The additional dialogue helps the most in scenes of character confrontation, the net result being an exciting audio experience.

RETURN OF THE JEDI

More than a decade would pass after the radio adaptation of *The Empire Strikes Back* before the third film in the *Star Wars* series would be brought to the air on NPR. But while *Empire* had been restricted to ten episodes, as opposed to the thirteen given to *Star Wars, Return of the Jedi* would experience an even greater indignity, with only six episodes provided to expand upon the film. Thus *Jedi* turned out to be less than half the length of the *Star Wars* radio adaptation. It was scripted again by Brian Daley, who unfortunately would never live to hear the production, as he passed away in March 1996 — on the day the cast completed the recording of their lines and months before the radio drama would be edited for airing.

To many people, *Jedi* is the least favorite entry in the trilogy, lacking the originality of the first two films. Probably the most

original sequences are the rescue of Han Solo and the confrontation between Luke, Vader, and the Emperor. Conversely, the attack on the Death Star is essentially a reprise of the original film's climax.

Some odd notes about this adaptation: Mark Hamill doesn't reprise his Luke Skywalker role. A young actor named Josh Fardon takes over. Also missing in action is Billy Dee Williams, with Lando portrayed by Ayre Gross (a Caucasian, incidentally); Jabba the Hutt is played by Edward Asner, which is odd because Jabba doesn't speak English. His lines would better have been picked up from the film, where at least that familiar voice would be heard. As it stands, Anthony Daniels is the only actor from the films who appears in this radio drama.

Episode one of this radio adaptation opens with scenes we had assumed took place but that are "shown" to us here. First we see Luke completing the construction of a lightsaber to replace the one he lost in Cloud City during his duel with Vader. A brief scene has the Emperor discussing Luke, then dispatching Vader to Endor to see to it that a project there is completed more rapidly. Everything else is pretty straightforward.

Early in episode two, there's a dungeon scene in which, for no particular reason, we can hear Boba Fett showing up to talk to Han. This may have been done because — inexplicably — Fett is a big deal with many fans despite the fact that he was barely seen in *Empire* and was disposed of quickly and effortlessly in *Jedi*.

Another improvement is that Brian Daley actually has Leia warn Luke about the trapdoor in front of Jabba's throne. Apparently droids can't talk when someone else is speaking, or at least that's the impression one gets from watching the film when Luke falls victim to this trap without anyone providing a warning.

An amusing scene in the movie, in which the rancor's two keepers weep and console each other over the gigantic body of their charge, does not appear in the radio show. Too bad, because it was one of the only offbeat moments in the film. Oddly enough, the episode ends in the *middle* of the battle on the sandbarge after Luke has obtained his lightsaber and freed Han.

On Dagobah, Luke has the same strange double-talk conversation with Ben Kenobi when Obi-Wan tries to explain that when he told Luke that Darth Vader had killed his father, he was speaking metaphorically.

The speeder-bike chase is fairly effective, although action scenes like this only serve to call to mind the imagery from the film. What few may realize is that in the movie *Return of the Jedi* the word *Ewok* is never spoken. But here, in episode five, they are actually referred to by their race's name.

The conclusion, like much of this adaptation, proceeds with very little in the way of new material, owing to the truncated length of the story. There are other concluding remarks of interest, such as Leia's telling Luke that Han is going to make him an uncle (which takes Han by surprise) and Luke's referring to the disembodied images of Obi-Wan Kenobi, Yoda, and Anakin Skywalker as meaning that the Jedi have returned (hence the title of this installment).

Amazingly, in some ways this comparatively scaled-down adaptation of the story is better than the movie.

THE STAR WARS TRILOGY RADIO DRAMAS

ADVENTURES
IN THE COMICS

"LUKE SKYWALKER — Will He Destroy the Galaxy or Save It?!?"

With those immortal words (featured on the cover of the first issue of *Star Wars*), Marvel Comics launched what was destined to become the most successful movie spin-off comic book series in history. In hindsight, this curious tag, intended to grab one's attention at the newsstand or in a comic shop, actually sums up Marvel's initial attempt at producing original *Star Wars* story lines — they just didn't get it (at least not at first). This, however, was not entirely the fault of the creative team working on the series. The series was rushed into production in order to coincide with the release of the movie; thus no one on the staff was as familiar with the characters and settings as fans would come to be in the following years.

The first issue, part one of six of the movie adaptation, was actually rushed onto the newsstands so fast that the initial printing had an erroneous price on the cover that was five cents less than it should have been (this was quickly caught and rectified, making copies with the incorrect price rare and worth far more these days than their corrected counterparts). The movie adaptation itself is pretty faithful to the final cut of the film — with the added bonus of including scenes cut from the movie, such as the Biggs and Luke scene on Tatooine, the Han and

Jabba scene in Mos Eisley, and the Biggs and Luke "reunion" scene on Yavin 4. The script for the comic was based on a slightly earlier draft of the screenplay that included these scenes, but since Lucas didn't actually end up completing the Han and Jabba sequence until twenty years later, Marvel had no photos of Jabba to supply the artist with when penciling the scene. To get around this, one of the various aliens seen briefly walking around the streets of Mos Eisley was chosen as the basis for Jabba, resulting in a two-meter-tall, bipedal orange humanoid alien with whiskers who was subsequently used two additional times in the Marvel series. This created an inexplicable continuity problem when the more familiar sluglike Jabba finally appeared in the *Return of the Jedi* adaptation.

Actually, this was just the first of a string of continuity problems that plagued the Marvel series owing solely to the fact that the writers and artists were working in a near vacuum as far as developing the characters because they had absolutely no idea what Lucas's plans were for the two sequels. The only help they had from Lucas was the occasional story line that he would not approve, although many times it was not clear if he didn't approve because it touched on something that would be contradicted in the sequels or if he merely felt that it did not fit in the *Star Wars* universe he had created.

After the *Star Wars* adaptation was completed, the Marvel crew moved on to completely original story lines picking up where the movie left off. The first story line involving Han and Chewbacca was nothing more than a reworking of the *Magnificent Seven*, as Han and Chewie recruit a band of gunslingers and outlaws to protect the local farmers on a backwater planet from a gang of pirates and, later, a Godzilla-like creature. The cast of characters that was created to make up Han's team were far from fan favorites. Most notable among them was Jaxx, short for Jaxxon ("which he ain't!"), a six-foot-tall green rabbit; Don-Wan Kihotay, a Don Quixote–like character; and "the Starkiller Kid," a young farm boy carbon copy of Luke (which is interesting, since in an earlier draft of the screenplay the family the movie centered around was originally named Starkiller rather than Skywalker). Not helping the situation was a continual rotation of the comic's art team, which only locked into place beginning with issue 11, when Archie Goodwin and Carmine Infantino took over. The duo provided a distinctive style that continued with only a few interruptions until the adaptation of *The Empire Strikes Back*. It was at this point that the series began to come into its own and started building a continuing story line that included a variety of recurring characters. Admittedly, Infantino's art took a bit of getting used to, as half the time the characters had a very Asian look to them, while the other half of the time they were as pumped up as the recent line of action figures from Kenner (Luke and Han look like they can take on Arnold Schwarzenegger, while Princess Leia's proportions make a Barbie doll look realistic).

The first of these story lines concerned an ocean world in which the local inhabitants live on giant city-size ships (much like the recent Kevin Costner movie *Waterworld*) and ride giant sea-serpent creatures. The Han/Leia/Luke love triangle began to be played upon and was continued throughout the series until the adaptation of the second movie. Infantino's run was interrupted for two issues, which proved to be very interesting stand-alone story lines. The first issue, 16's "The Hunter!" was drawn by Walt Simonson and Bob Wiacek and introduced one of the most original characters in the early issues of the comic: bounty hunter Valance, an Imperial stormtrooper until an explosion destroyed half of his body. He was rescued from death by the use of cybernetics and now feels that he is less than human. Indeed, he has developed a bizarre hatred of droids because they remind him of his cyborg nature, while at the same time he despises organic beings that treat droids as if they are sentient life-forms (saying a lot for his mental state, given his physical makeup). As he tracks down Luke Skywalker, whom he has become obsessed with because of Luke's friendship toward Threepio and Artoo, he mistakes the Starkiller Kid for Luke and a tale unfolds involving some of the characters from the earlier Han and Chewie

story line. The true success of the story is that Valance's revelation that he is a cyborg is kept hidden until the very last panel, thus fueling the reader's interest in finding out why he's on such a vendetta.

The next stand-alone story was issue 17's "Crucible!" a flashback to Luke's life on Tatooine shortly before the events of *A New Hope*, in which we are treated to the story of his race through Beggar's Canyon, as mentioned in the first movie. While the events

aren't nearly as entertaining as the similar story told in the first episode of the *Star Wars* National Public Radio drama, "A Wind to Shake the Stars," it was a treat to see a story that was set in an earlier time period. It was something Marvel tried again in issue 24's "Silent Drifting," which portrays a much younger Obi-Wan Kenobi in the pre-Empire days of the Old Republic. While it was exciting to see Obi-Wan as a dashing hero figure, the story itself was fairly weak.

The Goodwin/Infantino team resumed once again with a long string of entertaining story lines that finally brought Darth Vader (who hadn't been seen since the movie adaptation) back into the series.

Some of the more intriguing stories include "Return of the Hunter" (issue 27), featuring the return of Valance, who tracks Luke down and confronts him, only to finally understand why Luke has befriended these two droids; "Whatever Happened to Jabba the Hut?" (issue 28), a story in which Han and Chewie are forced to work with Jabba the Hutt (once again appearing in the humanoid form shown in the adaptation of the first movie and once again with *Hutt* being erroneously spelled *Hut*); and "Dark Encounter" (issue 29), a showdown between Vader and Valance that ends in the bounty hunter's death. After a brief stand-alone story featuring Princess Leia on a solo mission in issue 30, which comes across flat compared with the three previous stories, issue 31 features a return to Tatooine and kicks off a very entertaining story line centering on Baron Tagge, an evil Jedi who was blinded in a duel with Vader, and his evil scientist brother Orman Tagge. The remaining issues before the adaptation of the second film begin to read much like a soap opera as the story line kicks into high gear and culminates in a lightsaber duel between Luke and Tagge in issue 39, "In Mortal Combat!" (although Luke is duped into thinking he is fighting Vader because of a Force illusion created by the Dark Lord). Delays in getting the *Empire* adaptation completed resulted in issue 38's stand-alone story, "Riders in the Void," one of the most original stories in the entire run of the series. Michael Golden's unique art style created a truly alien setting for a bizarre tale involving an alien life-form from another galaxy.

At the same time the regular series was running, the first *Star Wars* annual ("The Long Hunt") appeared, with a fresh look thanks to artist Mike Vosburg and an intricate story line incorporating a short flashback to Han's life prior to *A New Hope*. There is also a reference to a trio of Jedi heroes — Obi-Wan Kenobi, Darth Vader, and Luke's father, which, of course, caused no end of continuity problems when it was later revealed that Vader *is* Luke's father.

On the other side of the Atlantic, the U.K. *Star Wars Weekly* comic was publishing the U.S. comics in multiple parts, but because it was being published four times as often as its U.S. counterpart, some filler stories needed to be produced specifically for the United Kingdom. These stories, which were later reprinted in the United States in paperback form, proved to be some of the best stand-alone stories to date. Two of the stories provided flashbacks into certain characters' lives in a time before *A New Hope*. The first, "Way of the Wookiee!" which ran in issues 94–96 of *Star Wars Weekly*, centers around Han and Chewie. We learn why Han was forced to dump Jabba's load of spice, which gained him a price on his head, and the story also deals with the issue of the Empire's use of Wookiees as slave labor. The other flashback story, "The Weapons Master!" (running in issues 104–106), tells how Leia was trained in self-defense use of a blaster by a weapons master who proves to be the perfect mentor but ends up betraying her. The story that appeared between these two, known as "The Day after the Death Star!" (issues 97–99), dealt with Luke's adventures the day after the Rebel celebration on Yavin 4 and is notable if only for the fact that

Chewbacca is finally shown receiving a medal of his own — something that was definitely lacking from the closing scene of *A New Hope* (of course, Leia has to climb up on a table to get the thing around his neck!). A fourth U.K. story, in issues 107–115 (collectively known as "World of Fire!"), was based in the present and proved to be a more traditional, and mediocre, story.

Around the same time, further comic book adventures began appearing in a syndicated newspaper comic strip throughout the world. The strip was initially written and drawn by Russ Manning, whose simplistic style seemed to fit the early days of the *Star Wars* phenomenon. At first the strip had separate story lines running on Sundays and on weekdays until six months into its run, when it switched to chronicling one story seven days a week. There were successful stories, such as "Tatooine Sojourn," which brought Luke back to the planet he grew up on, and "The Frozen World of Ota," which featured Boba Fett — already proving to be a fan favorite. Naturally, there were also disappointments, such as the now infamous "Princess Leia, Imperial Servant."

In 1980 *The Empire Strikes Back* hit theaters and Marvel published their adaptation of the movie in a few different formats. The earliest version appeared in a paperback-size book, followed by the magazine-size *Marvel Super Special* #16, and then in regular comic book form in six parts, beginning in issue 39 of the regular *Star Wars* series. The paperback version has a major difference from the others in that Al Williamson, the artist, originally had only a preproduction sketch of Yoda to work with and thus drew him as a much smaller and much grizzlier-looking purple creature. He redrew the panels with Yoda in the other two versions, although he was stuck with him looking smaller than he should have in many of the scenes. The artwork reached a new high, with Williamson penciling and Carlos Garzon inking likenesses of the characters that had an accuracy never before seen in the series. The majority of the panels drawn by Williamson are based on stills from the movie, which helped him achieve the near-perfect likenesses.

The string of comics that appeared between the time of the

adaptations of *The Empire Strikes Back* and *Return of the Jedi* varied greatly — some were excellent and others were horrendous. It was evident from the outset that the writers were somewhat at a loss about what they should do with the characters when the second film basically ended on a cliff-hanger to be resolved in the third. They had three years' worth of stories to tell before they themselves found out what would happen in *Jedi*, yet they wanted to avoid creating any major continuity errors with the pending third film.

The first set of stories were stand-alone tales penciled by Infantino, whose artwork, in comparison with Williamson's efforts on *Empire*, suddenly seemed subpar. In addition, they were written by a variety of writers who were unable to rise to the occasion. It seemed that with the dark tones of *Empire*, the *Star Wars* universe had suddenly "grown up," and the comic book took a little time getting used to this. The new post-*Empire* adventures didn't start picking up until issue 50, "The Crimson Forever!" which incorporated Domina Tagge, sister of Baron Tagge (giving a nice connection back to the earlier story lines); many of the bounty hunters seen in *Empire;* and the use of flashbacks to bring Han Solo into the story (who is, at this

point, still frozen in carbonite). This double-size special issue marked a turning point in the series. With issue 51, Walt Simonson came onboard as the regular artist, lending a new consistent look to the series, and the story lines, being written largely by David Michelinie, began stretching out into multiple parts once more.

Around this time, the newspaper strip began having some problems, as Russ Manning became too ill to continue to work on it. In fact, he was assisted in completing the artwork for his last story, "The Frozen World of Ota," by Don Christiansen, Alfredo Alcala, and Rick Hoberg. When this story ended, Alfredo Alcala took over the artwork for two subsequent stories, "Planet of Kadril" (generally considered the worst of the newspaper strip stories) and an adaptation of the book *Han Solo at Stars' End*. Alcala's artwork style never

quite seemed to fit *Star Wars* and never remained consistent throughout a story (the best example is how many of the characters in the *Han Solo at Stars' End* adaptation changed in appearance throughout the story).

In February 1981 Archie Goodwin came onboard as the writer, and Al Williamson, who had proved how well he could draw the *Star Wars* characters with his artwork on the *Empire* adaptation, took over the artwork. This team remained on the strip throughout the remainder of its run and produced some of the best *Star Wars* comics in any medium to date. The strip had been grounded in the period between *A New Hope* and *The Empire Strikes Back,* so as not to conflict with anything that would occur in *Return of the Jedi,* and it had taken on a soap opera feel as one story continued into the next.

The plight of the Rebellion is followed from the evacuation of the base on Yavin 4 through to the establishment of the base on Hoth, with a multitude of exciting adventures along the way involving a large cast of characters from the *Star Wars* universe. Among them: Boba Fett, Jabba the Hutt, Admiral Ackbar, and a crew of new characters that became regulars in the strip. Even after *Return of the Jedi* was released, the strip continued to remain in the pre-*Empire* period, since it provided so much more potential for story lines.

The story lines themselves in the strip were thoroughly engaging. Some of the stronger plots involved a sting operation arranged by Darth Vader to expose a group of Imperial officers preparing to move against him because of his habit of using the Force to choke the life out of his underlings when they failed him; the construction of Vader's new Super Star Destroyer *Executor;* the apparent reappearance of Obi-Wan Kenobi (who turns out to be an actor employed by Vader to trap Luke); and a mission to Mon Calamari, which introduced Ackbar before *Jedi* hit the theaters. These comic strips have recently been reprinted by Dark Horse in an abridged format so they read like regular comics (the panels that served as a recap of the prior day's events were removed), but something was lost in the transition from newspaper strip to comic book. The stories are much more rewarding if read in their original format as individual comic strips, as they feel more like an ongoing serial. Goodwin and Williamson's efforts are also much more impressive when one is reminded that the planning that goes into a running daily comic strip is no easy task and that they are unable to go back to edit strips that have already been printed to tighten up or alter the story line. It is unfortunate that of all the *Star Wars* comics, the newspaper strips are often the most overlooked, even though they are the best of the lot.

Back in the Marvel comic book series, the once-again homeless Rebel Alliance searched for a new base after fleeing Hoth, finally arriving at Arbra. In a move that foreshadowed the use of the "cute" furry Ewoks in *Jedi,* Plif and his fellow Hoojibs are introduced in issue 55, "Plif!" and become recurring characters. The Hoojibs are a race of docile rabbitlike creatures that are actually extremely intelligent and use telepathy to communicate. Instead of supplying the book with a bit of comic relief, however, Plif and company detracted from the recent more-serious story lines and took the series a few steps back in the progress it had made since its earlier days. Luckily, with the bad came the good: a new character named Shira Brie was introduced in issue 58, "Coffin in the Clouds," as a potential love interest for Luke. We soon discovered that she was really a double agent for the Empire sent to infiltrate the Rebel Alliance, but her destiny is sealed when she is apparently killed when Luke shoots down a TIE fighter, not knowing that she was the pilot. She is reborn later in the series as a female version of Darth Vader named Lumiya (first introduced in the post-*Jedi* story "Figurehead" in issue 88, but not revealed to be Shira until issue 96, "Duel with a Dark Lady") and proved to be one of the most interesting characters to come out of the Marvel series.

Another interesting character, introduced in issue 68, "The Search Begins," was the Irish-accented Fenn Shysa. Capitalizing on the popularity of Boba Fett, Shysa has an identical suit of Mandalorian armor that he puts to use fighting to free Mandalore from the Empire's slavers. As Shysa explained to Leia, he had been part of a

group of armored supercommandos who fought on the Emperor's side in the Clone Wars. Only two other commandos besides him had survived — one of whom was their chief officer, Boba Fett, who went on to become the most ruthless bounty hunter of all. Years later, in the new line of *Star Wars* role-playing game adventures, short stories, and Dark Horse comic books, a similar character named Jodo Kast appears wearing a suit of Mandalorian armor identical to Fett's, leaving the reader to wonder just how unique Fett's armor really is.

As if the nauseatingly cute Plif weren't enough, Marvel deemed it necessary to introduce another furry little alien race — the Lashbees — in issue 73, "Lashbane." The Lashbees appear to be cute little Ewok-like creatures, although once they go through puberty they transform into huge, fearsome monsters called Huhks. Like Plif, they primarily serve to provide comic relief as they continually fawn over Chewbacca.

Many of the later story lines involved Lando and Chewie's attempts to track down Fett, who still had Han's frozen body in his possession. One of the most notable, "The Stenax Shuffle" (issue 70), incorporated a great flashback involving Han and the others shortly after the destruction of the first Death Star, in which they run afoul of a trio of smugglers on Stenos led by Han's old acquaintance Rik Duel. This led nicely into a two-part "present day" story line on Stenos in which Lando, Chewie, and Luke track down Bossk and IG-88 with hopes of finding out where Fett took Han, and then run into Rik Duel once again. An interesting note of trivia in the final two-part story before the post-*Jedi* tales began was Lando's disguise in "The Big Con" (issue 79), which was a carbon copy of Japanese Anime icon Captain Harlock (complete with an unruly lock of hair, an eyepatch, and a scar!). As the series approached the theatrical release of *Return of the Jedi*, Lando and Chewie seemed to get closer and closer to tracking down Fett, but of course they were always just a little too late to catch him.

A few interesting stand-alone stories appeared during this time as well. Wedge Antilles, a relatively minor character in the movies who has become a major player in the recent line of novels and comic books, had an entire issue devoted to him in "Hoth Stuff!" (issue 78). The U.K. comic (now retitled *The Empire Strikes Back Monthly*) once again featured new short stories that did not appear in the United States until Dark Horse recently reprinted all but one of them in a two-issue special titled "Star Wars — Devilwords." These stories, while featuring the writing talents of Steve Moore and Alan Moore, paled in comparison with the earlier ones. For the most part, they seemed to be in total contrast to the rest of the stories going on in the *Star Wars* universe and read more like the short *Twilight Zone*–like comic stories that appeared in the old pulp comics from decades earlier.

The adaptation of *Return of the Jedi* was published in Marvel Super Special #27 and in a separate miniseries, once again penciled by Al Williamson and inked by Carlos Garzon. This time, however, the adaptation was restricted to only four issues (the events of the movie take place between issues 80 and 81 in the regular series). The Marvel stories taking place after the third movie seem to wander aimlessly at times, as if the creative team were at a complete loss about where to take the series. Lucasfilm, as usual, had certain restrictions on what they could and could not do, but as the current line of comic books and novels has shown, the possibilities were endless. Instead, the Rebels remained on the forest moon of Endor with the Ewoks, more talking about establishing a new Republic than actually doing anything about it. Many plotlines, however, actually mirror plotlines from the current novels and comic books. Luke, as would be expected, began recruiting Jedi trainees to teach the ways of the Force to. A group of never-before-seen alien assassins called the Nagai caused problems for the Rebels until they united with them to fend off another group of invading aliens. The Nagai have

many similarities in name and appearance to the Noghri, introduced in Timothy Zahn's *Heir to the Empire* novel, and both races ended up joining the Rebels.

The first post-*Jedi* story, "Jawas of Doom," saw the return of Boba Fett as he makes his escape from the Sarlacc pit; however, unlike the Fett in the recent novels and comics, he ends up right back in the Sarlacc's belly by the end of the comic. This is unfortunate because it deprived the Marvel series of a popular character that they could have made good use of, and it made his escape from the Sarlacc all the more ridiculous, since it was only temporary.

The writers and artists on the comic rotated frequently until the team of Jo Duffy and Cynthia Martin became the regulars. Martin's artistic style brought an entirely fresh look to the series, but the story lines began leaning more toward a comedic style. First off, there was "Small Wars," issue 94, in which an inept Hiromi agent posing as Admiral Ackbar's aide attempts to divide the Alliance so his race can conquer the galaxy by maneuvering the Ewoks into a battle with the Lashbees — guaranteed to annoy any serious-minded *Star Wars* fan no end. A race of red-skinned aliens called the Zeltrons had been introduced early in the series, and in an attempt to provide more comic relief, a group of four male Zeltrons arrived and continually followed Leia around, fawning after her and worshiping the ground she walked on. While this nonsensical plotline alienated a lot of the readers, the stories did have many creative high points, such as the return of Lumiya, the dark Jedi, with a new exciting look to her.

As the original movie trilogy came to an end, so did the current line of *Star Wars* comics. The syndicated newspaper comic strip wrapped up its impressive run on March 11, 1984 — exactly five years to the day after it began. Archie Goodwin and Al Williamson continued to deliver top-quality story lines through to the end and left us on the doorstep of *The Empire Strikes Back* with the Rebels establishing a base on Hoth. The last Marvel comic was published in September 1986, a little more than three years after the release of *Return of the Jedi. Ewoks* and *Star Wars Droids,* the two other short-lived Marvel *Star Wars* series aimed at young readers and released under the "Star Comics" banner, also wrapped up around the same time (*Ewoks* ended in July 1986, *Droids* in June 1987). Aside from a very short-lived 3-D *Star Wars* comic released by Blackthorne in 1987 and 1988 that lasted for only three issues, it seemed that there was no longer a life for *Star Wars* in the comic book venue (or any venue for that matter).

Years later, interest in *Star Wars* slowly began to resurface as West End Games released a *Star Wars* role-playing game with incredibly detailed sourcebooks on the characters and planets (so detailed, in fact, that they have become somewhat of a bible for recent writers). *Star Wars* didn't fully catch the public's eye once more until the release of the first of Timothy Zahn's novels, *Heir to the Empire*, in June 1991. This was shortly followed by a six-issue comic book series called "Dark Empire" released by Dark Horse beginning in December 1991. The new twist, which seemed to prove popular with all *Star Wars* fans, is that, with a few minor exceptions, *all* subsequent *Star Wars* tales, regardless of the medium in which they would be told, were part of the same chronology.

This has become a nightmare for authors in recent days because they need to be aware of everything that has been published to date in order to avoid continuity conflicts (nonetheless, as is to be expected, there have been some), since the stories being published jump around on the established *Star Wars* time line. It creates an incredibly exciting vehicle for readers, who are introduced to characters in one story and then given glimpses of their pasts in subsequent stories, and thanks to the painstaking attention to detail and continuity by the authors and editors, it allows one to fit the pieces of each story into one large tapestry of events.

From the outset, Dark Horse took a more serious view of *Star Wars* than Marvel did. Many fans, including the creative teams at Dark Horse, began to dismiss the Marvel stories as being, for the most part, rubbish, since they did not fit in the new time line. It is interesting, however, how Dark Horse continually lambasted the early Marvel stories and then churned out a good helping of juvenile

story lines, such as the "Droids" and "Jabba the Hutt" series, that were completely farcical. They did, however, start out with a bang with "Dark Empire." The story line, as denoted in the title, is decidedly dark and somber as Luke crosses over to the dark side of the Force. The artwork by Cam Kennedy gave a fresh, "adult" look to the series, made even more dramatic by the original coloring style. The plotline starts abruptly as we are thrown into the middle of an

Imperial civil war on Coruscant. This caused a bit of a continuity problem with Zahn's novels, as they take place immediately prior to the series and they have the New Republic firmly established on the former Imperial Center. Continuity is smoothed over with a brief intro, presented in the familiar scrolling-text style that the movies opened with, which explains that after Thrawn was defeated, the different factions within the Empire managed to retake Coruscant and force the New Republic to beat a hasty retreat. The only real weakness of the story line, scripted by Tom Veitch, is that he resorted to an age-old comic book cheat of resurrecting a popular dead character — in this case Emperor Palpatine. Through the use of clones, Palpatine is once again the antagonist; however, this time he is in the forefront of the action as never before. The ultimate resolution of the story sees him defeated but not killed — leaving it open for a sequel (or two). . . . The one character whose apparent resurrection is easily forgiven is Boba Fett. Everyone's favorite bounty hunter, bumped off so ungraciously in *Return of the Jedi,* is back in full force to provide endless trouble for Han and the rest. In the years to follow, Fett's popularity increased exponentially with each subsequent appearance.

Dark Horse decided to stick to the miniseries format for future *Star Wars* comic book projects and began experimenting with different types of stories. Some proved to be more successful than others. Among the first of the new series was "Tales of the Jedi," which takes place approximately four thousand years ago during the height of the Old Republic. At first the stand-alone tales of Nomi Sunrider and Ulic Qel-Droma seemed to be interesting stories on their own but "forced" into the *Star Wars* universe, since they were so far removed from the more "current" events taking place in the novels and in "Dark Empire." Soon, however, as subsequent "Tales of the Jedi" stories were conceived, the characters were shown to have many links with the present, as their actions in the past had ramifications that lasted more than four thousand years. The artwork in the different "Tales of the Jedi" series ranged from excellent to subpar, as did the story lines. Overall, they prove to be an interesting diversion but never as exciting as the original series involving the more familiar *Star Wars* characters.

A series of "Droids" miniseries soon began appearing that seemed no different from the young-reader series published by Marvel almost a decade earlier. The story lines were exceedingly juvenile, as "humor" rather than drama seemed to be the main thrust of the plotlines. Hearing Dark Horse editors speak badly of the Marvel comic series in their letter columns and editorials began to wear thin as they tooted their own horns about such series as "Droids," which doesn't come close to measuring up to some of the better stories produced by Marvel. With the recent nostalgic feelings surfacing in most longtime *Star Wars* fans, Dark Horse has seemed to change its tune: it now embraces the Marvel series as a part of *Star Wars* history and has plans to reprint selected issues in a "best of" series that gives Marvel all the recognition and credit it is due.

The "Tales of the Jedi" miniseries really started kicking into high gear with the release of the six-part "Dark Lords of the Sith" story line, followed shortly thereafter by the six-part "The Sith War." These series incorporated all of the characters previously established in the prior "Tales of the Jedi" series in an all-out war with dark Jedi utilizing Sith magic. Much akin to the tale of Darth Vader's fall to the dark side and eventual return to grace, the story line focuses mainly on Ulic Qel-Droma's plight as he is led to the dark side by Exar Kun and eventually betrays his friends and allies.

It seems that Tom Veitch, Kevin J. Anderson, and Cam Kennedy

didn't feel that the dark side was intrinsically tempting enough to lure a great hero like Ulic, so he was "helped" along by Exar Kun, who injected him with a Sith poison that affected his moral center enough to allow Kun to bring him over to the dark side. This not only makes Anakin Skywalker look bad, as he must not have been as strong as Ulic if he fell to the dark side without the use of foreign substances (although the exact circumstances of his fall have not yet been told), but it diminishes the overriding themes established by George Lucas in the (eventual) six movies of how one's choices can affect one's entire life as well as those of the individuals a person comes into contact with, and how everyone has within him or her the potential for great good and great evil. In essence, it is the choices a person makes in life that determine which will be played upon. Here it seems that Ulic would not have been able to fall to the dark side on his own and required an outside controlling force to cause his fall. Aside from the fact that the theme imbedded within the story line appears to be diametrically opposed to the theme established by Lucas, the two miniseries remain an enjoyable read, if only to learn the story of Exar Kun, who causes no end of trouble for Luke and his fledgling Jedi Academy in Anderson's *Jedi Academy* trilogy novels. The final series in the saga, "The Redemption of Ulic Qel-Droma," did not see print until recently, in 1998.

The inevitable sequel to Dark Horse's first miniseries appeared soon after, aptly titled "Dark Empire II," and was once again written by Tom Veitch, and illustrated by Cam Kennedy. The story starts as abruptly as the first series did, with a character named Kam Solusar training with Luke. A graphic novel titled *Lightsider* was planned to be published that would have told the story of how Luke rescued Kam from the dark side and took him on as a student, but the project fell apart and now looks like it will never be published. In the series the Emperor is once again causing trouble for the New Republic; however, there is no real direction for the plot this time. Ridiculous subplots such as that of the Ganathans — who travel through space in steam-powered ships — detract from the seriousness of the story line and weaken the overall narrative. The Emperor's fate is once again left to be resolved in a sequel, which came to pass several months later in the two-part "Empire's End." Tom Veitch once again scripted the story, along with Mike Beidler, but Cam Kennedy was replaced by Jim Baikie in the art department. Baikie's art style is completely different from Kennedy's and much less dramatic. This, combined with a very weak plot, causes the series to look like an afterthought instead of a resolution. Palpatine's eventual defeat is extremely anticlimactic, making one wish it had been resolved much earlier (like in the first "Dark Empire" series).

A four-issue miniseries titled "River of Chaos," set between *A New Hope* and *The Empire Strikes Back,* began in June of 1995. While entertaining, the series failed to create the interest that many of the other miniseries had and seemed more like a run-of-the-mill Marvel story line.

That same year also saw the start of one of the most logical *Star Wars* spin-off series, "X-Wing Rogue Squadron," which centered around Wedge Antilles, now captain of the famous Alliance fighter squadron that Luke once belonged to. The thirty-five-issue series was broken up into eight four-issue miniseries, one two-issue miniseries, and a double-size special that chronicled the adventures of Rogue Squadron during a period shortly after *Return of the Jedi* up through the first of the *X-Wing* novels (which began two and a half years after *Jedi*). The stories varied significantly in plot and artwork, with some succeeding more than others. At first the individual story arcs were more self-contained, but as the series progressed each subsequent one built on the last and began to tie in to the novels more closely (especially when Michael Stackpole, author of the first four and the eighth *X-Wing* novels, moved from merely outlining the stories to scripting them). The most interesting character to come out of the series by far is the former Imperial ace pilot Baron Fel, who happens to be married to Wedge's sister. Issue 25, "The Making of Baron Fel," is one of the best Dark Horse *Star Wars* comics to date, as it manages to reference and tie in to a multitude of other *Star Wars* comics and novels, with cameos by Thrawn (who was not yet a grand admiral), Han Solo (in his days at the Imperial

Academy), and Evir Derricote (the Imperial scientist responsible for creating the Krytos Virus in the *X-Wing* novels). The two-part "Family Ties" story gives us a glimpse of Corran Horn (who would go on to become one of Rogue Squadron's top aces in the *X-Wing* novels) in his days with CorSec. Two X-Wing specials were also published. The first was a short comic that took place very shortly after *Jedi* and was available only in a mail-away offer from Apple Jacks, and the second was "X-Wing" #1/2, available from American Entertainment, which was scripted by Michael Stackpole and told a story set during *A New Hope* with the original Rogue, including Biggs Darklighter and Jek Porkins.

A few months after the debut of the "X-Wing" series, Dark Horse published the first of their adaptations of novels — "Heir to the Empire." The six-part series was beautifully drawn by Oliviet Vatine, whose fresh and original style really brought the characters (especially Grand Admiral Thrawn and the mad Jedi Jorus C'Boath) to life. Adaptations of *Dark Force Rising* and *The Last Command* followed in 1997 and 1998, both with different artistic teams. An adaptation of *Splinter of the Mind's Eye,* the most popular of the early *Star Wars* novels, appeared in late 1995, with stunning artwork provided by Chris Sprouse. Dark Horse is currently developing plans to adapt the novel *Truce at Bakura,* which is, unfortunately, one of the weaker of the new novels. One hopes they will continue this line of adaptations while still providing exciting new series.

Late 1995 also saw the start of a series of Boba Fett comics. The first story line, "Twin Engines of Destruction," appeared in four parts in the *Star Wars Galaxy* magazine and dealt with Boba Fett catching up with Jodo Kast, who had been impersonating him with the use of an identical suit of body armor. Fett's justice is both swift and harsh, reaffirming that his reputation is not something he views lightly. In December 1995 "Boba Fett — Bounty on Bar-Koda" appeared, illustrated by Cam Kennedy, whose dark style fit the "Dark Empire" series so well. The Boba Fett series continued on with "When the Fat Lady Swings" in 1996, "Murder Most Foul" in 1997, and the American Entertainment exclusive Boba Fett #1/2 story,

"Salvage." Although it was great seeing everyone's favorite bounty hunter in solo adventures, the story lines were a bit tongue-in-cheek, with ludicrous-looking alien adversaries and comical plotlines. This didn't mesh well with Fett, who is one of the darkest characters in the saga.

Nineteen ninety-six saw the launch of the multimedia event *Shadows of the Empire.* This story, set during the short period between *The Empire Strikes Back* and *Return of the Jedi,* was told in multiple formats (a novel, a comic book series, and a Nintendo game), each with a slightly different perspective. The six-issue comic book series, stunningly drawn by newcomer Kilian Plunkett, dealt mainly with Boba Fett's trials and tribulations (something severely lacking in the novel). All the bounty hunters seen in *The Empire Strikes Back,* with the exception of Dengar, make appearances as they each try to steal Han's frozen body from Fett before he can deliver him to Jabba. The new antagonist, Prince Xizor, quickly became a fan favorite even though he is seemingly killed at the end. *Shadows* spawned two comic book sequels: "Shadow Stalker," a six-part short story that ran in the *Star Wars Galaxy* magazine and dealt with Vader's connection to his special agent Jix (which actually ties in directly to a story line from the *Star Wars* newspaper comic strip), and "Shadows of the Empire: Evolution," a six-part full-length comic series that deals with Xizor's replicant-droid Guri attempting to get her programming altered so she will no longer be an assassin.

Later in 1996 two more "Tales of the Jedi" miniseries began, this time taking the story back an additional millennium to five thousand years before *A New Hope,* when the Republic was charting new hyperspace routes and stumbled upon the Sith race. Because of its setting, the story line is removed from the "current" events that the more familiar *Star Wars* characters are involved in, but the story moves at a fast pace and quickly engages the reader's interest.

A new series of miniseries was begun in December 1997 when "Crimson Empire" hit the stands. The series unravels much of the mystery surrounding the Emperor's royal guard and follows two former guards as they culminate a personal vendetta against each

other. The antihero of the story is Kir Kanos, who seems to differ from the rest of the guards in that he has some semblance of a conscience; however, as the first miniseries ends he callously kills one of the New Republic agents assisting him and loses any sympathy the reader has developed for him. Because of the series' popularity, Dark Horse is following it up with two sequels in the near future.

Projects planned by Dark Horse for late 1998 and early 1999 include a miniseries called "Vader's Quest" set immediately after *A New Hope* in which Vader uncovers information naming Luke Skywalker as the pilot who destroyed the Death Star; a miniseries called "The Leviathan of Koribos" set shortly after the *Jedi Academy* trilogy novels in which two of Luke's students go out on their first mission as Jedi Knights; "Mara Jade — By the Emperor's Hand," a miniseries covering the events in Mara's life between *Return of the Jedi* and "Heir to the Empire"; and "Boba Fett — Enemy of the Empire," in which Vader hires Fett for an important assignment.

Currently it seems *Star Wars* is more popular than ever, and the new series of interconnected comic books and novels will undoubtedly carry on throughout the new trilogy of prequel movies, which will open up a whole new time period for stories to be set in (which is currently off-limits until Lucas is done with the new movies). The trend by Dark Horse to use the miniseries format gives greater flexibility in changing the setting of the story lines and catering to everyone's favorite characters. At the same time, the ongoing soap opera style of story lines that pervaded the Marvel comic book series and the newspaper comic strip are sorely missed. Still, no fan who ever wondered what had happened to the comic book adventures of *Star Wars* during the period from the mid-1980s through the early 1990s has any reason to complain — *Star Wars* comics are back and they are back in style!

THE FICTION GUIDE

AN INTRODUCTION

IN DECEMBER 1976, almost half a year before the
explosion into the theaters of one of the most in-
fluential movies ever, a book written by a relatively
unknown author quietly made its way onto the
bookshelves across the country. Unbeknownst to
anyone, this book, titled *Star Wars — From the Adventures of Luke Skywalker,* would be the first in a
long line of novels telling the adventures of what are
now a familiar group of science fiction icons.

Surprisingly, even with the massive inundation of
Star Wars merchandise following the success of the film
series, until 1991 only seven original full-length adult
novels were written, in addition to the three novelizations
of the films released between 1976 and 1983. It wasn't until
eight years later, when Timothy Zahn's number-one best-
seller, *Heir to the Empire,* appeared in stores, that a new line
of novels in which continuity was to play a major role began
appearing. Zahn's trilogy of novels set the example for subsequent writers to follow, simultaneously renewing the world's
interest in *Star Wars,* which had been quietly subsiding since
the mid-eighties.

While the writers of the original seven novels were not concerned with whether their story lines contradicted the other novels or even the movies, this new range of novels has attempted to
fit into a single, consistent *Star Wars* universe that includes recent
comic book series by Dark Horse, a range of computer games put

out by LucasArts, and a series of role-playing game adventures produced by West End Games. The novels themselves have even influenced Lucas's recent tinkering with the movies in the Special Edition releases, as evidenced by the inclusion of a swoop bike in the *Star Wars* Special Edition (first seen in *Han Solo's Revenge* and later in *Shadows of the Empire*) and Imperial Center in the *Return of the Jedi* Special Edition (the planet's name was given as Coruscant by Timothy Zahn in *Heir to the Empire* and was used by Lucas in the storyboards for the new scene, most likely to be used again in the upcoming new trilogy of prequel movies). What we now have is a complicated tapestry of events that unfold in a completely random order. The exciting thing about this is that we are introduced to new characters in one novel and then learn more about the history of these characters in later stories that take place earlier in the *Star Wars* time line. While this is infinitely more complicated when it comes to avoiding continuity errors, the end product is much more enjoyable when the pieces are put together in order. The earlier novels, with some latitude, can still be included in this time line and are counted as part of the true "canon" of *Star Wars* material by most fans and many of the subsequent authors.

What follows is a look at the *Star Wars* novels and short stories that center on the pivotal characters. There were many that simply could not be included in detail because of space limitations.

Some notes on presentation:

- The novels and short stories are, with some exceptions, presented in the chronological order of the stories they contain as opposed to the order in which they were published.
- The publishing dates are used as opposed to the street dates (which are usually one month prior to the publishing dates).
- The dates used in placing the books in a time line are best guesses in many cases. Dates are given in relation to the movie trilogy (which itself spans a period of approximately four years from the beginning of *A New Hope* to the end of *Return of the Jedi*). While the newer novels have generally stated exactly the

year in which they take place in relation to the movie trilogy, the original novels and many of the short stories are open to speculation.

- ✦ Stories that span a period of time that overlaps that of other stories are placed in the order of when the story finishes (for example, the short story "The Last One Standing: The Tale of Boba Fett," which spans a period ranging from approximately twenty-five years before *A New Hope* to fifteen years after *Return of the Jedi*, is placed after "Vision of the Future," which takes place fifteen years after *Return of the Jedi*).

- ✦ A quick summary of each story is given, followed by a review, notes, and a rating based on a letter grade (A to F). Both the synopses and the reviews contain major spoiler information.

- ✦ To distinguish the novels from the short stories, the titles of all novels are given in italics, while the titles of all short stories are given in quotes.

"MIST ENCOUNTER"

(from *The Official Star Wars Adventure Journal*, vol. 1 no. 7) (approximately twenty-five years before *ANH*) by Timothy Zahn (August 1995)

SYNOPSIS: An enigmatic alien smuggler known as Mitth'raw'nuruodo is at first pursued by the Empire but ultimately brought into its folds. In the end, the smuggler takes on a new name: Thrawn.

REVIEW/NOTES: A treat for any fan of Timothy Zahn's Grand Admiral Thrawn. Zahn's *Heir to the Empire* trilogy leaves the reader wanting to learn more about this villain whom you admire and respect despite his being committed to killing our heroes and destroying the New Republic. This story also serves as a great example of how enjoyable it can be to have the short stories and novels presented to us in a random order along the *Star Wars* time line. We are introduced to a character in one story and then, in another, we're given the opportunity to look into his past, knowing exactly where he or she will end up in the future.

Thrawn still remained somewhat of an enigma by the end of Zahn's trilogy. The simple fact that he rose to the rank of grand admiral despite the strong antialien prejudices of the Emperor implies that there is a lot more to the man than is apparent.

What's fascinating about this story is the fact that it takes us back to a time when "President" Palpatine has just declared himself emperor and we are witness to his initial, and ruthless, conquest of the galaxy. While the *Star Wars* features have made the interaction of various species a common fact, "Mist Encounter" lets us see how this situation began as the Empire begins reaching the Rim worlds, encountering myriad alien races unknown to the Old Republic or long forgotten over the millennia. Even so, it's amusing to see the Empire encounter someone of such cunning and pure genius who simultaneously appears so primitive and yet is able to outmaneuver and outwit the greatest force in the galaxy. What doesn't work, however, is Zahn's attempt to disguise the true identity of this new alien until the last few lines of the story. It isn't long before his identity becomes known to the reader.

The true high point of the story is Parck's confrontation with Mitth'raw'nuruodo on the *Strikefast*. Parck's ability to see past Thrawn's appearance and ignore his own wounded pride speaks highly of the man. On the other hand, Barris's inability even to begin to figure out what was going on during Thrawn's attacks let alone recognize Thrawn's usefulness to the Empire foreshadows his eventual fall in Michael Stackpole's "Missed Chance" story.

Accurately dating this story is a bit difficult without having the definitive version of the events surrounding Palpatine's rise to power and Vader's fall, as will be told in the new trilogy of prequel movies. We know that Palpatine has just recently claimed the title of emperor, which would place it approximately twenty to twenty-five years before *A New Hope* (depending on whether this event occurs in the second prequel, set twenty-five years before *A New Hope*, or the third prequel, set five years later). We also know that the events on Honoghr concerning Vader's manipulation of the Noghri, which are mentioned in this story, occurred twenty-five years before *A*

New Hope (Khabarakh claims that it happened forty-four Imperial years before the events in *Dark Force Rising*). One thing that may end up being contradicted in the new movies is the timing of Anakin's transformation into Vader in relation to Palpatine's becoming the emperor. Like many stories that deal with or refer to the time setting of the prequels, a good portion of them will most likely be contradicted in some manner. Despite this possibility, they're exciting to read because so many pivotal events occurred back then that shaped the galaxy into what we were introduced to in *A New Hope*. **(A+)**

HAN SOLO TRILOGY:
BOOK 1 – THE PARADISE SNARE

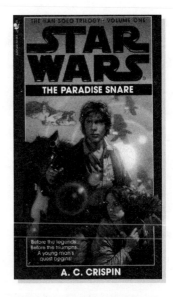

(ten years before *ANH*, with flashbacks during the period from twenty-five years before *ANH* to twelve years before *ANH*) by A. C. Crispin (June 1997)

SYNOPSIS: Han Solo's "origin" is told as readers are taken through his formative years.

REVIEW/NOTES: The book is a double-edged sword as it peels away the mystery surrounding Han's past. While it's exciting to learn about Han's formative years, some of the edge is taken off the character, as he's shown less as a heroic icon and more as a normal human being.

A. C. Crispin does a great job in taking on the burden of trying to tie together all the bits and pieces we have thus far learned about Han's past (some of which stems from casual offhand remarks made by different characters in the course of a story). She succeeds almost impossibly in tying together Han's past and accomplishments, while at the same time weaving a tale of his past that parallels *Oliver Twist* (even the droid that sends out the pickpocketing children is named F8-GN, a play on the character Fagin from the Dickens classic). Crispin does not stop at merely tying together the pieces we already know, she also takes the opportunity to fix a few other continuity glitches, such as why Leia's adopted father Bail Organa was referred to as "Prestor" in the National Public Radio *Star Wars* dramatization. She also sprinkles cameo appearances by other well-

known characters such as Hal Horn, member of CorSec on Corellia (the father of Corran Horn from the *X-Wing* novels), and even a ten-year-old Princess Leia.

Obviously Crispin did a lot of research before tackling such an ambitious project. Han's obsession with becoming an officer in the Imperial Navy nicely foreshadows his eventual desertion (unfortunately, Crispin was not allowed to touch on that segment in Han's life — possibly because Lucas has other plans to tell this story). The only real drawback in the story is that the main thrust of the plotline is not nearly as exciting as the frequent brushes with continuity. The character of Muuurgh is not much more than a temporary substitute for Chewbacca, and Bria's character never really justifies the intense feelings Han develops for her so quickly. Han's character is not consistent throughout the story, as he continues to drift back and forth from arrogant and cocky to naive and immature.

All in all, Crispin does a decent job of portraying a younger Han who is trying to find his place in the galaxy and make his mark while at the same time learning important life-changing lessons. **(A−)**

LANDO CALRISSIAN AND THE MINDHARP OF SHARU

(four years before *ANH*) by L. Neil Smith (July 1983)

SYNOPSIS: Lando Calrissian, a character barely illuminated despite his roles in *The Empire Strikes Back* and *Return of The Jedi*, has his background explored in this novel, which takes him from winning the *Millennium Falcon* to finding himself in a struggle between two factions of an alien race.

REVIEW/NOTES: L. Neil Smith definitely has the most distinct writing style of any of the *Star Wars* authors to date. In fact, the majority of the book is handled in a very lighthearted manner, never taking itself too seriously. While this may put off many readers, it provides a nice change and suits the younger Lando. Lando's character is very different from the somewhat hardened character we are accustomed to in the movies. Thankfully, Smith didn't make him another Han Solo carbon-copy smuggler. Instead, Lando comes across as a sort of Bret Maverick–style gambler whose love for card games tends to lead him into serious trouble wherever he goes.

Neil's trilogy is extremely different from Brian Daley's previous trilogy of Han Solo novels in many ways. While Daley's novels were almost completely unrelated to each other, Neil's trilogy is closer to one continuous story with three chapters. As with Daley's efforts, they suffer slightly from the fact that they were written prior to the resurgence of popularity in *Star Wars* that occurred in the early nineties and were not written with the intent of fitting into a much larger Star Wars universe. The aliens encountered by Lando are, for the most part, created by Smith and are not familiar faces from the movies. This was also the case in Daley's novels, and it causes the stories to feel slightly removed from the "real" *Star Wars* universe.

Conversely, the characters introduced by Smith are just as interesting and entertaining as any encountered in the other novels. Vuffi Raa is a unique droid as is evidenced by the fact that he so quickly becomes Lando's best friend, even though Lando won him in a card game. This also says a lot for Lando, since the majority of humans seem either to harbor a strong prejudice against droids or else merely to think of them as property or equipment. The ongoing joke in the novels is the fact that Vuffi Raa continues to call Lando "master" no matter how many times Lando screams at him not to call him that. The two characters work very well together, and it proves the point that not every team of rogues or adventurers needs to be made up of a smuggler and his large towering alien partner — something that few other authors have realized. The sorcerer Rokur Gepta, the new antagonist created for the trilogy, is also a fascinating character. He remains primarily behind the scenes in the first novel, which makes him more intriguing than the stereotypical Imperial commander who provides the opposition in many of the other novels and comics.

The plotline involving the mystery behind the Sharus' disappearance is engaging and never predictable. What makes the story line even better is that Lando remains completely uninterested in

solving the mystery, to the point where he takes a nap inside one of the massive Sharu structures while the race's history is being played out before him. The offbeat quality of the writing does get a bit too odd at times, and on occasion there seems to be a lack of motive for the actions of certain characters. For instance, it is never really explained why Lando so quickly puts his trust back in Mohs after the elder Toka so unexpectedly steals the key to the Mindharp and engages in a fistfight with Lando when trying to escape with it. What is even more confusing is that Mohs once again betrays Lando, this time by tying him to a tree trunk and leaving him to die of exposure, but Lando yet again forgives Mohs for no apparent reason after he escapes. Even though the novel has its flaws, it makes a good read if only for the fact that it breaks away from the "standard" type of *Star Wars* story while remaining within the confines of the established *Star Wars* universe. **(B+)**

LANDO CALRISSIAN AND THE FLAMEWIND OF OSEON

(four years before *ANH*) by L. Neil Smith (October 1983)

SYNOPSIS: Lando tires of the "straight" life but finds himself in intergalactic trouble as he returns to his old ways.

REVIEW/NOTES: L. Neil Smith manages to maintain the tongue-in-cheek style that was such a highlight of his first Lando Calrissian novel without moving too far toward the absurd. The plot is an effective continuation of the first, the return of Rokur Gepta as the antagonist providing a nice feel of continuity. The greatest strength in Smith's storytelling is that the majority of the characters in his novels continue to change throughout the story line and many times turn out to be completely different from how they are initially portrayed.

A good example is Rokur Gepta, the Sorcerer of Tund. In the first novel he appears to be nothing more than an individual in possession of some sort of magic who is out to subjugate the galaxy through power and fear, much the same way the Emperor has. In this second novel, however, we learn that there is a lot more to Gepta than meets the eye.

The most intriguing thing set up in this novel, however, is the mystery surrounding Vuffi Raa, although this plot thread is left dangling until the third novel. Lando and Vuffi Raa also continue to develop as characters, Lando's piloting skills showing marked improvement, as does his use of the weapons on the *Falcon*. Vuffi Raa exhibits more humanlike traits because of his time with Lando, and the two develop an even closer friendship.

The main plot of the story is a bit reminiscent of the first novel, as Lando finds himself in trouble with the law and railroaded into doing their dirty work. This doesn't detract much from the story line, however, since it once again puts Lando in the middle of things without a clue about what is really going on. Figuring out everyone's true motivations proves entertaining.

The traitor onboard the *Falcon* sequence was also familiar from *Han Solo at Stars' End,* but the ultimate revelation of the traitor's identity was more rewarding in this novel. Instead of Lando figuring it out (as Han did) and killing him, there is a satisfying series of twists. At the same time, the storyline is far less complicated than the first novel and suffers a bit in comparison. It still provides a fresh change from the standard style of writing utilized by the other authors. **(B–)**

LANDO CALRISSIAN AND THE STARCAVE OF THONBOKA

(four years before *ANH*) by L. Neil Smith (December 1983)

SYNOPSIS: While Lando and Vuffi Raa attempt to help a race known as the Oswaft, they find themselves trapped by enemy troops and must con their way out of the situation.

REVIEW/NOTES: The final installment in the Lando Calrissian trilogy of novels proves to be even more tongue-in-cheek and irreverent than the first two, yet stands out above the others for the same reason.

L. Neil Smith walks a fine line between comedy and farce in his novels, telling a good science-fiction story at the same time. He does so in such a manner that you forget how serious a place the *Star Wars* universe typically is, yet never once do you feel that his stories are so different that they couldn't possibly occur within it. The character of Rokur Gepta reaches the peak of his insane obsession with enacting his revenge on Lando in this novel. Even though he is such an ancient creature, he has managed to completely lose touch with reality thanks to Lando continually escaping from each trap he has laid. He finally reaches the point that he is willing to sacrifice the lives of however many beings it takes in order to kill Lando. All of this contributes to the final irony when the true Gepta is finally revealed.

The characters of Lehesu and his race are interesting — a definite break from the usual humanoid aliens that make up the majority of the galaxy portrayed in the novels. The addition of "the One," "the Other," and "the Rest" was a great way of showing that size is relative (Lehesu first appeared to be unbelievably huge to Lando and Vuffi Raa; then we learn that he is young for his race and the Elders turn out to dwarf him in comparison; then this new race appears and makes the Elders look tiny).

The way Lando uses his skills at sabacc and his con artist talents to take control of the situation in this first-contact scenario is very funny and unprecedented in a *Star Wars* novel. The ongoing joke concerning Lando's continuous pleas for Vuffi Raa to stop calling him master comes to a head at the end of the novel. The unique friendship Vuffi and Lando developed is almost unheard of between droids and organic beings. The revelation about Vuffi Raa's true origin is skillfully withheld until the very end, as Smith makes it appear that "the One" may be after Rokur Gepta. All in all, Smith's trilogy is a great departure from the more serious story lines in the other novels and proves that *Star Wars* stories do not have to fall into a standard format in order to be accepted as part of the *Star Wars* universe. **(A–)**

HAN SOLO TRILOGY:

BOOK 2 – THE HUTT GAMBIT

(five years to four years before *ANH*) by A. C. Crispin (August 1997)

SYNOPSIS: In this second chronicle of Han Solo's life he is dishonorably discharged from the Imperial Navy, finds himself teamed up with Chewbacca, and begins to live the life of a smuggler.

REVIEW/NOTES: Although it's unfortunate that Crispin was forced to skip over Han and Chewie's first meeting, she begins the second novel in her trilogy immediately after Han is drummed out of the Imperial Navy and still unsure of what he will do next. As the novel begins, he is annoyed by Chewie, but then a deep friendship develops between them, culminating in Han's thinking of Chewie as a brother by the end. The main recurring theme throughout the novel concerns the development of Han's relationships with others — both good and bad.

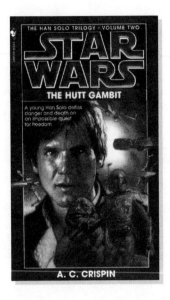

First there are the many smugglers that Han and Chewie become involved with. Crispin manages to integrate nearly every "old smuggling friend" of Han's mentioned in all of the other novels and comic books. Another significant relationship that Han builds in the novel is with Lando. Their first meeting was a nice treat, as it also involves Han's initial meeting with bounty hunter Boba Fett. Han's escape from Fett helps explain why Fett despises Han so much later on.

Not all of Han's relationships are good ones. Aside from crossing paths with Fett, Han becomes involved with the Hutts — Jabba in particular. Han quickly proves himself to be an extremely useful and capable employee to Jabba and develops a stronger relationship with him than most of the Hutts' employees do. This is most likely why Jabba gives Han some slack in paying him back in *A New Hope*. At the same time it is probably the thing that fuels the vendetta he develops against Han, as he feels personally betrayed by someone he relied on and came to trust (something that is not in the nature of a Hutt to do).

Interestingly, Crispin clarifies why Jabba's size increased so

much in the four years between *A New Hope* (as seen in the Special Edition) and *Return of the Jedi* (Hutts, it seems, undergo spontaneous growth spurts throughout their lives).

Not all of the relationships dealt with in the book are new ones. Han meets up with Bria twice in the novel, and both times he gets the wrong idea about what she is doing.

Overall, the novel is extremely enjoyable and especially rewarding for anyone who has read the other novels and comic books that it is tied in to, and nonetheless an entertaining read for those who haven't. **(A+)**

HAN SOLO AT STARS' END –
FROM THE ADVENTURES OF LUKE SKYWALKER

(two years before *ANH*) by Brian Daley (April 1979)

SYNOPSIS: Han and Chewie are hired to locate a secret detention center and rescue the prisoners within.

REVIEW/NOTES: The idea of reading about the adventures Han and Chewie had in the *Falcon* prior to meeting Luke and Ben and getting caught up in the Rebellion is very enticing. The problem with the three books written by Brian Daley, however, is that they were written in the late seventies — a time when science fiction was still viewed by most people as something geared toward children. Daley never set out to write a series of *New York Times* best-sellers but instead wanted to present straightforward plotlines with a multitude of aliens and spaceships set in the *Star Wars* universe.

As any reader of some of Daley's later works, such as the series of *Robotech* and *Black Hole Travel Agency* novels (which were both cowritten with James Luceno under the pseudonym of Jack McKinney), knows, he is more than capable of creating a story line with myriad subplots that at first seem to be unrelated but eventually are revealed to be interconnected with such complexity that the reader is forced to reread large sections of the books in order to completely grasp the implications of the latest revelation in the plot. That being the case, one must approach these novels much less critically than the newer ones.

The first of the three, *Han Solo at Stars' End,* has an extremely linear plotline with little to catch your attention and make you want to read through it in one sitting. About the only true sense of drama comes when it is discovered that there is a traitor onboard the *Falcon,* but that traitor is exposed almost immediately, quickly putting an end to any real tension. The characters of Bollux and Blue Max are very dry substitutes for Threepio and Artoo, but at least they have their own unique personalities instead of merely being carbon copies of the well-known protocol and astromech droids.

The real villain of the story, Vice-President Hirken, is not even introduced until the last third of the novel. Hirken is nothing more than a petty bureaucrat who revels in the small amount of power he wields. His bodyguard, Uul-Rha-Shan, had the potential to pose a somewhat more serious threat to Han but remained nothing more than another gun-toting lackey.

The fact that Daley created a new threat in the Corporate Sector Authority instead of using the Empire made the story seem a little too removed from the *Star Wars* universe. One also has to wonder how the Authority, which is nothing more than an incredibly large corporation, has managed to maintain control of such a large portion of the galaxy that is uninhabited and rich in untapped resources. It seems the Empire would be quick to force the Authority out in order to exploit the resources in their conquest of the galaxy. The climax, in which the tower of the prison complex is launched into near orbit by an explosion, is nothing short of ludicrous. In the end, an unstoppable self-destruct sequence in the complex would have provided the same level of drama without having to bend the laws of physics and strain credibility. **(B–)**

HAN SOLO'S REVENGE –
FROM THE ADVENTURES OF LUKE SKYWALKER

(two years before *ANH*) by Brian Daley (November 1979)

SYNOPSIS: When Han and Chewie, desperate for credits, take on the job of shipping an unknown cargo, they come to realize that the

cargo in question actually consists of slaves in transport. The duo conspire to turn the tables on the slave traders.

REVIEW/NOTES: The second novel, *Han Solo's Revenge,* is a major improvement over the first. The plotline is engaging and more complex in nature, with none of the characters turning out to be what they initially appear. Fiolla is an interesting shipmate for Han, simultaneously providing both a potential love interest and an adversary.

The characters of Bollux and Blue Max come across much stronger in this story, turning out to be valued crew members aboard the *Falcon* by saving Han's and Chewie's lives. With the respect Han develops for these droids, it's a wonder that he subsequently develops such distaste for droids by the time he meets Threepio. Perhaps there is just something about Threepio himself that annoys Han. An interesting point to note about this story is the use of swoop bikes, which come to play a large part in *Shadows of the Empire* and actually predate the speeder bikes from *Return of The Jedi* by a few years. The character Spray is also an interesting enigma, seemingly a bumbling collections agent who turns out to be the Authority territorial manager.

Once again, Han meets up with a fellow sharpshooter in Gallandro; however, Gallandro is put to much more use than Uul-Rha-Shan, the alien gunslinger from *Han Solo at Stars' End*, was. It's also amusing to see Han's bullheaded perseverance getting him out of yet another scrape.

All in all, the plotline of this novel bore quite a number of similarities to the first, but in a way it seemed designed to correct missteps in its predecessor. **(B+)**

HAN SOLO AND THE LOST LEGACY – FROM THE ADVENTURES OF LUKE SKYWALKER

(two years before *ANH*) by Brian Daley (September 1980)

SYNOPSIS: Han and Chewie meet up with an old smuggling acquaintance named Badure and are talked into accompanying him on a treasure hunt to recover the lost treasure of the infamous Xim the Despot, who ruled in the pre–Old Republic era.

REVIEW/NOTES: The third of the Han Solo books written by Brian Daley falls back into the same style as the first — a straightforward plot with practically no twists or turns. Even the main thrust of the story line isn't enough to keep the plot interesting.

Daley attempts to interweave a few side stories, such as a battle between two sauropteroids that pull ferries across a river, to provide a change of pace, but it serves as little more than a mild diversion. We are treated to a piece of *Star Wars* history, however, when we learn how Han got the scar on his chin. The return of Gallandro adds a little spice and the only real drama. We also see that Han is not the best sharpshooter in the galaxy, as he is outdrawn and almost killed.

Once more we have a female character who is initially put off by Han's arrogant demeanor but who slowly warms up to him and eventually falls hard. Thankfully, the story ends with the departure of Bollux and Blue Max, so readers aren't left wondering whatever happened to them. It would have been much more rewarding, however, if the ending had also tied in to events that led into *A New Hope,* such as setting up the spice smuggling job with Jabba. Of course, if Brian Daley had attempted to address this story line back in 1980 when this book was written (before *Return of the Jedi* came out), there would no doubt have been many continuity problems with facts revealed in the third movie. Perhaps it is best that Daley kept his three novels as isolated as possible from established events in the *Star Wars* universe, as it made A. C. Crispin's job of tying everything revealed to date about Han's past into one cohesive series of events a bit easier. It also left the story line of Han's ill-fated spice smuggling job to be told at a much later time when more facts surrounding it have been established and much more is known about the Hutts — Jabba in particular.

Of the three novels, this one is by far the weakest. None of them ever truly captures the right feel of the movies or the characters. On

the other hand, bearing in mind that this trilogy was written just prior to the release of *The Empire Strikes Back,* which is when Han's character was really developed, it isn't such a bad attempt to flesh out everyone's favorite scoundrel. **(C–)**

STAR WARS –
FROM THE ADVENTURES OF LUKE SKYWALKER

(recent printings have been retitled *Star Wars — A New Hope*) by George Lucas (with Alan Dean Foster) (December 1976)

SYNOPSIS: This is the novelization of the first film, *Star Wars Episode IV: A New Hope.*

REVIEW/NOTES: While containing many minor deviations from the movie (some of which create inconsistencies with facts stated in later novels), the novelization of the first film contains many interesting additions to the story line. The most notable is the prologue to the novel, stated as being an excerpt "from the First Saga: *Journal of the Whills,*" which gives a brief recounting of Palpatine's rise to power and creation of the Empire. It also mentions the Clone Wars and the extermination of the Jedi.

In the latest Special Edition printing of the novel, Lucas states in the foreword that the prologue is basically an outline for the new trilogy of prequels. It will be interesting to see how much the final movies resemble this passage. The novelization was written using the next-to-final version of the screenplay and therefore incorporates some scenes that were filmed but cut from the final film. Two of the most famous scenes are the early Tatooine sequences between Luke and Biggs Darklighter, and the Mos Eisley scene with Han and Jabba. Lucas was forced to add the Biggs and Luke scene by the people at Fox, who were getting concerned that the main character of the movie wasn't even introduced until twenty minutes into the film, but Lucas felt the scene came at an awkward point and disrupted the natural flow. Apparently he still felt this way twenty years later when producing the Special Edition of the first movie and opted to leave it out once again.

The Jabba scene, however, was cut because of budgetary constraints. Lucas was finally able to realize the scene in the Special Edition as he had originally envisioned it. The scene in the novelization, however, is slightly different in that Jabba is described as "a great mobile tub of muscle and suet topped by a shaggy scared skull" who speaks Basic instead of Huttese. Other differences between the movie and its novelization range from trivial items such as Luke's being Blue Five during the attack on the Death Star instead of Red Five as he was in the film to larger continuity goofs such as Blue Leader's recognizing Luke at the Rebel Base on Yavin's moon and stating that he met Luke's father once when he was a boy. How can Blue Leader know who Luke's father was if Vader himself didn't find out that Luke was his son until after *A New Hope*?). The Special Edition has also created a few more minor changes to the *Star Wars* universe as portrayed by the novels, such as the slightly different scene where Greedo confronts Han in the cantina. The novelization is worth reading primarily for its historical significance in that it was the first piece of *Star Wars* merchandise released and has a very different feel to it than many of the novels to come later. **(A−)**

HAN SOLO TRILOGY:
BOOK 3 − REBEL DAWN

(three years before *ANH* to during *ANH*) by A. C. Crispin (March 1998)

SYNOPSIS: Among his other adventures in this novel, Han wins the *Millennium Falcon* from Lando and gets on the wrong side of Jabba the Hutt when he is forced to betray him.

REVIEW/NOTES: A. C. Crispin delivers an incredible wrap-up to her Han Solo trilogy that brings us within seconds of Han's fateful meeting with Luke and Obi-Wan — a meeting that would change his life forever.

The final pieces of Han's life before *A New Hope* fall into place with this story — the first of which is how Han won the *Falcon* from Lando. Until now, most people have assumed that this was the act that drove a wedge in Han and Lando's friendship, but Crispin shows that this was not the case. The fact that Crispin chose otherwise allowed her to use Lando throughout the entire novel instead

of effectively writing him out early in the story, not to make contact with Han again until *The Empire Strikes Back*. The intervening scenes between Han and Lando — from the time Han gets the *Falcon* until their falling out — help develop their friendship even further and make their falling out and eventual reconciliation all the more believable.

Another character who is developed beautifully is Boba Fett, who makes numerous appearances and crosses paths with both Lando and Han more than once. Their interaction serves to give the reader a better understanding of the "relationship" between the three characters during *The Empire Strikes Back* four years later. This is also the first novel or short story to reaffirm Fett's true identity as Jaster Mereel, former Journeyman Protector as disclosed in "The Last One Standing: The tale of Boba Fett." In fact, the bizarre moral code of ethics by which Fett operates is utilized to its fullest in this novel as he continues to surprise the others — who know him only as a ruthless bounty hunter — with his actions.

We're also given some background on Chewbacca, whose family life is revealed in detail. Throughout the novel, Han and Chewie seem to make trips to Kashyyyk at least once a year, which, if kept up, explains how Chewie was able to reconcile his life debt to Han with his responsibilities to his family. Crispin also utilizes the method of conveying the Wookiee language in plain English first used by Michael P. Kube-McDowell in "Tyrant's Test," albeit only for a few sentences. Still, for the most part we are left with only a third-person account of what Chewie has said, or we have to figure it out on our own based on Han's responses.

The story line concerning Bria and the slave camp on Ylesia expertly comes to an end and serves to make the three books, which span a period of more than ten years, come together as one solid trilogy. Crispin also nicely weaves the original Han Solo trilogy of novels by Brian Daley into this novel by having Han and Chewie disappear to the Corporate Sector for about a year while the narrative shifts to Bria and Lando. Crispin wisely interjects short accounts of Han's activities that occur at the finish of each of Daley's novels, further integrating them into the larger story line of her novel. Bria is also directly involved in transmitting the plans for the Death Star to Princess Leia on the *Tantive IV*, a scene that occurs before the opening of *A New Hope* but that is detailed in the third episode of the *Star Wars* National Public Radio drama, which gives her death in the process a lot more weight. The account of the procurement of the plans, however, conflicts with "Dark Forces: Soldier for the Empire."

With her three books, Crispin has managed to do the seemingly impossible and seamlessly pull together all the fragments told about Han's past from every movie, book, comic book, and short story while at the same time remaining completely fresh and original and telling a hell of a story. She has rapidly risen to be one of the *Star Wars* continuity experts and one hopes she will get a chance to further showcase her literary talents with another *Star Wars* novel in the future. **(A+)**

"COMMAND DECISION"

(from *The Official Star Wars Adventure Journal*, vol. 1 no. 11) (shortly after *ANH*) by Timothy Zahn (November 1996)

SYNOPSIS: A continuing look at the rise of Thrawn and his role within the Empire.

REVIEW/NOTES: This story shows us another exciting chapter in Thrawn's early career. We also finally get a better idea about why the Emperor had banished Thrawn to the Outer Rim when he is one of the best military leaders in the fleet.

What we are led to believe is that the Emperor felt that Thrawn's powers of deductive reasoning and his uncanny ability to figure out an adversary's true motivations through a series of assumptions would best serve the Empire by exploring and conquering the Rim worlds. It always appeared as though the Emperor showed a strong lapse of judgment in assigning Thrawn so far away from the Core, but now we see that he had a much better reason. One of the best things about Thrawn is his style of leadership. It is refreshing to see that not all Imperial commanders are driven by greed and power and that some, like Thrawn, actually put a value on their troops

instead of thinking of them as expendable. Parck has obviously not regretted his decision to bring Thrawn into the Empire, as his loyalty to the admiral has no bounds. **(A−)**

SPLINTER OF THE MIND'S EYE −
FROM THE ADVENTURES OF LUKE SKYWALKER

(shortly after *ANH*) by Alan Dean Foster (February 1978)

SYNOPSIS: When Luke, Leia, and the droids are forced to land on Circarpous V to make repairs while en route to Circarpous IV, Luke finds himself on a quest for the Kaiburr Crystal, which supposedly increases one's perception of the Force to powerful levels.

REVIEW/NOTES: The story line in this novel is both fast-paced and exciting. It makes use of certain parts of earlier drafts of the first movie's screenplay in which Lucas incorporated the Kaiburr Crystal as a focal point for the Force. While the actual story line is a great read, it contradicts the movies in numerous ways. The most important contradiction to the movies is Luke's ability to control the Force. In the novel, Luke is able to levitate large objects and seems to have mastered the lightsaber. In *The Empire Strikes Back* he has trouble even levitating his lightsaber while trapped by the Wampa on Hoth.

The other major deviation is that Luke confronts Vader — and defeats him, slicing his arm off in the process! Although it is never explicitly stated, it is obvious in *The Empire Strikes Back* that Lucas intended this to be Luke and Vader's first meeting and Luke is obviously the weaker opponent in their duel. Ignoring these facts, the story is very entertaining and it would be a shame to discount it as noncanonical because of these inconsistencies. The fact that Dark Horse (whose stories to date are all considered canon) recently published a comic book adaptation of the novel (with all of its inconsistencies intact) further presses the issue that the story should be incorporated into the current *Star Wars* universe in some manner. It would also be very interesting for another author (or even Alan Dean Foster himself) to bring back Halla and the Kaiburr Crystal in order to look further into the Crystal's origins and its powers. **(A)**

THE EMPIRE STRIKES BACK

(three years after *ANH*) by Donald F. Glut (May 1980)

SYNOPSIS: This is the novelization of the second film, *Star Wars Episode V: The Empire Strikes Back.*

REVIEW/NOTES: The novelization of the second film has very little more to offer than the movie. Unlike the novelizations of the other two movies, there are no scenes cut from the movie but included in the book, nor are there any real expansions on scenes that give new information not obtained from viewing the movie. While the writing style is adequate, it is basically nothing more than a straight novelization. **(C)**

"THE EMPEROR'S TROPHY"

(from *Star Wars Galaxy* magazine, issue 11) (immediately after *TESB*) by Peter Schweighofer (May 1997)

SYNOPSIS: Vader brings Luke's recovered severed hand and lightsaber to the Emperor, who thinks of the items as trophies, but Vader is reminded of the loss of his own hand. As the Emperor prepares to further the plans to construct a second Death Star, Vader has his own plans to deal with a potential conflict with Prince Xizor.

REVIEW/NOTES: This short story clears up a lingering plot thread from Timothy Zahn's trilogy regarding how Luke's hand and lightsaber ever made it into the possession of Jorus C'Boath. The real highlight of the story, however, is that the growing conflict within Vader concerning his son is so well played upon. It is rare that Vader features in a *Star Wars* story at all, but it is rarer still that we are made privy to his private and personal thoughts. More authors should be encouraged to write short stories such as this that fill in little holes in the tapestry of stories woven through the different mediums. The story is incredibly short, yet it manages to tie together plotlines from *The Empire Strikes Back, Shadows of the Empire, Return of the Jedi,* and the Timothy Zahn trilogy in such a simple manner that we end up feeling as if we were let in on what was, until this point, a big secret. **(A)**

THE FICTION GUIDE

SHADOWS OF THE EMPIRE

(during TESB and shortly thereafter) by Steve Perry (May 1996)

SYNOPSIS: As the search for Han continues, Darth Vader meets with Prince Xizor but is ignorant of Xizor's desire for vengeance. His devised plan of revenge is to kill Luke and make it look like Vader's doing.

Luke and company find themselves pawns in a political battle between Vader and Xizor that concludes just prior to the events of *Return of the Jedi.*

REVIEW/NOTES: *Shadows of the Empire* was preceded by an intensive marketing campaign stressing the multimedia aspect of the story. We were given a novel, a comic book, and a Nintendo game (later also released as a computer game) as the main storytelling mechanisms; however, with all of the buildup it was hard not to be a little disappointed with the final product.

The story itself is very well written and the new villain of the story, Prince Xizor, is an interesting and multifaceted character. His schemes against Vader and his attempts to make himself second in power to the Emperor evoke a completely new side of Vader. The new hero, Dash Rendar, however, is nothing but a clone of Han Solo and seems to be there only because, owing to the setting of the story, Han cannot be. The most interesting parts are those that expand on things that we saw in *Return of the Jedi.* Author Steve Perry obviously loved being able to use Darth Vader in his novel, owing to the time it is set in, something that few other authors have been able to do. He makes good use of the Dark Lord and gives us an interesting look into Vader's perception of his relationship with the Emperor. The threat to him posed by Xizor isn't one that he can eliminate with sheer power or even through the use of the Force. Vader is forced to go behind the Emperor's back to deal with Xizor, which helps show that Vader is not completely under the Emperor's control and foreshadows his eventual betrayal of the Emperor at the end of *Return of the Jedi.*

On the flip side we see that the Emperor is far from completely honest with Vader and prefers to keep the Dark Lord on his toes. We see right in the opening of the book that Vader is not privy to all that goes on where the Emperor is concerned. Perry also gives us a Luke who is still impulsive and quick to anger, unlike the melancholy Jedi Master who is always in full command of the Force whom we see in all of the later novels. This allows Luke to be a much more interesting character because you are never sure exactly how he is going to deal with a situation.

The main thing lacking in the novel is Boba Fett, who plays only a very minor role. The comic book adaptation, on the other hand, uses Fett and his bounty hunter rivals to a great extent. Another exclusion from the novel version of *Shadows* is Dash's ultimate fate. All of the versions of *Shadows* also leave the fate of Xizor shrouded in ambiguity. **(A−)**

RETURN OF THE JEDI

(one year after TESB — shortly after the events in *Shadows of the Empire*) by James Kahn (June 1983)

SYNOPSIS: This is the novelization of the third film, *Star Wars Episode VI: Return of the Jedi.*

REVIEW/NOTES: This novelization does not add as much to the story as the novel form of *A New Hope* did, but it adds much more than the novelization of *The Empire Strikes Back.* The main example is the scene in which Ben tells Luke how his father, Anakin, became Darth Vader. We are also given a short explanation of the Battle of Taanab that Lando cites in the film as the reason he was given the rank of general in the Rebel Alliance.

Also included here (as in the novelization of the first movie) is a scene cut from the film — the Tatooine desert sandstorm that takes place right after Jabba is killed. With the new additions come a few inconsistencies, such as the statement that Han had been frozen in carbonite for a six-month period, when it had been previously established in *Shadows of the Empire* that it was closer to a year. **(C)**

THE TRUCE AT BAKURA

(immediately after *ROTJ*) by Kathy Tyers (January 1994)

SYNOPSIS: Luke leads a small fleet to help the Bakurans and Imperial forces in the sector defend themselves against the invading alien race, which has developed a means of transferring a human's life force into the body of a droid.

REVIEW/NOTES: While there is nothing particularly wrong with this book, there is little to keep one enthralled with it. The overall plot concerning the truce that the Imperials are forced to make with the Alliance is not nearly as dramatic as it would have been if this book were set before the Emperor had died. It would have been more effective had the Imperials been in combat with the Alliance when the Ssi-ruuk attacked them both, putting them in a situation where they had to make a hasty truce or both would be destroyed.

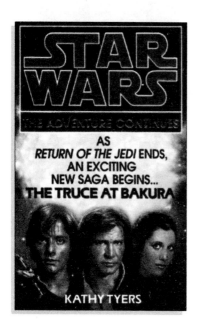

The fact that the story takes place the day after the celebrations at the end of *Return of the Jedi* leaves one hoping that it will deal a lot with the aftermath of the Rebel victory: what the costs were, where the Alliance must go from there, and so on. Instead, we are given a few brief scenes on Endor and then we are thrown right into the situation on Bakura, which is on the other side of the galaxy. In effect, the story is extremely anticlimactic.

The one scene that makes the book worth the read, however, is when the ghostly image of Anakin Skywalker appears to Leia.

The character of Imperial Commander Thannus is extremely well developed. Imperials are much more interesting when they are portrayed as realistic individuals instead of the more common power-mad megalomaniac villains.

The Ssi-ruuk are an extremely two-dimensional race of aliens bent on conquest and domination and their entenchment process is the only thing threatening about them. The scenes in which Luke touches the human mind inside one of the battle droids is very chilling and manages to portray a real feeling of loss and captivity experienced by the individual undergoing the entenchment, bearing some similarity to the assimilation process of the Borg, an alien adversary in the *Star Trek* universe. Dev Sibwarra is supposed to be portrayed as a sympathetic character, but he comes across merely as a pathetic, simpleminded fool.

If this story had been set either much earlier or much later in the *Star Wars* time line it would most likely have been a much better read. It never comes close to living up to the preceding dramatic and emotional resolution of the Luke/Vader father/son plotline in *Return of the Jedi*. **(C–)**

"A BARVE LIKE THAT: THE TALE OF BOBA FETT"

(from *Tales from Jabba's Palace*) (immediately after *ROTJ* and one year after *ROTJ*, with flashbacks between *TESB* and *ROTJ*) by J. D. Montgomery (January 1996)

SYNOPSIS: Boba Fett awakens to find himself in the belly of the Sarlacc that swallowed him in *Return of the Jedi*. There he is tortured by a being named Susejo. Fett ultimately escapes and returns periodically to torment both the Sarlacc and Susejo.

REVIEW/NOTES: Finally, the story of how Boba Fett escapes from the Sarlacc is told. After his surprise appearance in the *Dark Empire* comic book series by Dark Horse, fans were left to speculate about how their favorite bounty hunter escaped his fate. J. D. Montgomery does a great job in portraying a Fett who is, for once, not at all in control of the situation.

Throughout all of Susejo's attempts to break him, however, Fett singlemindedly plots his escape and refuses to let the visions deter him, although those same flashbacks allow the reader to get a real handle on the character.

This story was a long time coming but definitely ends up being worth the wait. **(A)**

THE COURTSHIP OF PRINCESS LEIA

(four years after *ROTJ*) by Dave Wolverton (May 1994)

SYNOPSIS: Leia finds her feelings torn between Han and Prince Isolder from the rich and powerful Hapes Cluster. But it doesn't take more than an intergalactic adventure for Leia to realize that there's only one scoundrel for her.

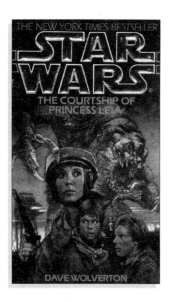

REVIEW/NOTES: Dave Wolverton deserves praise for successfully capturing the personalities of the characters better than many of the other writers, especially in his portrayal of Han, as he achieves the proper balance of flippancy and seriousness when Han deals with situations. Some fans might be put off by Leia's near betrayal of Han when she suddenly falls out of love with him and begins developing feelings for Isolder, but this kind of thing occasionally happens in the real world. Truth be told, we don't exactly know what their day-to-day life has been in the years in between. There must have been some reason that they waited four years to get married. Perhaps they both needed some form of confirmation about their love for each other before making it permanent.

Isodler is an interesting character because he isn't the arrogant show-off that Han initially believes him to be. Luckily, Leia makes the right choice and Isolder conveniently falls in love with Tenenial, which allows Han and him to become friends.

The Luke we see portrayed in the novel is still gaining confidence in his Jedi powers and has not yet reached the stoic Jedi Master level that he achieves in later stories (and, thus, still remains an interesting character).

A few things in the novel, however, are a bit curious. This one is minor: Why, when Luke listens to the recording of Yoda from a few decades ago, does Yoda speak like a normal person instead of in the odd manner we are used to from the movies? Did he purposely start speaking like this afterward when he went into hiding to further prevent people from realizing that he is a great Jedi Master? Maybe he was getting a bit senile in his old age.

In the end, this book is a very good read and, thankfully, ends before we are subjected to reading the play-by-play of Han and Leia's wedding ceremony. **(B)**

HEIR TO THE EMPIRE
(five years after *ROTJ*) by Timothy Zahn (June 1991)

SYNOPSIS: Grand Admiral Thrawn has begun preparations for a master plan to wipe out the Rebellion for good. Luke must deal with the hateful Mara, who seeks vengeance against him for ruining her life. Thrawn is temporarily forced to retreat, though everyone is startled to learn that Admiral Ackbar has been arrested and charged with treason.

REVIEW/NOTES: *Heir to the Empire* marked the end of what seemed like an eternity since an original *Star Wars* novel had been released (even though it was only eight years). Just when the flame of *Star Wars* fandom seemed to be smoldering out, the novel came out of nowhere and became an instant best-seller. Not only was *Star Wars* back, but it was back with style.

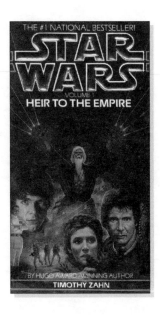

Zahn's trilogy showed the utmost respect for the movies and the intricate back story that George Lucas had hinted at throughout them. The story line he wove wasn't merely a run-of-the-mill science fiction story that could have been told with any set of characters and had the *Star Wars* logo slapped on the cover. Instead, we are reacquainted with all the familiar faces we knew and loved, interacting with the same personalities we saw in the movies, and we're introduced to a bevy of new exciting characters who have since become just as popular among fans.

The first and most enthralling of these new characters is Grand Admiral Thrawn. Thrawn is the complete opposite of Darth Vader, relying on his tactical genius instead of his position of power to wage his campaign against the Rebellion. His fairness toward his crew and his respect for Captain Pellaeon actually cause the reader to root for him at times. Even though he is committed to the utter destruction of the Rebellion, he comes across as amoral rather than immoral, resulting in a bit of begrudging respect for him.

Also introduced is Talon Karrde. Instead of replacing Jabba with just a slight variation of the greedy immoral crime boss, Zahn gives us another sympathetic character that we can sink our teeth into. Karrde is primarily out to better his own position and that of his employees; however, he realizes that from a moral standpoint the Empire has to be stopped and quickly allies himself with the Rebellion. Mara Jade is another intriguing character who goes through a major reevaluation of her past, present, and future in the trilogy. She has to

come to terms with the fact that her previous life as the Emperor's Hand is over and she must decide whether she should let go of it and begin to make a better life with the Alliance. Luke proves that he has the makings of a true Jedi Master as he shows an incredible amount of patience with this woman who repeatedly tells him that she is going to kill him.

Zahn approaches Luke in the series in a very delicate manner, not wanting him to get out of every predicament he is thrown into by using the Force, a crutch that many subsequent writers seem to rely on. As various other novels have shown, the more powerful Luke is, the less interesting his character becomes. The Jedi Master Jorus C'Boath is an extremely fun character, especially during those numerous points where his insanity comes to the forefront.

The first book of the trilogy wastes no time in plunging right into the action. We are kept in the dark about the full scope of Thrawn's plans, as we are given, instead, an effective slow reveal. One of Zahn's greatest skills as a writer is his ability to give all the main *Star Wars* characters (plus his originals) a fairly equal share of the story line without forcing any of them to take on roles that betray their established personalities for the sake of furthering the narrative. The reader never doubts that these are the same people as in the movie trilogy. **(A+)**

DARK FORCE RISING

(five years after *ROTJ*) by Timothy Zahn (June 1992)

SYNOPSIS: Thrawn makes his next move and appears to be unstoppable once Luke discovers that he has obtained cloning cylinders and is planning on creating the galaxy's ultimate army.

REVIEW/NOTES: The middle act of the trilogy works well to build up the tension for the climactic final act. The Noghri, who appeared to be nothing but ruthless killers in the first novel, are revealed to be a very honorable race with a tragic history. We also begin to understand just how insane C'Boath is as he teaches Luke the ways of the Force based on his own twisted perspective. At times, Luke comes across as a bit dense: he accepts C'Boath's tutelage even though the mad Jedi exhibits far more traits of the dark side than the light.

The character of Fey'lya is a great addition created by Zahn. The character is utterly despicable yet has the ability to use his master skills as a politician to maneuver his way into a very powerful spot in the New Republic.

Zahn comes into his own with this installment by capturing the real personalities of all the familiar characters from the movies. They have undergone a logical progression from their development at the end of the movie trilogy to where we would expect them to be five years later. It is very easy to imagine that Zahn's trilogy is actually a sequel to the movies themselves instead of just a story using the same characters. Indeed, it was the ease with which readers were able to refamiliarize themselves with their favorite characters through these novels that caused the incredible resurgence of interest in the movies over the past number of years.

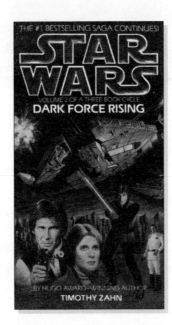

Zahn also fleshes out the personalities of minor characters from the movie trilogy, such as Admiral Ackbar and Mon Mothma, who take on roles of considerable importance in the novels and comics. The new characters introduced all turn out to be incredibly successful, with no exceptions, primarily because he creates characters who are neither good nor evil but exist in a state of gray. Prime examples are Karrde and Thrawn, the former being a smuggler with a conscience, while the latter is an enemy with a strong sense of honor and a lack of malice.

The final revelation about the use of clones in Thrawn's plot will whet the appetite of all *Star Wars* fans who have had their curiosity piqued by the mention of the Clone Wars throughout the movie

trilogy. At the close of the second novel, Thrawn has his fleet and his army and is poised to attack the New Republic, while C'Boath has his own plans involving Luke nearing fruition. Not bad for a cliffhanger! **(A+)**

THE LAST COMMAND

(five years after *ROTJ*) by Timothy Zahn (May 1993)

SYNOPSIS: Thrawn's final assault on the Alliance is intermixed with Leia giving birth to twins; Luke battling his own clone, generated from DNA taken from his severed hand on Bespin; Mara's changing allegiance; and the truth about C'Boath.

REVIEW/NOTES: The final book in the trilogy neatly ties all the threads together more seamlessly than *Return of the Jedi* did the films.

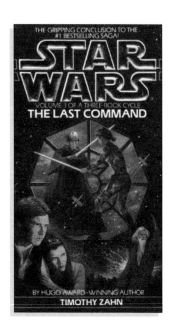

C'Boath shines in this final installment as he sheds any pretense of being sane, and the revelation of his being a clone of the original Jedi Master Jorus C'Boath is set up well. However, Zahn's original idea of C'Boath's being an insane clone of Obi-Wan would have been infinitely more entertaining — it's a pity Lucas nixed the idea at an early stage. One hopes that nothing Zahn described in the cloning process using the spaarti cylinders will be contradicted by the new movies, but with the increasing amount of information that has been provided in novels and comic books about the time period in which the next movie trilogy will take place, it seems inevitable that many things will be contradicted.

Mara also comes to the front in this novel as she proves how much potential she has in the Force by defeating both the clone of Luke (annoyingly referred to as "Luuke" in the book) and C'Boath. Unfortunately, Mara's use in future novels has, for the most part, been wasted and very little is ever done with her Jedi abilities.

The only real disappointment in the novel is the ease with which Thrawn is dispatched, although the fact that such a powerful leader went out with a whimper instead of a bang makes the story all the more realistic. The new two-part *Hand of Thrawn* story by

Zahn (*Specter of the Past* and *Vision of the Future*) deals with an imposter Thrawn. Unfortunately, Zahn has sworn that Thrawn will not turn out to be alive, as this is too much like an overused soap opera trick and is a bit insulting to the reader. Most readers would no doubt forgive him for such a "cheap" trick if it meant reading more about the character. **(A)**

THE JEDI ACADEMY TRILOGY:
VOLUME 1 – JEDI SEARCH

(seven years after *ROTJ*) by Kevin J. Anderson (March 1994)

SYNOPSIS: Han and Chewie, acting as ambassadors for the New Republic, travel to Kessel and find themselves prisoners. At the same time, Luke is trying to find candidates for a Jedi Academy he wants to start. In between all this they discover that the creator of the Death Star has also developed the Sun Crusher, which can cause a sun to go supernova, essentially destroying an entire star system at one time.

REVIEW/NOTES: Kevin J. Anderson is one of the driving forces behind helping the multitude of *Star Wars* tales spun in a variety of formats by different authors fit more coherently into a single universe.

By setting this trilogy immediately after the Dark Horse comic trilogy "Dark Empire," "Dark Empire II," and "Empire's End," Anderson smoothes out the continuity between the comics and Timothy Zahn's trilogy that preceded it. Despite the perception that paperbacks are less prestigious than hardcovers, these novels mark a major turning point in the lives of many of the characters. Luke makes his progression from Jedi Knight to Jedi Master, Leia replaces Mon Mothma as chief of state of the New Republic, Wedge gives up being captain of Rogue Squadron for a promotion to general, Talon Karrde has retired from the smuggling business, and for better or for worse, Han and Leia's children start taking a more active role in the story lines.

The tone of Anderson's writing is more akin to the over-the-top

style of a comic book or Saturday morning serial than the more serious and intricate plotlines of Timothy Zahn or Michael Stackpole; however, this is no less a proper *Star Wars* tale. The best thing about the *Star Wars* universe is that both styles can coexist harmoniously, since the movie trilogy itself is a blending of the two different styles.

Anderson fleshes out many of the planets and races mentioned or seen briefly in the movies.

The other main plotline in the book running concurrently with Han and Chewie's problems on Kessel is that of Luke's quest to find Jedi disciples to teach. The choice of Yavin 4 for the site of the Jedi Academy was a nice touch by Anderson, retaining a connection with the movie trilogy as Luke returns to the place where he first joined up with the Rebellion and solidified the new path his life was to take.

The introduction of Admiral Daala is a much-needed asset to the novels. Much like Thrawn before her, Daala is completely dedicated to the Emperor's New Order and is above personal desires of greed or power. Unlike Thrawn, however, she is extremely ill-tempered and her actions are often dictated by rage instead of well-thought-out tactical planning. Her past love affair with Grand Moff Tarkin, her mentor, is yet another strong tie to the movie trilogy. Anderson recognized the lack of female superiors in the Empire and took advantage of this by creating such a powerful leader as Daala (something that was repeated by Michael Stackpole in creating Yssane Issard in the *X-Wing* novels). She proves to be a worthy adversary to the New Republic.

Anderson also delves into the planning and testing of the Death Star and explains how this was pulled off with such secrecy that the Rebellion learned of it only shortly before it became operational. Overall, Anderson's writing style is easy to warm up to and he unfolds the plot in a successfully unrelenting manner — more than enough to engage one's interest in the remaining books of the trilogy. **(A)**

THE JEDI ACADEMY TRILOGY:
VOLUME 2 — DARK APPRENTICE

(seven years after *ROTJ*) by Kevin J. Anderson (July 1994)

SYNOPSIS: Admiral Ackbar is ready to resign following a devastating accident that, unbeknownst to him, was the result of sabotage. Meanwhile, Luke has begun training students in the way of the Force and comes up against an apprentice, Kyp, who immerses himself in the dark side and plummets Luke into a coma.

REVIEW/NOTES: This plotline of the novel tends to move a bit slowly as we are subjected to quote after quote from Yoda (by the end of the trilogy, the "There is no try — do or do not" line may actually have replaced "I've got a bad feeling about this" as the most often quoted line from the movies). The monotony starts to break once Kyp discovers the spirit of Exar Kun and begins his dark descent.

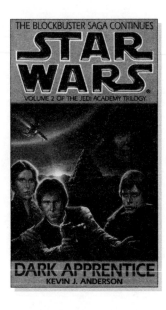

Anderson cleverly uses the character of Exar Kun to tie the novel in with the "Tales of the Jedi — Dark Lords of the Sith" and "Tales of the Jedi — The Sith War" comic series he scripted (along with Tom Veitch). Since the first issue of "Dark Lords of the Sith" was released at the same time as this novel, our real introduction to Exar Kun is as the spiritual embodiment of the dark side portrayed in the novel. The comic series, however, shows many parallels between Kun's path and that which Kyp is headed on in the novel. Both were strong students in the Force who felt that their powers grew to be greater than those of their Jedi Masters. Kun ended up killing his master and succumbing to the dark side of the Force. Kun's fate shows what will happen to Kyp if he continues along the path he has begun to walk.

Kyp's progression to the dark side dominates the majority of the novel, although Anderson does interject many subplots into the story line in order to mix things up. The true standout is the sabacc game Han and Lando play, with the *Falcon* once again at stake. This time, however, Lando comes out the victor (luckily for Han, however, he eventually wins it back). The trilogy is also filled with various relationships developing between the characters —

some interesting (Lando and Mara) and some bizarre (Ackbar and Winter). The one that contributes the most to the plotline is the budding relationship between Wedge Antilles and Qwi Xux. It's good to see Wedge finally finding someone (he and Luke are the two most eligible bachelors in the series, seeming to prefer to remain celibate), and it gives Wedge more to do than just show up in a battle scene commanding Rogue Squadron and then quietly disappear afterward. Their relationship also provides the basis for a great feeling of tension between Wedge and, first, the New Republic, then Kyp after Kyp forcibly extracts the knowledge of the Sun Crusher from Qwi's mind.

The novel ends with more of a cliff-hanger than the first, but it basically serves as a buildup for the climax, leaving a lot of pressure on the final novel to deliver. **(B-)**

THE JEDI ACADEMY TRILOGY:
VOLUME 3 – CHAMPIONS OF THE FORCE

(seven years after *ROTJ*) by Kevin J. Anderson (October 1994)

SYNOPSIS: Luke's students play a major role in thwarting the mounting threats, which now include a new prototype Death Star, while Kyp struggles between the light and dark sides of the Force.

REVIEW/NOTES: The final chapter in the *Jedi Academy* trilogy succeeds in justifying the somewhat drawn-out buildup of the first two novels by being packed with cover-to-cover action. As it starts out, we see that Kyp has not yet fully fallen to the dark side, and the scene in which Kyp fails to save his brother and watches as he is disintegrated by the force of the exploding sun is by far one of the most powerful in any *Star Wars* novel.

The defeat of Kun by the Jedi students is somewhat disappointing. The "champions of the Force" theme is a bit trite and serves to further the belief that anything is possible in the Force if the individuals can open themselves to it sufficiently. While this plays upon the spiritual side of the Force and provides a good "moral" for the story, it lacks drama and provides an easy resolution to a difficult problem. While Timothy Zahn approached the Force as an obstacle to generating true drama and eliminated it with the ysalimiri, the subject of Anderson's trilogy forces him to deal with it head-on. Anderson goes overboard in the other direction by making the Force an even greater source of power than ever before.

Many have criticized Anderson's use of the Death Star in the novel as unimaginative, but it is realistic that the Empire would continue to try to use such a weapon, especially since it was only Luke's connection with the Force that allowed him to fire the shot that destroyed the original one. The only thing unbelievable was that they never fixed the one major weakness in the station's design when they built the second one, which was destroyed at the end of *Return of the Jedi* in much the same manner. Thankfully, Anderson does not subject the Death Star prototype to a carefully aimed destructive shot from an X-Wing and instead comes up with a new way to destroy a Death Star — shove it into a black hole! The only irritating thing about this Death Star is the group of inane Imperials commanding it who are useless when their operations manual does not cover every potential situation that they will encounter. Anderson is obviously trying to make a comedic comment about upper management in an organization; however, the timing in the novel detracts from the dramatic tension being built up in the finale.

Kyp's redemption at the end is believable, as he never seemed to give in fully to the dark side in the first place. It seems that one piece of advice Yoda gave Luke in *The Empire Strikes Back* was far from accurate, when he told him that once you start down the path to the dark side it will forever dominate you.

Looking at Anderson's trilogy as a whole, it is definitely an en-

tertaining read but not nearly as deep as Zahn's trilogy or Stackpole's *X-Wing* novels. Much as Zahn set the stage for future novels with his trilogy by reintroducing us to the characters in a completely new setting, Anderson has ushered in a new direction for the subsequent stories to take by making drastic changes in the lives of certain characters. With a few notable exceptions, the novels that have come after this trilogy have successfully furthered the themes established by Anderson, Zahn, and the various comic series by Dark Horse. **(A−)**

I, JEDI

(seven years after *ROTJ*) by Michael A. Stackpole (May 1998)

SYNOPSIS: Desperate to rescue his kidnapped wife, Mirax, from the Empire, Corran Horn infiltrates a pirate vessel and gradually moves up the ranks to get into a position where he can actually do something.

REVIEW/NOTES: Michael Stackpole takes on the nearly impossible task of writing a full-length *Star Wars* novel from a first-person perspective — something that had previously not been done (although there have been numerous short stories using the first-person perspective). The trick is to somehow maintain the reader's interest in the story line without having the luxury of jumping around between characters and settings to keep things fresh. Luckily, Stackpole did such a great job developing Corran Horn throughout the first four *X-Wing* novels (in fact, the majority of those novels were told from Corran's perspective) that Corran makes the perfect candidate to attempt such a feat with.

The final product comes out a winner. It does take a bit of getting used to at first, as the story line makes many dramatic stylistic changes throughout to keep it fresh and exciting. The first phase of the novel is the Jedi training sequences, which are concurrent with the events in Kevin J. Anderson's *Jedi Academy* trilogy. The motivation for getting Corran to accept Luke's offer to train him, which he had previously declined, is a bit weak. Mirax's predicament of being trapped in stasis conveniently allows Corran to run off and train for

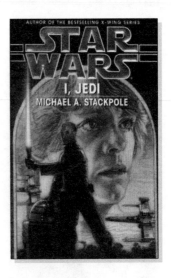

a few months before being pressed into action, but this never comes off as more than a contrived plot device.

The next phase of the novel comes when Corran infiltrates the fighter squadron of pilots in order to work his way onboard the star destroyer *Invidious*. This is a slow process that takes a number of months, but it allows us to see the Corran Horn we have come to know from the *X-Wing* novels in his element once again. The over-riding theme of the novel is a journey of discovery for Corran. He goes through many changes before finally discovering exactly who he is and who he was meant to become.

Stackpole has obviously worked closely with Timothy Zahn while writing the novel in order to incorporate a lot of crossovers to Zahn's *Specter of the Past* and *Vision of the Future* novels in an attempt to create more bridges of continuity. The most notable example is the inclusion of a Caamasi character, a race that plays an important role in Zahn's novels. While *I, Jedi* doesn't consistently reach excellence from cover to cover, Stackpole should be praised for successfully pushing the envelope of the standard *Star Wars* format and spinning yet another highly entertaining yarn at the same time. **(A)**

CHILDREN OF THE JEDI

(eight years after *ROTJ*) by Barbara Hambly (May 1995)

SYNOPSIS: Luke and two of his students — Cray Mingela and Nichos Marr — encounter the *Eye of Palpatine*, a warship disguised as an asteroid and designed to take prisoners and brainwash them into believing they're stormtroopers. Once onboard, Luke comes into contact with an entity within the ship's computer, a Jedi named Callista.

REVIEW/NOTES: Barbara Hambly is a very talented writer, but her writing style does not seem to fit the *Star Wars* universe. While doing justice to and showing us a previously unseen side of Luke, her portrayal of the other major characters is very weak, and the overall plotline is so far removed from the typical *Star Wars* story that it accentuates their uncharacteristic behaviors.

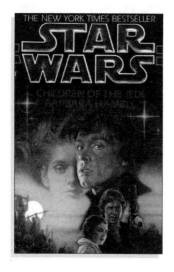

The main thrust of the story — dealing with a huge warship created by the Emperor that was programmed to pick up troops stationed on backwater planets for a devastating sneak attack — is a bit unrealistic. The Emperor never seemed to have a problem with building the Imperial fleet in the public's eye before. In fact, his reign of terror depended on having the fleet visible in order to deter Rebel uprisings. Therefore the plotline exists primarily to contrive a means of trapping Luke alone on a ship, and the notion that this ship is headed to destroy a planet where Han and Leia are is improbable at best.

Hambly also feels the need to make the story seem more "otherworldly" by using alien names for things, like topatoes (instead of potatoes) and coffienne (instead of coffee). Coffienne has been used before in the Lando novels, but at least they were written at a time when the novels weren't so seriously considered part of the *Star Wars* universe. Instead of making it seem more alien or futuristic, it brings back bad memories of seventies sci-fi shows that used to go crazy doing the same thing (remember the "microns" and "centons" in *Battlestar Galactica*?!).

At least the author can be credited with finally proving that Luke is interested in having some semblance of a sex life by creating a worthy love interest for him and not writing her off at the end (well, at least not at the end of *this* novel . . .). **(D–)**

DARKSABER

(eight years after *ROTJ*, with flashbacks shortly before *ANH*) by Kevin J. Anderson (November 1995)

SYNOPSIS: While Luke and Han are enroute to finding the spirit of Obi-Wan Kenobi on Tatooine, in the hope he will be able to return to Callista, now in human form, the power of the Jedi, they learn that the criminal Hutts are constructing a new Death Star named Darksaber. At the same time, Admiral Daala returns with a plan to destroy the Jedi Knights.

REVIEW/NOTES: Once again Kevin J. Anderson delivers a fast-paced, over-the-top tale that makes a quick, easy read. Unfortunately, this time out he strays a little more toward the comedic side by having many tongue-in-cheek scenes such as the flashbacks of the Emperor executing a character named Lemelisk each time he fails him, only to resurrect him in a clone body to serve him again. Fortunately, Anderson offsets the less than serious aspects of the book with some startlingly dramatic plotlines, most notably the return of not only Admiral Daala, still hell-bent on destroying the New Republic, but also Pellaeon from Timothy Zahn's trilogy.

The most dramatic part of the book by far is the surprising death of General Madine. Never a major player in the *Star Wars* universe, Madine did, however, have the honor of being immortalized as an action figure and therefore taking on the status of a noteworthy character. His death was a nice touch of realism, since so few of the "good guys" ever get killed in the novels. That speck of realism, however, is marred by a multitude of completely ludicrous scenes in the novel. First off, with all we have been told about the cloning process in the past novels and comic books, it seems that only a powerful Jedi would be able to transfer his or her "spirit" into a cloned body the way the Emperor did after his apparent death near Endor. How is it then that Lemelisk is able to do the same not once but a number of times?

There are also minor annoyances, particularly anticlimactic plot resolutions, such as when the Darksaber falls apart because of shoddy workmanship when it is supposed to take out the New Republic fleet. Anderson also goes too far in trying to utilize all of the information he compiled and created for some of the planets in the galaxy in his *The Illustrated Star Wars Universe* book, squeezing in a trip to just about every one of them while Luke attempts to reawaken Callista's connection to the Force. At first it seems like a nice touch, but after the story takes us to four different planets, the plot device seems too contrived.

Anderson also goes overboard in the magnitude of power in the Force that the students end up tapping into. Continuing his idea that if he can't avoid using the Force as a main part of the story line, he has to use it more than ever before in order to make it interesting,

the author now has the students using their power to hurl Star Destroyers out of the solar system!

Nonetheless, Anderson should be applauded for turning the character of Callista, which was created by Barbara Hambly, into a more interesting companion for Luke. A lot of this has to do with the fact that she is "in flesh" now instead of being a bodiless voice communicating with Luke. Her departure at the end of the novel to get closer to the Force actually leaves one interested in the resolution of her relationship with Luke. Unfortunately, the resolution that comes in *Planet of Twilight* is less than satisfying. **(B)**

PLANET OF TWILIGHT

(nine years after *ROTJ*) by Barbara Hambly (April 1997)

SYNOPSIS: As Luke attempts to respond to a distress signal from Callista, Leia finds herself taken political prisoner by warlord Seti Draconis, who plots the annihilation of a race known as the Therans.

REVIEW/NOTES: This much-anticipated novel was expected to be the big resolution to the Luke-Callista relationship, particularly necessary since she isn't in any of the subsequent novels. Primarily because of that anticipation, this novel fails miserably, as Callista does not even appear until the end of the book! Instead we are left with an angst-ridden Luke chasing down every clue that *might* lead him back to her. In the process, he coincidentally involves himself directly in the alternate plotline running throughout the novel concerning Leia.

Unfortunately, the Leia plotline is even less interesting, as she spends the majority of it as a drugged-up prisoner. Added to this, Hambly's writing style has become increasingly awkward as she consistently breaks in midsentence, goes off on a tangent, and then tries to shift back, expecting it to flow smoothly. Once again the story line is sprinkled with references to topatoes and coffienne, making the plotline appear to be farcical at times.

There are points of interest in the story that may actually justify reading the book, such as our finally being given an explanation of where the heck the Noghri have been since the end of *The Last*

Command. We also are treated to a completely original portrayal of Threepio who, along with Artoo, is stuck on his own, cut off from friendly faces, and actually makes his way back to the New Republic using a cunning and devious side of his programming that has rarely been seen. This is much more satisfying than having him bumble his way in and out of one mess after another.

The use of Han and Chewie in the story, on the other hand, seems more of an afterthought, as they provide no impact whatsoever on the plot. Even worse is the use of Daala, who returns as a completely different character from what we have seen before. Her appearance comes too late in the novel to explore sufficiently the reasoning behind her change of heart, and it is therefore unrealistic.

Unfortunately, it seems that the majority of the single-story novels set in the post–*Return of the Jedi* time period haven't captured the true essence of *Star Wars,* while the multibook series seem to have enough time to explore the characters in new ways and still remain truthful to the movies. **(D–)**

THE CRYSTAL STAR

(ten years after *ROTJ*) by Vonda N. McIntyre (December 1994)

SYNOPSIS: The Solo children are kidnapped by slave traders. It is up to the core group of characters to free the children while simultaneously dealing with an enigmatic creature known as Waru, who apparently has the ability to heal.

REVIEW/NOTES: *The Crystal Star* is a perfect example of a decent story line that might have worked well in a different venue but fails to resemble a *Star Wars* story in the slightest. First off, the topic of the story line, religious shams and brainwashing cults, seems a bit

out of place when compared with the style of stories we are familiar with in the *Star Wars* universe. McIntyre should not be faulted for trying to explore a new subject in a familiar setting, but in order to do so properly she should have made sure that the portrayals of the characters were true to those in the movies. This is where the book ultimately fails to deliver.

While Han and Leia are not too far off, Luke is considerably different from the strong-willed, impetuous youth in the movies or even the wise, stoic Jedi Master in the previous books. Instead, he comes off as being weak-minded and unsure of himself, which leads to his being taken in by Waru. This works to alienate any true fans of Luke's, since he doesn't even have the strength of mind to save himself at the end. It's only the intervention of Han, Leia, and the children that stops him from giving his life to Waru.

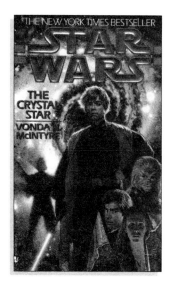

The children are the other problem in the novel. Science fiction has seemed to be plagued by the genius child characters as much as by the quirky robot sidekicks. Lucas, thankfully, left out the kids from the cast of characters in the movies, yet he still managed to present a story that children could easily relate to. He also created interesting robots in C-3PO and R2-D2 that had just the right mix of comic relief and serious contribution to the plotline. It will be interesting to see if he can successfully pull off revolving a full movie around a "brainy kid" in the first of the prequel films, in which Anakin Skywalker is only ten years old.

The natural progression of events from where *Return of the Jedi* left off was to have Han and Leia start a family. All was well and good until now, when their children are old enough to start becoming actual characters in the story lines. Unfortunately, they are still too young to contribute significantly unless their remarkable intelligence and uncanny powers in the Force are played upon throughout. So once again we are left with the brainy little kids who surprise everyone with their ability to take matters into their own hands and even help save others. Along with this, naturally, come large portions of the book written from the children's perspective, which never prove as interesting as the rest of the "adult" scenes. To make matters worse, we not only have the twins and Anakin to deal with, but they find themselves held captive with a bevy of other children!

Even Xaverii, Han's old love interest, fails to come across half as interesting as A. C. Crispin made her in *The Hutt Gambit*.

The interesting parts of the plot dealing with Hethrir's plans to start a new faction of the Empire seem to take a back burner to the plotlines involving the children and the religious cult set up around Waru. While Vonda McIntyre has written some great *Star Trek* books in the past, it seems she should have familiarized herself more with the *Star Wars* characters and how they have been handled in the other novels before contributing a story of her own. **(D–)**

THE BLACK FLEET CRISIS:
BOOK 1 – BEFORE THE STORM

(immediately after *ROTJ* and twelve years after *ROTJ*) by Michael P. Kube-McDowell (April 1996)

SYNOPSIS: While Luke goes to his mother's homeworld in a quest to find her people, Lando becomes involved in a mission that takes him into contact with a ghost ship of advanced technology. At the same time, Leia finds herself going up against the leader of the Duskhan League, who seems determined to launch a genocidal war that threatens the New Republic.

REVIEW/NOTES: The *Black Fleet Crisis* trilogy is the most peculiar set of *Star Wars* novels because of its lack of consistency throughout the three books. It starts off with a bang in the first novel, slows down to a snail's pace in the second, and just when it seems to be redeeming itself in the third, it falls flat on its face.

The first novel sets up the history of the Yevetha, who are shown to be enslaved by the Empire until shortly after the battle at Endor. This helps establish how powerful a threat the Yevetha are to the New Republic when, in twelve short years, they have become one of the most powerful entities in the galaxy.

Kube-McDowell's pacing in the first novel is flawless. He quickly engages the reader's interest in Leia's dealings with the Yevetha

threat while simultaneously cutting back and forth between the two other plotlines running concurrently concerning Lando and Luke. Rarely seen aspects of each of the three main characters' personalities are emphasized and explored throughout the story line. For instance, Leia's naïveté is taken advantage of by the devious Nil Spaar.

Meanwhile, Luke is similarly led around by Akannah with the promise of being reunited with his mother. Both Luke and Leia are normally portrayed as extremely strong characters who are in control of most situations and rarely able to be manipulated in such a way. The way the chinks in their respective armors are exposed and played upon makes their characters all the more human. Lando, on the other hand, emerges as a capable leader throughout his dealings with the vagabond as he continually works his way past increasingly difficult obstacles and seems to be in control of every situation — even when unexpected problems continue to arise.

The introduction of Hyram Drayson makes for a welcome addition to the cast of characters, since he represents a side of the New Republic that we haven't yet been privy to.

Leia's character seems to mature throughout the novel as she sheds her naïveté and becomes a much stronger leader. Her actions show that she is starting to worry less about the politics of office and more about doing the *right* thing.

Luke seems to be reaching a crossroads in his life in which he must decide whether he should continue on in his current function as a Jedi Master or remove himself from the public eye and live his life as a hermit. He brings up an interesting question about whether Obi-Wan and Yoda ended up living life as hermits by choice or if that is the natural progression for a powerful Jedi when his powers increase to the level that makes it difficult to block out the thoughts and emotions of nearby people. Luke seems to be searching for a greater purpose in his life or at least an affirmation that the life he has chosen is an important one.

Akannah's arrival comes at a time when Luke is most vulnerable and thus makes it more believable that Luke would follow her on such a wild-goose chase.

Overall, this entry provides one of the strongest starts to a series of novels and gives every sign that it will develop into one of the most powerful story lines to date. **(A)**

THE BLACK FLEET CRISIS:
BOOK 2 – SHIELD OF LIES

(twelve years after *ROTJ*) by Michael P. Kube-McDowell (September 1996)

SYNOPSIS: All story lines from the previous novel continue, with Leia attempting to develop a diplomatic solution to the aggression of the Yevetha; Lando and company trapped aboard the alien vessel, which has become a "runaway"; Luke continuing to seek out the truth about his mother and the nature of the Force; and Han going on a secret mission to infiltrate Yevethan space.

REVIEW/NOTES: After the first novel built up such a good foundation, the second book goes absolutely *nowhere*. The biggest failing of the second installment is not that there is little progression of the story line (admittedly a major problem) but that it is divided into three separate sections: "Luke," "Leia," and "Lando." The lack of intercutting between the different plotlines makes it very boring, especially the long section concerning Lando and company walking around on the deserted alien spaceship. The Lando story line is extremely similar to Arthur C. Clarke's *Rendezvous with Rama,* in which a mysterious alien ship appears near Earth and is explored by a team trying to unlock the secrets it holds within it. The reason that Clarke's book worked so well and yet Kube-McDowell's similar story line fails is that *Rama* takes place in the near future when the secrets of interstellar travel have not yet been discovered and contact with alien life-forms has not yet occurred. The possible knowledge and secrets that an alien craft might provide in this setting are staggering. The Lando story line, however, takes place in a setting where interstellar travel is the norm and interaction with aliens is an everyday occurrence.

The plotline is also a bit similar to the first book in L. Neil Smith's Lando Calrissian trilogy, *Lando Calrissian and the Mindharp of Sharu.* Lando's intelligence also seems to have jumped to

new heights during this trilogy. While Lando has always been intelligent, he seemed to rely more on his card-shark skills to gain control of a situation than on an incredible storehouse of knowledge. Suddenly, Lando is able to figure out complex intelligence-based puzzles set forth by the vagabond, when all of the scientists and military tacticians around him cannot. This makes the portrayal of Lando seem out of character at times and further detracts from an already weak story line.

The other two sections of the book, dealing with Luke and Leia, fail to progress their respective story lines far enough to warrant an entire third of the book each. After reading the second novel in the trilogy one is left with little in the way of anticipation. **(C-)**

THE BLACK FLEET CRISIS:
BOOK 3 — TYRANT'S TEST

(twelve years after *ROTJ*) by Michael P. Kube-McDowell (January 1997)

SYNOPSIS: Essentially, the story lines of the two previous books are wrapped up in this adventure that focuses on the New Republic's efforts against the Yevetha.

REVIEW/NOTES: The third book makes up for the slow read of the second, rushing, as it does, at breakneck speed to what looks to be a full resolution. One problem: it comes too early.

Of the three separate plotlines being told in the book (the Yevethan threat, Luke's search for his mother, and Lando's investigation of the vagabond), only two come together in the end. The final discovery of what the vagabond really is has no bearing whatsoever on the other story lines and takes place after the resolution of the story, making it seem extremely out of place. It seems that Kube-McDowell had a few very different ideas for story lines and tried to mesh them together into one. If the vagabond story line had been dropped and the trilogy were tightened up to two books, it would most likely have been on a par with Timothy Zahn's and Michael Stackpole's series. Kube-McDowell also attempts in this third book to do something that no other author has: show Chewbacca with his family (yes, the same family from the dreadful *Star Wars Holiday*

Special) and reveal exactly, word for word, what they are saying. We find that Chewie is actually a very eloquent speaker in his native tongue! No doubt many fans will not be able to accept having Chewie "speaking," although it never made sense why, out of all the aliens ever presented in the novels, the Wookiee tongue was one of the very few never translated for the reader.

Thankfully, Kube-McDowell doesn't opt for the picture-perfect ending by having the Imperials defect to the New Republic after taking care of the Yevethan threat, choosing instead to leave an effective dangling plot thread revealing that the remnants of the Imperial Navy are now stronger than they have been in years owing to the liberation of the Black Sword Fleet. It is to be hoped that another author will pick up on this and offer a new threat to the Republic.

The resolution of the plotline involving Luke's quest for his mother leaves the reader with a somewhat ambiguous answer concerning her final fate. The woman Akannah, who claims to be his mother, does not prove her identity, thus avoiding any possible continuity conflicts with the upcoming prequels.

The trilogy on the whole excels with its superb characterization, yet fails with a story line that is full of padding and lacking an ending justifying the use of three books to tell the tale. **(B−)**

THE NEW REBELLION
(thirteen years after *ROTJ*) by Kristine Kathryn Rusch (December 1996)

SYNOPSIS: The dark Jedi Kuellar unleashes his plan to kill Luke Skywalker and become the most powerful Jedi in the galaxy. It begins with him and his apprentice, Brakiss, setting off a series of explosions that kill millions of Je'har and threaten the very fabric of the New Republic.

REVIEW/NOTES: *The New Rebellion* is a great treat for those who enjoy a lot of continuity references. Kristine Kathryn Rusch ties together aspects from many of the other novels, including the *Young Jedi Knights* series. Until now, Kevin J. Anderson seemed to be the only author who strove not only to tell a good story but also to make it fit as tightly as possible with the rest of the stories to date.

Rusch creates an interesting multilayered adversary with Kuellar. He is not the normal megalomaniacal villain that is all too common in *Star Wars* and in science fiction in general. He is at once convinced that he is one of the most powerful men in the galaxy and unsure of his strength as a leader.

A subplot involving Artoo and Threepio's mission to the droid world brings up a very interesting argument for the belief that a droid can evolve beyond its programming into a truly sentient being. This line of reasoning begs the question of whether the two can actually be considered sentient or if they are still merely "acting" human as designated by their programming. It also gives a lot more meaning to the scene in *A New Hope* when Luke's uncle tells him to take the droids into town the next day to get their memories wiped.

Another nice touch in the novel occurs when we learn that even after almost fifteen years, Lando still hasn't forgiven himself for the part he played in Han's ordeal in carbonite, even though everyone else, including Han, has.

Overall, the book is not up to the caliber of the majority of the other novels, but it makes a very entertaining read. **(B–)**

AMBUSH AT CORELLIA –
BOOK 1 OF THE CORELLIAN TRILOGY

(fourteen years after *ROTJ*) by Roger MacBride Allen (March 1995)

SYNOPSIS: Han returns to his homeworld of Corellia for a trade summit just as civil war is about to break out between the five planets making up this sector of the galaxy.

REVIEW/NOTES: Roger MacBride chose one of the most-referenced and least-known areas in the *Star Wars* universe as the focal point for his trilogy — the Corellian Sector. A multitude of major characters hail from Corellia, including Han Solo, Wedge Antilles, and Corran Horn. References are constantly being made to the planet, but until now no one has provided a good understanding of what the planet and its surrounding star system are truly like. This also gives MacBride an excuse to explore Han's past in a little more detail (all of which is flawlessly incorporated into A. C. Crispin's *The Paradise Snare* novel). By far the most interesting bit of information we learn is that the origin of the system itself is surrounded in mystery, as it appears that it may have been constructed ages ago by an advanced race.

MacBride begins his trilogy at full speed as we are thrown into a tangled web of intrigue and deception with only hints about who the true antagonists are. The overall plot encompasses a variety of themes, of which the one in the forefront is racism. The author manages to get his message across clearly without resorting to preaching as he shows the futility in each of the separate racist movements happening within the Corellian Sector (the Human League, the Drallists, and so on) and the way in which their hatred is easily manipulated by a much greater power. Naturally, Han is the main driver in the story line, although by the end of the trilogy the focus shifts dramatically to his children. In fact, much of Corellia and Drall is shown to us through their eyes.

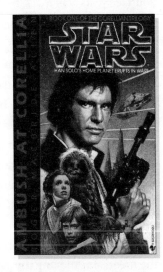

The other main plotline unfolding concerns Lando's search for a potential bride/business partner. His quest for a bride based on the level of capital that he will be provided for investment gives a bit of comic relief. It also, however, brings up an interesting issue. At first Luke is appalled that Lando would marry for money and not love, but Lando brings up a good point: that this has been an accepted tradition in numerous cultures throughout history. Just because Luke does not believe in it does not mean that it is wrong. The true irony is that his pursuit of deep pockets ends with his falling in love and starting a relationship with Tendra that proves to be more serious and mature than any he has ever had in the past.

The greatest surprise, however, comes at the end when the leader of the Human League is exposed as Han's cousin Thracken Sal-Solo. The story ends with many unresolved questions and properly sets the stage for the second installment. **(A)**

ASSAULT AT SELONIA — BOOK 2 OF THE CORELLIAN TRILOGY

(fourteen years after *ROTJ*) by Roger MacBride Allen (July 1995)

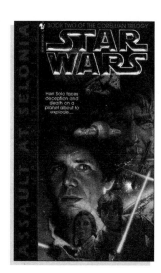

SYNOPSIS: The struggle between Han and his cousin heats up as Thracken plots to restore the Imperial system and gain ultimate power. Han's only means of stopping him seems to lie with a female alien being named Dracmus.

REVIEW/NOTES: Book two begins with an all-too-familiar scene as Han is — once again — held captive. What makes this more interesting, though, is that the aggressor is Han's own flesh and blood with a personal grudge against him. It's not until A. C. Crispin goes back in time to explore Han's dealings with Thracken as a teenager in *The Paradise Snare* that we fully understand why Thracken despises Han so much.

Han's capture and subsequent escape provide MacBride with the means for moving the plot to Selonia in order to explore the culture of the Selonians. More interesting, however, is Luke's mission to Bakura to request the aid of the Bakuran fleet for an attack on the Corellian Sector.

While the excuse for the unavailability of the New Republic fleet is extremely weak (it is unlikely that such a large portion of the fleet would be undergoing a refit at the same time, especially with the Imperial Black Sword fleet, as seen in the *Black Fleet Crisis* trilogy, still posing a threat), it is great to revisit Gaeriel Captisan some fourteen years since we last saw her. MacBride does an excellent job in handling the reunion between Luke and Gaeriel, as Luke wonders whether the many accomplishments he has achieved in his life were worth the sacrifices.

The Bakuran device MacBride devises for punching through an interdictor field is very original and shows that he did his research before writing the trilogy. The battle near Selonia is brief but serves to bring together most of the players for the final chapter in the trilogy. The plotline moves at a steady clip throughout the book and once again builds up nicely to a cliff-hanger ending. **(B+)**

SHOWDOWN AT CENTERPOINT —
BOOK 3 OF THE CORELLIAN TRILOGY
(fourteen years after *ROTJ*) by Roger MacBride Allen (October 1995)

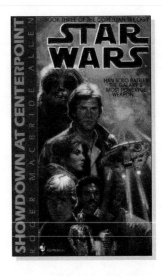

SYNOPSIS: All things come to a dramatic head when the leaders of the Corellian rebellion announce their demands: the New Republic must withdraw all claims to power over this sector or millions of lives will be lost when they use the "starburster" to make the sun go supernova.

REVIEW/NOTES: The trilogy comes to a grand finale that is a bit anti-climactic after such a steady buildup. At first it continues on at the pace established by the first two novels as we learn the secret of Centerpoint Station and the battle the Bakuran fleet finds itself immersed in starts to intensify. Toward the conclusion, though, the focus once again shifts to Han and Leia's children, and the story wraps up a bit too neatly. In many ways, this novel suffers the same fate that plagued the miniseries *"V"— The Final Battle,* the story line of which continued to build for ten hours but dissipated at the end when things were wrapped up thanks to the magic powers of the so-called Starchild. It's the same here: the fate of an entire world comes down to young Anakin's uncanny abilities in the Force and thus takes away from the struggles the rest of the characters have endured throughout the trilogy.

The only thing that saves the book from completely falling flat at the end is that MacBride provides a truly dramatic scene in which the wounded Gaeriel and Ossilege decide to give their lives in order to take out the enemy fleet. As mentioned earlier, a touch of realism is provided when not all of the good guys survive (which, aside from the nameless expendable Rebel/New Republic soldiers, is what normally happens). Even though Gaeriel is far from a main character, her loss is still touching, especially after the scenes where her young

daughter asks Luke to promise to protect her mother. The main antagonists, who have been revealed to be the Triad, remain faceless entities, which detracts from the revelation about their part in organizing the individual rebellions on different worlds. This leaves Thracken as the recognizable face of the enemy, although his defeat also comes a little too easily (and is once again due to the actions of the children!).

It seems that MacBride had all the proper ingredients for a great trilogy of books, but it never really reached its full potential, remaining merely an enjoyable read rather than a *Star Wars* classic. **(B)**

THE HAND OF THRAWN:
BOOK 1 – SPECTER OF THE PAST

(fifteen years after *ROTJ*) by Timothy Zahn (November 1997)

SYNOPSIS: Just as it seems that the Empire will finally, irrevocably, come to an end, a plan is unleashed to tear apart the New Republic, aided in no small way by rumors that Grand Admiral Thrawn has been cloned back to life.

REVIEW/NOTES: Timothy Zahn makes a long-awaited return to the *Star Wars* universe with his first full-length *Star Wars* novel in four years. Back again are most of the surviving characters he created in his first trilogy, including Talon Karrde, Mara Jade, Pellaeon, Bossk Fey'lya, and the Noghri. Joining them are other popular characters introduced in other novels, such as Corran Horn, Booster Terrik, and Mirax.

Unfortunately, even with such an impressive cast list, something in the novel seems to be missing. Perhaps the fact that Zahn's original trilogy has been elevated to the status of perfection in the minds of most readers makes it almost impossible to follow up with an equally strong story. Or possibly it is because of the hinted-at return of the most popular new character created by Zahn, Grand Admiral Thrawn, who nonetheless remains as dead as he was at the end of *The Last Command*.

Zahn himself has stated that he felt that bringing Thrawn back would be too much like the often-used trick in comic books in which characters rarely stay dead for long before some far-from-plausible means is used to explain how the character in fact cheated death. While Zahn should be commended for refusing to resort to such a Saturday-matinee-serial trick (since two main characters, the Emperor and Boba Fett, have already cheated what appeared to be their demise in *Return of the Jedi*), it seems in this case that the majority of readers would have quickly forgiven him this indulgence for a chance to read more about one of the most original characters to be created by any of the *Star Wars* authors.

What makes matters worse is that Zahn leads us to believe Thrawn has returned only for a paragraph or two before we are told that it is an impostor. It would have been far more interesting to have been left wondering throughout the novel if it was the real Thrawn, a clone of Thrawn, or an imposter. There are also many nuances of old age and futility throughout the novel, both as Pellaeon, now supreme commander of the Empire, begins to realize they have lost the war and that reclaiming the Empire has become a near impossibility and as, at the same time, the New Republic begins to unravel from within as increasing problems arise among its members.

Zahn's original trilogy was set in a time when the war was far from over and each side was a major power to be reckoned with. Now, however, it seems that both the Empire and the New Republic are fighting more against entropy than against each other.

Despite its faults, the novel is a very entertaining read and still excels over the majority of the other novels that have been published. Zahn continues to explore new sides of his well-established characters, especially Pellaeon, who now has to deal with deciding the fate of the last vestiges of the Empire (a task he never would have dreamed would be up to him), and Mara Jade, who still seems to be searching for a true purpose in her life. The progression of Pellaeon's character from the extremely "green" captain in Zahn's first trilogy to the master tactician in this novel is exciting. It gives a sense of full circle, as Pellaeon has now become a capable leader like Thrawn, while the captain on his Star Destroyer is in the position that Pellaeon was in back when he served under Thrawn.

Even Luke undergoes some major changes as he explores the ramifications of taking his powers in the Force for granted and using them in such a gratuitous and carefree manner as he has over the past number of years. He begins to realize that neither Ben nor Yoda ever used the Force while in his presence nearly as much as he has lately, and he begins to wonder if he is starting down a dangerous path. Even Han begins to notice how quick Luke has been to use the Force to accomplish the most trivial of actions.

While this is a theme explored in many similar ways in the "Dark Empire" comic book series when Luke actually crossed over to the dark side to learn its strengths and weaknesses, and in the *Black Fleet Crisis* trilogy when he begins to feel that he is becoming too strong in the Force to remain among crowds of people, Zahn approaches it from a slightly different angle and manages to keep it fresh.

The novel ends quite abruptly, with many unanswered questions concerning Mara Jade's fate and who was really behind the destruction of Camass. One hopes the final part of the story will have a bit more action now that the characters seem to be in place and that it will be a bit closer to Zahn's other novels in style. (A–)

THE SPECIAL
EDITIONS

ALTHOUGH THE TERMS *director's cut* and *special edition* may be commonplace in video today — where directors restore additional footage to their movies in an attempt to get closer to their own original conception — when George Lucas decided to perform an overhaul on his *Star Wars* trilogy it meant a visual reevaluation instead of a conceptual rethinking of the original movies: something certainly different from the standard restoration of excised scenes that one usually associates with the kind of "director's cuts" we've seen from the likes of Oliver Stone *(JFK, Natural Born Killers)* and James Cameron *(Aliens, The Abyss, T2)* over the years.

Bothered by special effects that, however "special" they may have been in 1977, were no longer cutting edge, Lucas and his Industrial Light and Magic team decided not only to restore the original print of *Star Wars* for its twentieth anniversary but also to add new special F/X footage, mainly of today's digital CGI (computer-generated imagery) variety, into the original film. The results would bring a twenty-year-old film back into theaters, where it would sport all-new, modern special effects from Industrial Light and Magic.

"I've wanted to do this ever since I made the movie," Lucas said at a press conference concerning the Special Editions. "If you go back and check the interviews from that time, you'll find that I said, 'Well, I don't think it turned out very well. It's only about 40 percent of what I wanted it to be. I'm really disappointed in it.' People were saying, 'What is he talking about? This guy must be crazy.' Obviously, people who work with me have been hearing this for twenty years. In fact, I think they were relieved. 'Finally! He's going to do it! We don't have to listen to this anymore!' The opportunity came along with the twentieth-anniversary celebration. Rather than do some of the other things that had been presented, everybody agreed that we should take the risk. We're reissuing the movies that have been on video and television a lot; this has never been done with a live-action film before, especially not on this scale. So I said, 'If you're going to put that much money into reissuing this movie, I want to get it right this time.' The idea of spending $5 million to noodle on a movie — you can't do that unless there is some chance of making that money back."

In describing the process and the vocation of filmmaking, Lucas explained that you begin with a script and a pocket full of compromises. "There's never enough time," he said, "never enough money, some things just aren't possible. So you have to rewrite, change, and in some cases, cut things out. Sometimes you cut things because they don't belong in the movie — an idea that didn't work — and the film works better. Sometimes, as in the case of the Jabba the Hutt scene, it was a scene that worked and could have been in the movie. But at that point in history, ILM was a brand-new company that was way behind schedule. To add that sequence — it was going to be a stop-motion sequence, which we hadn't done much of at that time — would just have broken the back of the operation.

"I figured that the plot part, the exposition, that Han Solo has a price on his head as his motivation, was handled in the Greedo scene just before that. So, plotwise, it wasn't essential that it be there. It was going to cost way too much money and take too much time. I did not know whether I was ever going to get to make the

> **T**he opportunity came along with the twentieth-anniversary celebration. Rather than do some of the other things that had been presented, everybody agreed that we should take the risk."
>
> — GEORGE LUCAS

other two movies, so if I did not make the third, the idea of introducing Jabba the Hutt really wasn't that important. I just figured it would expedite matters to cut it out. I was frustrated. I was disappointed that it couldn't be in the movie, but there were many things I was disappointed about. I never expected to be able to fix it. Almost any filmmaker can look

back and say, 'Gee, if only I had a few more days, or a little more money, I could really fix a lot of those things.' When the idea of reissuing films took hold, it was my chance to fix all those things. So I took it."

Lucas has always been a vocal proponent of preserving the original intention of films, battling against the notion of colorization or reediting the works of filmmakers who are no longer around to protect their efforts. Special editions, he feels, represent an entirely different situation.

"The idea of film as a dynamic, ever changing medium just puts film in the same category as all other art forms," he explained. "Artists are continually changing their work. Fine artists have the advantage of just leaving it in the corner. If you go into almost any artist's studio, you're going to find a wall of paintings. You might think they're finished and look great, but the artist will say, 'Well, I don't think they're completed yet.' But they can afford to keep the paintings there. It's the same thing with a novelist. You might say, 'You've been working on that for years, why isn't it finished? I read a draft four years ago, and I thought it was great.' But the writer keeps going on. Sometimes after a film has been finished, a book

> **A**lmost any filmmaker can look back and say, 'Gee, if only I had a few more days, or a little more money, I could really fix a lot of those things.' When the idea of reissuing films took hold, it was my chance to fix all those things. So I took it."
> — GEORGE LUCAS

THE SPECIAL EDITIONS

published, or a painting shown, the artist might take it back and doodle on it. It's a curse, I guess, a process in which you always see things you want to fix. I see imperfections; that's who I am. I see things that really bother me and make it less than what it could be. We've been given the opportunity, so we fixed it. It's like something in your house that's not quite right, you go by it every day for five years saying, 'I'm going to fix that next Saturday.' Eventually, it does bug you, or your wife, enough that you get out and fix it.

"It's the same thing with making movies," he elaborated. "It's very different for a filmmaker doing that than for a corporation or a group of executives to say, 'We're going to go back and fix all these movies. I can do this better than those guys can.' I'm a founding member of the Artists Rights Foundation, which is backing legislation to make sure it's the *artist* who is allowed to redo the work, rather than the so-called copyright owner, which is a corporation that gets sold from time to time, resulting in executives at studios who take our heritage and doodle with it. People are going to be able to do this more and more, not just colorization or panning-and-scanning — they are adding scenes, they are cutting things, they are changing the political content of the movies, the aesthetic content."

All of which raises the question of how director Irvin Kershner felt about Lucas "doodling" with *The Empire Strikes Back.* "I discussed it with him [and] he's very excited about the whole thing," Lucas said. "In this particular working relationship that I have with directors, I'm more like an executive producer in television. I'm much more creatively involved in the whole process than a normal producer would be. In the case of the *Star Wars* films, not only am I the producer, but I wrote the stories, a lot of the casting decisions are made by me, and I pretty much oversee all the special effects.

"With *Star Wars,* there was a low budget, we had this young director — me — and all kinds of problems. With Kershner and *Em-*

In this particular working relationship that I have with directors, I'm more like an executive producer in television. I'm much more creatively involved in the whole process than a normal producer would be. ➤

pire, we were in a much better situation. We had a lot more resources. Most of what we've changed is in the Cloud City sequence,
and Kershner was complaining on the set that he wanted to see
more. Digital backgrounds didn't even exist then. You wouldn't even
think about that. It was the same thing with the snow monster. We
built a snow monster, but it didn't look very good. It was Kersh who
said that thing couldn't stay in the picture. So we cut it out. We had
somebody else build a little tiny puppet and used that just to give an
impression of a snow monster. A lot of these things are situations
you have to have compromises for, and now you can say, 'We're
going to do it the way we wanted to do it then.' Much of it
comes from economic opportunities — somebody is
willing to put up the money. If you're a filmmaker,
you're restricted by your resources. They give you X
amount of dollars and you pretty much have to live
with it. You say, 'Well, I have so many days, and I
have so much money, I have to make it work within
reason.'"

> ➤ In the case of the *Star Wars* films, not only am I the producer, but I wrote the stories, a lot of the casting decisions are made by me, and I pretty much oversee all the special effects."
> — GEORGE LUCAS

The results of Lucas's special-edition edit speak
for themselves. The films — particularly *Star Wars*
itself — were a massive box office smash, enabling a new
generation of children to experience the movie on a big theatrical screen in THX digital audio, along with their parents, the
generation that had helped turn *Star Wars* into one of the greatest
attractions in the cinema some twenty years earlier.

Lucas's restoration of *Star Wars* cost some $10 million, and
while additional restorations were performed on both *The Empire
Strikes Back* and *Return of the Jedi,* neither went through as many alterations as the original film did. However, both were successes, and
altogether, the Special Edition rereleases grossed some $250 million
in North America alone.

What follows is a list of the changes performed on the three
films, and it should be noted that Lucas did not restore all the scenes
that had been cut, but rather simply updated the technology of the
three films. As Lucas said in a 1997 interview in *Cinefex* magazine,

"What I'm doing, I think, is what a lot of painters do, and some writers do — which is to go back and repaint or write." Major scenes that had been shot but cut from *Star Wars* in particular were not restored just because they had been edited out — indeed, as Lucas confirmed, these scenes were excised because they did not work in 1977, and they still don't fit within the framework of the films today.

The Special Editions of *Star Wars*, then, should not be seen as a thematic rethinking of Lucas's original material but rather as a technological update, one that viewers consumed with a passion during the winter and spring months of 1997.

STAR WARS

Original version, 121 mins.
Special Edition, 125 mins.

As noted earlier, George Lucas spent some $10 million restoring the original nitrate film and adding a plethora of new Industrial Light and Magic CGI effects into his then-groundbreaking 1977 sci-fi classic. Ben Burtt also was on hand to create a handful of new digital sound mixes for the film to play in theaters nationwide. In a bold stroke, Lucas decided to have the Special Edition films play only in theaters equipped with digital sound, hoping to ensure that all audiences saw his updated pictures in the best possible cinematic environment.

Some viewers were disappointed that legendary scenes involving Biggs Darklighter, Luke Skywalker's Tatooine friend who appears at the end of the picture, and friends of Luke and Biggs's, were not restored to the picture (scenes that had been criticized by those who saw them as being overly reminiscent of Lucas's *American Graffiti*), but some breathtaking new shots were added to a movie many felt did not need any changes.

- In the Tatooine desert, the lizardlike creatures called the dew-backs, which previously were puppets that stood motionless on the horizon in the original version, now move about on all fours thanks to new ILM effects.

- New matte paintings add a three-dimensional quality to the scene where Artoo heads down a Tatooine canyon, and new model shots of the Jawa sandcrawler heading over desert terrain combine to create a more realistic look and feel to the picture. New additional matte shots also include a long-range look at Obi-Wan Kenobi's dwellings.

- The effect of Luke's landspeeder has been cleaned up and now appears seamless; in the original release, Lucas put Vaseline over the camera lens in an attempt to fudge the effect of the speeder hovering over, but not touching, the ground. Curiously enough, the landspeeder footage for the original film had been reshot in Death Valley after principal photography was wrapped; a stand-in for Mark Hamill was used after the actor was involved in a severe car crash that resulted in Hamill's having to undergo plastic surgery for his injuries (an issue that was later addressed in *The Empire Strikes Back*'s opening scenes).

- In one of the major new sequences added to the Special Edition trilogy, the spaceport of Mos Eisley has been completely overhauled. New computer shots manifest the scope of the area, which Lucas had originally thought wasn't nearly as intimidating to the protagonists or as vast as his original conception. Overhead shots of the area are combined with new digitally enhanced creatures (robots, other beasts of burden) in footage that seamlessly blends the original shots of Luke, Ben, and the robots passing through town with brand-new backdrops and actors. The result is a completely successful new sequence that captures Lucas's original vision and his motive for creating the Special Edition in the first place.

- Han Solo's cantina encounter with the bounty hunter Greedo has been altered so that Greedo, not Han, fires the first shot at

A CRITICAL LOOK AT THE STAR WARS TRILOGY SPECIAL EDITIONS

by MARK A. ALTMAN

The box office performance of the Star Wars *trilogy Special Editions proved audiences couldn't wait to plunk down their eight bucks to check out what Forcemeister George Lucas had concocted for them. Interestingly, while every genre magazine fell over itself attempting to tell the "exclusive" story of the magic behind these extended versions,* Sci-Fi Universe *took its traditional lines on what was* really *motivating Lucas.*

Former Sci-Fi Universe *editor Mark A. Altman was probably* the *most outspoken person on this subject. Indeed, he was often quoted regarding the subject in such publications as* USA Today *and* Entertainment Weekly. *What follows are Mr. Altman's reviews of the Special Editions.*

Star Wars was back on the big screen where it belongs with some special modifications *Wars* guru Lucas made himself — and, as I feared, they do little to make this genre classic any better. Shattering the seventies documentary-life feel of the original *Star Wars,* which was as close as you got to an independent film sensibility in a big-budget genre offering of the era, the new bells and whistles provide an unwelcome coat of paint that proves both distracting and unwarranted.

How do I define "unwarranted"? Well, I'll tell you. One of my favorite scenes of all time is when Ben Kenobi uses the Jedi mind trick to deceive a party of stormtroopers upon arriving in Mos Eisley. It's a scene filled with suspense and dread, but in the Special Edition the scene is sabotaged by new footage of a cute flying robot passing the star warriors on screen, serving as a comic moment that undermines the drama. (It's a revision that's born of the same impulse that marred *Return of the Jedi* — the urge to turn a dark and weathered milieu into a kiddie theme park fantasia.)

Even in the much-heralded Jabba the Hutt scene, the state-of-the-art special effects don't do anything to more capably convey the drama of the story. Jabba reiterates everything Greedo has just told Han in the cantina. The scene is pointless, and the addition of a menacing Boba Fett — which proves a momentary visceral thrill — is equally ludicrous. Just because the fans have such a hard-on for the character doesn't mean you should cater to such a capricious and illogical whim. Boba Fett is a top-notch bounty hunter and mercenary; why would he be hanging around as part of Jabba's entourage in a spaceport? No reason, other than to get a rise out of the audience, a point hammered home by a long, lingering shot of Boba Fett in the scene's coda.

However, the most offensive addition to the original *Star Wars* film is having Greedo, a veteran bounty hunter, miss shooting Han at point-blank range. Lucas's desire to turn Solo into a kinder, gentler hero is not only absurd but unnecessary. Solo redeems himself by showing up at the Death Star and saving Luke's (and the entire Rebellion's) ass. He doesn't need to be toned down; he is a pirate, smuggler, and scoundrel, you know. The fact that he would shoot Greedo in cold blood makes his redemption even more powerful later in the film (although God knows he certainly had reason to splatter Greedo across the bar considering the ill-tempered Rodian was about to kill him anyway). Worse yet, the scene is ineptly realized, the editing is ruined, and the depiction of Greedo firing and missing is truly idiotic.

Unfortunately, much of the movie smells of "Where can we put an enhancement?" syndrome, with many fine original shots being replaced by new, lackluster CGI material. (It also serves to take people out of the film his opponent. It seems that Lucas must have thought that the original sequence of events, where Han shoots Greedo in cold blood, made Solo out to be more of a ruthless thug than planned; thus, here the creature shoots and misses Solo, while Han quickly returns the fire in self-defense. The scene is somewhat awkward, as there is a raggedness to the effect that makes it a bit unconvincing in relation to the other new shots created for the Special Edition.

Surprisingly, Lucas has revealed that the intention was there from the beginning that Greedo would shoot first. "In the original film you don't get that very well," he said. "Some people thought we should leave that ambiguous, but I didn't like the idea that practically the first thing Han Solo does is gun someone down in cold blood. We had three different versions of that shot. In one, Greedo fires very close to when Han fires. In another, [Greedo fires] three frames later, and in the third, three frames after that. We tried to figure out which one would be perceivable but wouldn't look corny. Many things are happening in and around that scene, so it's hard to perceive just what's happening there, even now. We tried to find that median ground. It's always this way in any film — what can the majority of the audience perceive, and what can't they perceive? I like movies and I like presenting some things in an almost surreal way. I'm caught between doing things that work for the audience, which I know is looking at the film for the first time, under circumstances that are different. So, it's a question of knowing where to draw the line. Perhaps I should have cut two frames later."

✦ One of the legendary scenes cut from the original film, where Han Solo meets Jabba the Hutt, has been restored to the Special Edition. Jabba was originally played by a large human actor, and during postproduction, plans were made to animate over the actor and put Jabba in his place. Unfortunately, technological limitations forced Lucas to trim the scene, but after having made *Return of the Jedi*, the filmmaker was more convinced

and into a game of "Where's Waldo?" Now viewers watch *Star Wars* not as a compelling dramatic story but as a game where the goal is to spot each and every marvelous technological revision or addition.) The new establishing shots of Ben's abode on Tatooine look like a bad matte painting. What's the point? I liked the ramshackle house he lived in before. He is a hermit, after all. Now they have him living in the Xanadu of the planet Pointless.

And while the destruction of Alderaan is suitably enhanced with a *Star Trek VI*–type shock wave, the ILM effects artists change the Death Star explosion itself in what I found to be among the most egregious additions to the movie. This is one of the most iconic images of contemporary cinema! In the original version, the camera lingers on the explosions as the embers slowly flame out for what seems like minutes. Now it's just another piece of pyrotechnic wizardry. So what? In fact, the entire revamp on the film's finale during the Death Star attack seems colored by the MTV mind-set in which the camera no longer follows the story but instead cuts even more rapidly between moments of kinetic action. Yes, there are some fine new additions here, but more is lost than gained. Marcia Lucas's Oscar-winning editing is ➤

destroyed, and since the battle is not rescored, Williams's stunningly effective music no longer works as powerfully as it once did with the original imagery.

Ironically, the most potent addition to the film isn't a special effect at all but real human drama. Preparing to depart Yavin for the hopeless attack on the Death Star, Luke is reunited with his old friend Biggs Darklighter. The two share a moment of rekindled friendship, trying to make up for lost time. Luke's credibility as a pilot is even questioned by one of the Rebel leaders. It's a real and affecting moment that makes Biggs's death far more wrenching to the audience. The scene is about genuine emotion, not the sheer artifice of new special effects, and is truly a *special addition*.

Only in a few notable exceptions do the effects serve as a storytelling device. Perhaps the most inspired is Han's run through the Death Star chasing several stormtroopers that ends in a room filled with Imperials, prompting his hasty retreat. Here's an example of the new technology embellishing the abundant wit and story line of *Star Wars*. This is in contrast to a moment on Tatooine when the stormtroopers first discover that droids were in the jettisoned escape pod. What was once a brief piece

than ever to put it back in. With new ILM technology, Jabba has been digitally animated into the sequence, which, as a result, now establishes a vital link to both the ending of *Empire* and the events in *Jedi*, which was the intention all along.

Explained Lucas, "I was very keen to put Jabba the

Hutt in. And with digital technology I had the power now, technologically speaking, to do it — to put him in there and to make it be the same Jabba the Hutt that was in *Return of the Jedi*. [But] one of the things that happened when I changed from a big furry Jabba the Hutt to a big sluglike Jabba is that the new Jabba had this big long tail. When I went to shoot the scene [and] I put the sluglike Jabba the Hutt in there, it's obvious that Han would have to walk over his tail in order to get to the other side. Jabba reacts to that as if somebody had stepped on his tail, and so it's really something that grows out of the reality of it. You have Jabba, you have Han walking around him, and what would definitely happen would be Han stepping on Jabba's tail. It would hurt."

✦ The blastoff from Mos Eisley contains new effects as the *Millennium Falcon* takes off, with more-detailed computer-generated shots.

✦ The destruction of Alderaan, Princess Leia's home planet, also is enhanced with a more breathtaking explosion.

✦ When C-3PO is at the computer terminal, watching R2-D2 plug into the Death Star's mainframe in an attempt to locate the tractor beam controls, he says, "The tractor beam is coupled to the main reactor in seven locations. A power loss at one of the terminals will allow [the *Millennium Falcon*] to leave." This dialogue, included in the original film and the initial video issues, was inadvertently excised from the 1993 "THX remastered" laser disc and video release, but has been restored here.

* One of the film's funniest bits has also been enhanced. Han Solo chases a group of stormtroopers down a Death Star runway, only to turn the corridor and see several more stormtroopers waiting for him. In the Special Edition, when Han turns, we see an entire docking bay of stormtroopers — virtually quadruple the number from before — standing before him.

* At the Rebel base on the planet Yavin, Luke meets Biggs before taking off to storm the Death Star. Additional dialogue, which had been cut from the original film, is restored as the two discuss their home on Tatooine and the old days.

* The Rebel ship takeoff from Yavin contains far more detailed effects work, perfectly incorporated into the original footage.

* The Death Star battle sequence, one of the classic set pieces in cinematic history, has been substantially enhanced with numerous new special effects shots. X- and Y-Wing fighters now move three-dimensionally past the camera, shooting down TIE fighters with far more realistic movement. The basic editing rhythm of the sequence, of course, remains the same, but the effects are now more a product of the nineties than the seventies, and the ships and the entire sequence look far more believable because of it.

* The destruction of the Death Star includes new animation and a more impressive explosion.

* Actual actors have been digitally inserted into the Throne Room celebration sequence, which previously contained cardboard-looking, matte-inserted stand-ins at the right and left edges of the frame (something that would not have been noticeable in non-wide-screen showings of the picture).

* The end credits now list James Earl Jones as having provided the voice of Darth Vader (only *Jedi* credited the actor previously), while additional credits list the contributors to the Special Edition. John Williams's music has been looped to pad the additional running time.

of narrative information with two stormtroopers now becomes a huge scene of swooping shuttles, running dewbacks, and a massive investigation. Sure, it looks nice, but what's the point? Like the visual effects trickery in Mos Eisley in which an abundance of creatures (including a number of dinosaur-type creatures called rontos) are added throughout the scenes set there, the additions serve to undermine *Wars'* incredible sense of internal logic. One reason *Star Wars* tapped into the popular consciousness in such a dramatic way the first time around was that you really believed you were in a galaxy far, far away because of Lucas's rigorous attention to detail. Now I ask myself, why would they have dinosaur creatures on a desert planet and how come there are so many people in a town on a world that even Luke admits is on the outer rim of nowhere?

To Lucasfilm's credit, the new print is truly stunning and most welcome. The new sound mix is less effective, with some obtrusive foley work and additional sounds being incorporated into the soundtrack.

But ultimately, what bothers me the most is that had Lucas embarked on a restoration of the film like Universal did with the beautiful new version of Hitchcock's *Vertigo,* ➤

restoring the print to its original luster and remastering the soundtrack, it would have been a truly marvelous experience. But, of course, a $2 million rerelease gross wasn't what the studio or Lucas wanted. They needed a film that had the potential to make $100 million, and a *Vertigo*-type restoration just couldn't meet those needs. As a result, the Special Edition, in my opinion, was born for the most crass and commercial of reasons. And if, as Lucas has said, the Special Edition is truly designed to supplant the original version of *Star Wars,* it is the greatest tragedy of all. (I pray it's nothing more than New Coke — and we all know what happened to that.) All I know is that one day when I have kids, I know which version of *Star Wars* they'll be seeing. Now if we can only get some extra flying monkeys into *The Wizard of Oz.*

There's a scene in George Lucas's last great masterpiece, *Raiders of the Lost Ark,* when the Nazi lieutenant tells Bolloq that he is "uncomfortable with the thought of this Jewish ritual" as they prepare to open the lost ark of the covenant and gaze upon the wonders within. Well, I'm pretty damned uncomfortable with the thought of the *Star Wars* Special Editions, but let's put that aside for a moment and

see how the new, retooled editions measure up against the originals.

Empire has deservedly spent the least time under the knife, with only some minor changes being made to the best film in the *Star Wars* trilogy. Some work, some don't. In the case of the enhancements on Cloud City, the changes do legitimately reduce the claustrophobic feel of Bespin and there are some beautifully rendered establishing shots that have been added. Less successful, however, is Darth Vader's departure. Did anyone really not understand the fact that Vader took a shuttle back to his Star Destroyer? We really didn't need to see this visualized. Unfortunately, it's a poorly realized addition with a new line of looped dialogue from Vader sounding like it was phoned in from a recording studio in Prague preceding his shuttle trip back to space. Worst of all is the use of some stock footage from *Return of the Jedi* for the scene where Darth Vader lands on the docking bay of his Star Destroyer. The *Star Wars* trilogy is among the most famous movie series ever made — you can't sneak stock footage in without people's noticing. It's obvious this is the Death Star docking bay. Also ineffective is the additional Wampa footage, which just calls more attention to how cheesy looking these

creatures are and helps to diminish some of the suspense in the original scene.

Like *Empire's*, *Jedi*'s new footage is a hit-or-miss affair (unlike *Wars'*, which is just plain miss). Certainly *Jedi* stood to gain the most from the upgrades, as it is, by far, the worst film of the trilogy. Unfortunately, none of the changes do anything to address the problems in the film's narrative. A new dance number in Jabba's palace is just a cutesy vignette attempting to inject some more adorable creatures into a film that is already overripe with marketing concepts rather than movie characters. Meanwhile, there's no attempt to clean up the dreadful-looking rancor scene, whose egregious matte lines and rear-projection work make it the film's most unconvincing set piece. Marking a striking contrast with this is the new sail barge and Sarlacc pit scenes, which look great. The addition of a migrating herd of wild banthas is probably the single most striking image added to any of the three films. And the Sarlaac pit no longer looks like a giant vagina, but instead seems to be a distant cousin of Audrey II, the man-eating plant from *Little Shop of Horrors*. While it's not an inspired design, it is integrated seamlessly into the live-action footage shot in 1982.

THE EMPIRE STRIKES BACK

Original version, 124 mins.
Special Edition, 127 mins.

Of the three films in the trilogy, *The Empire Strikes Back* had the least amount of changes made to its special-edition updating. This is ironic, since the original film had gone through more editing changes than either of the other films in the series, including even minor discrepancies between the 35mm and 70mm versions screened during the time of *Empire*'s original theatrical release (differences that involved minor musical changes, various alternate takes, and wipes/dissolves).

The picture's first act, set on the ice planet Hoth, saw at least one major subplot excised (involving the Wampa creatures), along with most of John Williams's original score from the opening Hoth scenes and Luke's battle with Vader at the end. Glimpses of these unused elements can be found on *Empire*'s Special Edition soundtrack album, which presents Williams's unexpurgated score, as well as in Fox Video's 1993 *Star Wars* Trilogy laser disc boxed set, where theatrical trailers reveal a shot of C-3PO tearing a "warning" sign off the Wampa containment door.

That said, there are a few noteworthy additions and alterations to the special edition of the second *Star Wars* film.

+ The Wampa creature, which had previously been seen only for a brief second as a hand puppet that attacks Luke and his tauntaun (the original creature design simply didn't work at the time), is now seen in newly shot footage eating in his cave and in new shots of the Wampa attacking Luke.
+ Matte lines around the snowspeeders and in the cockpit POVs have been cleaned up digitally by ILM for the Hoth battle sequence (similarly, brief new CGI elements have been added to the Rebel escape from Hoth and the *Falcon*'s escape from the Star Destroyer, while Boba Fett takes off in pursuit, later in the movie).

However, the most anticlimactic aspect of *Jedi* is the highly touted new ending, in which several worlds celebrate the demise of the Emperor. Boasting a beautiful new piece of music by John Williams (which doesn't really sound like a *Star Wars* cue at all, though), the film cuts between celebrations on Bespin, Mos Eisley, and Coruscant. The problem here is that it just seems like an experiment in which live action actors are composited into a CGI matte. There's no emotion here, only technology and artifice. And unless you're a *Star Wars* geek, you don't even know what Coruscant is. There's a neat image of the statue of Emperor Palpatine being pulled to the ground (a scene that recalls the end of the Cold War), but it's so far in the background you're likely to miss it on first viewing. We should get a pull-back from a close-up here to really emphasize the epic nature of what's transpiring. As it is, I have to wonder why the hell they are celebrating on the Emperor's home planet. Shouldn't they be pissed off?

Ultimately, what disturbs me the most about the Special Editions — if we are to accept them as the inevitable result of the triumph of all commerce over art — is the spottiness of their specialness. If they're going to go and "fix" the *Star Wars* trilogy, ➤

why has so much remained untouched? You have dramatic changes that have been made to *Star Wars* while even greater flaws remain untouched. Certainly this is the case with *Jedi,* where you don't get the sense that George Lucas ever sat down with his special effects artists and really watched the whole film, studying and really analyzing and exploring how to make it better. The Special Editions amount to a bunch of special effects touch-ups rather than a concerted effort to bring the film into the nineties. Ironically, the addition of some of the new footage makes some of the unenhanced material look that much hokier by comparison (for example, the matte paintings on Bespin in *Empire*). And while the digital imagery never seamlessly blends with the grain of the twenty-year-old Gil Taylor cinematography in *Star Wars, Empire*'s and *Jedi*'s new footage doesn't cut in as seamlessly either. The addition of some new Boba Fett footage in *Jedi* is particularly laughable as he flirts with Sy Snootles's backup singers. If you really want to indulge the Boba Fett sycophants who clap at his every appearance in the trilogy (and even Lucas admittedly remains mystified by the appeal of the character), then why don't we get to see Boba escape the Sarlacc pit instead of seeing this sup-

posedly formidable bounty hunter get swallowed in one of the most execrable moments of slapstick in the trilogy? (Frankly, I would have loved a postcredit scene where we see Boba crawling out of the Sarlaac pit. That would have been a treat.)

Ultimately, when watching the three films as a whole, one can't help but be struck by the incredible imagination of George Lucas's vividly realized universe. *Star Wars* remains a great movie, a masterpiece, its luster somewhat diminished by the Special Edition missteps. Even more remarkable is *The Empire Strikes Back,* one of the most unconventional sequels of all time, which widens the scope of *Star Wars* and shockingly tells a dark and fatalistic story full of chills and thrills. Its biggest action set piece occurs twenty minutes in and it ends with the villain revealed as the hero's father. This is not the stuff of traditional modern filmmaking. That's why *Jedi* is ultimately such a dramatic disappointment. Eschewing the bleak fatalism and atypical structure of its predecessor, *Jedi* is the most mindlessly by-the-numbers film one could imagine. It is a virtual remake of *Star Wars:* another Death Star, another infiltration of an Imperial stronghold, another space battle against overwhelming odds in order to blow up the baddies. Only

this time, it's colored by the cutesy antics of the Ewoks and some seemingly endless exposition that attempts to explain all the plot points left open in the first two movies. Some of the early going is interminable, as first Yoda, then Ben, then finally Luke (to Leia) explains the back story in some painfully slow and badly written scenes. The first maxim of moviemaking is "Show, don't tell," and *Jedi* just tells and keeps on telling. Never mind that the revelation that Luke and Leia are brother and sister is nearly as disappointing as Vader's conversion to good guy, or the subsequent revelation that the Dark Lord of the Sith is, in fact, Humpty Dumpty.

The fact is that the mythic quality that gave the first two films their epic scope is sadly lacking in the finale, which fails to introduce anything new to the mythos. Even the Emperor's a bit of a bore, constantly lamenting Luke's lack of vision and spewing cackling laughter while repeatedly echoing his "dark side" mantra. Despite the best efforts of Ian McDiarmid, the Emperor begins to sound like a used-car salesman after a while, as the depth and complexity of *Empire*'s characters are dispensed with in favor of the stick-figure characterizations of *Jedi*. There's a brief moment that only hints at the Emperor's venality: when he orders

- The *Millennium Falcon*'s arrival in the Cloud City of Bespin has been enhanced, much like the Mos Eisley scenes in *Star Wars*. New shots of the ship arriving through the metropolis in the sky have been added, along with additional John Williams music that had been virtually inaudible in (or cut from) the original version.
- Throughout the Bespin sequences, new digital backdrops and matte paintings — mainly of windows that overlook the Cloud City surroundings — have been added. Lucas had felt that the sets previously had a claustrophobic feel and did not take advantage of the unique setting that Bespin afforded.
- A brief exterior shot of Bespin's population listening to Lando's warning that the Empire has taken over their city has been created.
- As Vader confronts Luke at the climax, telling him that he is his father, the young Jedi-in-training yells in horror as he falls downward through a wind tunnel. In the original version, Luke lets go of his father's grasp and falls silently; why this unnecessary vocal scream was added is anybody's guess.
- Several inserts of Darth Vader walking to his shuttle and landing in an Imperial Star Destroyer (in footage that appears to have been culled from *Return of the Jedi*) have been intercut to scenes where Luke hangs from an antenna on the bottom of Cloud City.
- James Earl Jones is credited in the Special Edition, though not in the original release.

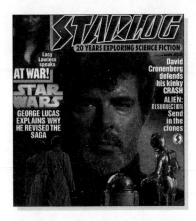

RETURN OF THE JEDI

Original version, 131 mins.
Special Edition, 135 mins.

The final chapter in the *Star Wars* trilogy had several new sequences created for its special edition. Criticism of the rather static puppets that Lucasfilm's now-defunct creature shop created for Jabba's

Vader back to his command ship and turns to his wizened advisers, here are three men who would sink to depths of evil that Darth Vader could only imagine. Then we cut away back to Endor, so that the Care Bears adventure can ensue. The true blackness of such mythical characters as Morgan le Fay and Mordred or *Lord of the Rings*'s Sauron is hinted at but never realized, replaced by cartoon wickedness. The Emperor does look like the wicked witch from *Snow White*, after all.

So are the Special Editions all that special? Not really. But it doesn't really matter, because *Star Wars* and *Empire* will always be among two of the most special movies of all time, upgrades or no. We can only hope that it is the original versions, not the Special Editions, that will be preserved for future generations to enjoy on the big screen rather than just on video, which only hints at their brilliance. ✦

palace was addressed by a new CGI musical number, while another new elaborate sequence was added for the film's celebratory finale. Aside from these new scenes, there are few changes in the Special Edition version; fans had hoped to see an excised scene with our heroes fleeing from a Tatooine sandstorm, but for the most part, Lucas opted to remain faithful to his original version.

+ The musical number "Lapti Nek" has been replaced by an entirely new sequence and musical number, "Jedi Rocks," written for the Special Edition by Jerry Hey. Singer Sy Snootles now moves about without the constraint of puppeteering wires and is joined in a duet by a new creature, a Yazim, while a chorus of singers provides backup and bandleader Max Rebo, one of the original creatures, joins in.

Noted Lucas, "Special effects don't make a movie; the story makes the movie. All special effects allow you to do is make a particular story. In the original *Jedi,* I wanted to do a musical number. The state of the art at that point was that I could get just barely fifteen or twenty seconds out of it, with a puppet that moved around a little bit. A big musical number was impossible. The new technology allows you to go one step further and make it what you originally envisioned it to be. It's not like writing a book, where you use words to create an imaginary world in the reader's mind. Film is very literal. You create a synthetic reality that can fool the audience, but at the same time you're stuck with a very literal interpretation of what's going on. You must create something to photograph that fools the audience into thinking this creation of an imaginary world allows them to function in this make-believe environment. How do you create the illusion that something exists on the screen? If you're doing it in words, it's easy. You can just write, 'The earth falls apart.' You can describe it in as much detail as you want, but to actually show it is really hard."

> **S**pecial effects don't make a movie; the story makes the movie. All special effects allow you to do is make a particular story."
>
> **— GEORGE LUCAS**

- Just as the musical number concludes, a girl is shown inside the rancor pit.
- An establishing shot of the Tatooine desert, showing a herd of banthas, has been added.
- The Sarlacc pit monster has been digitally enhanced to include a mobile beak and additional tentacles in an attempt to make it appear more menacing.
- The celebration sequence that constitutes the picture's finale includes another new musical piece, "Victory Celebration," composed for the Special Edition by John Williams. (The cue it replaces, "Ewok Celebration," has been entirely eliminated from this version.) Newly produced special effects shots of crowds around the galaxy celebrating while the music plays have been added, and the trilogy concludes with our heroes celebrating on Endor, while the original Jedi (Obi-Wan, Yoda, and Luke's father, Anakin Skywalker) proudly look on.

> I feel there's a certain advantage to being constrained, for the artist. Without limits, you can go berserk, you can't end it. It's very helpful for an artist to say to him, 'Here is the circle. Draw in the circle.'"
> — GEORGE LUCAS

Lucas is, admittedly and finally, pleased with the trilogy, and is a realist in terms of the limitations of time and budget.

"I'm a very strong believer in discipline," he has said. "Though most of the films I've directed have been under very difficult conditions, on low budgets, I feel there's a certain advantage to being constrained, for the artist. Without limits, you can go berserk, you can't end it. It's very helpful for an artist to say to him, 'Here is the circle. Draw in that circle.' And many of the great artists, even Pablo Picasso, if you say [picking up a notepad on the table], 'Here is the yellow pad, and here is the blue pen,' he can work within that. Without those limits, it can be very hard to be self-disciplined enough to get them done. On the other hand, there's a lot of fun in self-indulgence, and I really enjoyed this process of fixing the movies. But of course, no matter how you do it, there are certain constraints — the film does have to come out. Creatively, I think the films are pretty much the way I want them now."

THE SPECIAL EDITIONS

REBIRTH

GENERALLY SPEAKING, every time there is a phenomenon within the entertainment industry, it is the quintessential flame burning twice that burns half as long.

Remember Coonskin hats? Barnabas Collins? Disco? Power Rangers? Dear Lord, who could forget the Barney phenomenon? Well, by 1985 it seemed as though *Star Wars* was completely falling by the wayside, Lucasfilm being unable to give away licenses to the property.

Although every now and then George Lucas would drop hints that "some day" he would return to that galaxy of his, everyone took his words with a grain of salt, and the general perception was that while there would always be a cult following of the films, the mainstream audience had left him for the likes of (ugh!) *Independence Day*.

"We always felt that *Star Wars* was much deeper than simply a toy property," Howard Roffman, vice president of licensing for Lucasfilm told *Not of This Earth* magazine. "Obviously the films have affected hundreds of millions of people, and not just kids. We felt that it would be a classic, but that it needed to be nurtured and developed as a classic."

When Roffman segued from Lucasfilm general counsel to his position in licensing in 1986, *Star Wars* merchandise had come to a virtual standstill. "We had gone through this tremendous period with *Star Wars*," he said. "When it was new, *Star Wars* was a mass market phenomenon and toys were by far the majority of the product being sold and [from which] revenues [were] being generated. Things like that normally have a limited lifespan and the question always is, is there something about them that makes them more enduring or are they a one-shot phenomenon? But in 1985, the toys were over. You couldn't even mention *Star Wars* to retailers. There simply wasn't a whole lot happening."

In an attempt to begin rectifying the situation, Roffman struck a deal with Western Games, which developed various role-playing games based on the *Star Wars* trilogy that were enormously successful. Said Roffman, "What we've begun to do is look at a program that would take *Star Wars* into new territory. It was not an attempt to repeat what had been done before when *Star Wars* was hot in 1977, and we've been slowly building it. It started with the novels."

"The novels" in question have been published by Bantam Books, beginning with Timothy Zahn's 1991 effort *Heir to the Empire,* which was the first in a trilogy. That book, like those that have followed, was on the national best-seller lists.

"I think the success of the novels surprised everybody," Bantam editor Tom Dupree told journalist Edward Gross. "The first *Star Wars* novel that we did hit number one on the *New York Times* best-seller list, which is almost unheard of for a science-fiction novel. We were stunned to hear stories about customers in Waldenbooks helping the clerks to open boxes to find the books."

Lucas, for his part, never seemed to doubt his saga's continued commercial viability. In the late eighties, as he began to gear up (slowly) for the prequel trilogy, he decided that the time had come to bring in established sci-fi novelists and let them loose in his universe. Said Lucas, "After [the movies were] released, it became apparent that my story — however many films it took to tell — was only one of thousands that could be told about the characters [from the movies]. But these were not stories that I was destined to tell. It

> **W**e always felt that *Star Wars* was much deeper than simply a toy property. Obviously the films have affected hundreds of millions of people, and not just kids. We felt that it would be a classic, but that it needed to be nurtured and developed as a classic."
>
> — **HOWARD ROFFMAN,**
> vice president of licensing,
> Lucasfilm

is an amazing, if unexpected, legacy of *Star Wars* that so many gifted writers are contributing new stories to the saga."

Added Roffman, "One of the things obvious about *Star Wars* is that, like *Star Trek*, it's a very rich universe with very well-defined characters and situations and creatures and politics. Timothy Zahn's first book turned out to be a smashing validation of the theory that people would be interested in good new fiction based on the *Star Wars* universe. George did, however, give us certain limits so we didn't interfere with anything he would have to say in the new movies. That's why [the books] focus on events after *Return of the Jedi*."

One of the things that Bantam has done has been to spend a great deal of time making sure that the films and novels all fit together to make a cohesive universe.

"That's a key difference between our book program and, say, the *Star Trek* program," said Dupree. "*Star Trek* is episodic, while ours is part of a larger mega-story. In a typical *Trek* novel, everything's okay at the beginning, there's a problem, they fix it and then everything is okay at the end — just like an episode of the TV show. We're making our stories work together in the larger *Star Wars* universe, so if Han and Leia get married in Zahn's book and you write a book that happens after that, they are married. Each publication adds a little bit to the mythology."

"Continuity is an important issue to us," said Roffman. "We feel there has to be an integrity to the program or it's not worth doing."

The success of *Star Wars* merchandise continued to snowball following the launch of the novels. Next up was Dark Horse comics, which offered a six-issue miniseries titled "Dark Empire," a limited series known as "Tales of the Jedi," and many others. "We knew we had to get very good comic book artists and writers, which is why we went into business with Dark Horse," said Roffman. "We felt that they had the commitment to quality we were looking for, and we're thrilled with what they've done."

> The first *Star Wars* novel that we did hit number one on the *New York Times* bestseller list, which is almost unheard of for a science-fiction novel. We were stunned to hear stories about customers in Waldenbooks helping the clerks to open boxes to find the books."
>
> **— TOM DUPREE,**
> editor, Bantam Books

Particularly successful have been the efforts of LucasArts Entertainment, which has marketed several video and computer games that have broken all sales records, followed by a wide-ranging series of action figures, vehicles, and the like.

"The idea was that if we were going to bring *Star Wars* back as a classic, we had to give people something that adds value to the property," Roffman pointed out. "It's not just putting the name on something in an effort to pump up a mass-market success. Everything has to have a reason for being. You really need to be sensitive to the quality demands of your audience. In everything we're doing, that's a big concern. And we've approached toys very cautiously. We had no idea if you could sustain any kind of toy presence at mass market, because the two things that seem to drive toys very much are either television and movie exposure or television advertising. What we learned is that there is a pretty big pent-up demand for *Star Wars* in the toy category. Overall, we have two different goals. We want to treat *Star Wars* the way it deserves to be treated, preserving its status as a classic. That is what we're entrusted with right now and that's a long-term goal regardless of the sequels. The other is making sure that everything kind of leads into the marketing of the sequels and trying to make them as successful as possible. It's an interesting challenge because it's combining something old and something new while continuing to make it relevant to people today."

*S*tar *Trek* is episodic, while ours is a part of a larger mega-story. In a typical *Trek* novel, everything's okay at the beginning, there's a problem, they fix it and then everything is okay at the end — just like an episode of the TV show. ➤

That relevancy was proven in 1994 when Lucas issued a boxed set of the trilogy, digitally remastered for sound and picture quality. The fact that these films — which were still widely available on video and are on television constantly — sold 22 million boxed units proved two things: (1) George Lucas ain't no dummy, and (2) *Star Wars* was here to stay.

"We're seeing more and more the impact those tapes have had," said Roffman. "What it's told us in a big way is how perennial — how enduring — the films are, and how they hold up. What I hear over and over again is that people who were kids or teenagers and just loved it, when they see it again today, after they haven't seen it for a while and are looking at it through the eyes of an adult, they're seeing it on a whole other level of meaning that really turns them on. To me, that's very exciting because it says you have created something that will last through the ages."

Although the box office success of the Special Edition trilogy (discussed elsewhere in this book) would prove just how enduring *Star Wars* really was, there was still one barometer left to be tested.

SHADOWS OF THE EMPIRE

The familiar *Star Wars* music swelled, the Emperor, Darth Vader, and Luke Skywalker filled the screen as the audience was barraged with a montage of images, including X-Wings and TIE fighters.

Although this sounds like a trailer for a new *Star Wars* movie, it was, in actuality, merely a collection of clips from the original three movies designed to prime fans for the marketing onslaught from Lucasfilm and its licensing partners of *Shadows of the Empire*.

When a new *Star Wars* was still several years away, Lucasfilm introduced a new licensing program under the *Shadows of the Empire* umbrella, taking place between the events of *The Empire Strikes Back* and *Return of the Jedi*. The *Shadows* story revolves around the galactic underworld's attempts to assassinate Luke Skywalker and get closer to the Emperor in order to take control of the Empire, as well as to deal with feuding bounty hunters. *Shadows* involved the simultaneous release of a novel by Steve Perry from Bantam Books; a video game for Nintendo Ultra-64; a six-part Dark Horse Comics series by John Wagner, Kilian Plunkett, and Hugh Fleming; a trading-card series from Topps featuring art by the Brothers Hildebrandt, who created the famous one-sheet for the original *Star Wars;* the Mark Cotta Vaz trade paperback, *The Making of Shadows of the Empire;* and a

> ➤ We're making our stories work together in the larger *Star Wars* universe. Each publication adds a little bit to the mythology."

— TOM DUPREE
editor, Bantam Books

soundtrack album (!) composed by Joel McNeely. Insofar as Lucasfilm was concerned, the trick was to make sure that all of the spin-offs were different enough from each other that they would, in the end, cover every aspect of the story imaginable.

"We had been using three different media to spin new stories in the *Star Wars* universe," said Howard Roffman, referring to novels, comics, and games. "And the fans were really enjoying them; it was all working really well. Even though we were paying a lot of attention to continuity, so that they weren't contradicting each other, it hit us: Wouldn't it be interesting if they all complemented each other, so that we had all these media united into a single, galvanizing story? To do that, it had to be a very special story . . . set in the time period of the original trilogy. We looked to the movies to give us our clue as to what would be interesting to explore in that time period. That's where we came up with the idea of the underworld, the organized crime empire within the *Star Wars* universe. We glimpsed it in *Empire,* where Vader hires bounty hunters.

> **W**e want to treat *Star Wars* the way it deserves to be treated, preserving its status as a classic. That is what we're entrusted with right now and that's a long-term goal regardless of the sequels."
>
> **— HOWARD ROFFMAN**
> vice president of licensing,
> Lucasfilm

"When we thought it through," he added, "it just got more and more interesting, because if there was a head of an organized crime world, he would most likely need to exercise great influence with the Emperor. So, suddenly you have a shadowy figure who is all-powerful, head of the immensely powerful criminal organization, and who has the ear of the head of the Empire. Naturally that person could be an ally of Darth Vader — or a political infighter. It's more interesting to have him as a political infighter."

Author Steve Perry picked up the scenario. "The time between *Empire* and *Jedi* is probably anywhere from several months to a year," he related to *Cinescape* magazine. "A lot of stuff could have gone on. Still, it was kind of scary because I couldn't help but think, 'I'm getting into some territory here that has to be nailed down pretty tight.'"

With the events bookending *Shadows* "nailed down pretty

tight," Perry turned his attention to character. Though he wasn't able to use Han Solo, who spends the course of the book as Jabba's prized wall ornament, the author took advantage of the opportunity to flesh out the other primary characters, particularly Darth Vader.

"I think Vader is more interesting in this book than he's ever been before," Perry said. "I got to play with his motivations and reveal why he's doing what he's doing. I also had to show the transition of Luke from where he was in *Empire* to the beginning of *Jedi*, where he is a good enough Jedi to walk into Jabba's palace unarmed and come out alive."

The creative highlight of the book, according to Perry, was the development of the new villain, Xizor, who he knew had to be on a par with Vader. Perry sat down with members of Lucasfilm and developed a history for the character and his Cosa Nostra–like organization, Black Sun.

"He's kind of like Marlon Brando in *The Godfather*, though more physically capable than Brando was in that movie," explained Perry. "He wants to be the number-one man in the galaxy, but he's about number three. Obviously, he's got a couple of major impediments in Vader and the Emperor in his effort to get to the top. If you've seen the third movie, then I don't think it's ruining anything to say that he doesn't quite make it to the top."

Probably the strangest offshoot of *Shadows of the Empire* was the soundtrack album by Joel McNeely — a soundtrack to a film that doesn't exist, coming off the legendary work of John Williams.

The soundtrack project originated with Lucasfilm's Lucy Wilson and Varese Sarabande Records VP Robert Townson. From the beginning, Townson saw McNeely (who had been recommended by John Williams himself to score episodes of *The Young Indiana Jones Chronicles*) as the perfect man for the job, although the project nearly fell through when one of McNeely's film-scoring assignments encroached on the narrow window of opportunity assigned for writing and recording the *Shadows* CD.

> **I** think Vader is more interesting in this book than he's ever been before. I got to play with his motivations and reveal why he's doing what he's doing."
>
> — **STEVE PERRY**, author, *Shadows of the Empire*

"I called Bob up and said, 'I'm really sorry but I'm not going to be able to do this,'" McNeely reflected to writer Jeff Bond. "I couldn't get off of the movie. Then he said, 'Well, then we're not going to do it.' There was a very tense week there when the whole thing was falling apart. And then my second movie just went away because that got pushed back, and I had to give up that movie."

With the project set, Townson and McNeely each tried to determine exactly what form this untried concept would take. "I read the book, Bob read the book and we independently made our own concept notes of what we thought it should be and then we got together and found out that they were almost identical," said McNeely. "In fact, there were a couple of additions of his that were great ideas."

McNeely then had to confront the biggest shadow engulfing the project: the specter of Williams. "I started to listen to the trilogy CDs and I thought, 'I have to put these away, I can't go there. John Williams did it better than anyone can ever do this, and if I start thinking about that I'll wind up in a ball and I won't be able to write anything, and what's the point anyway.' He did it so incredibly well. So I started to look at it as, 'This is a piece of music,' and I tried to forget about *Star Wars* and everything that's come before it and concentrate on the characters in the book — forget that it's Luke Skywalker and Princess Leia, just look at them as characters and pretend I'm writing a score to this thing as if none of this had been done before."

After negotiating between his own film composing schedule

> **X**izor is kind of like Marlon Brando in *The Godfather*, though more physically capable than Brando was in that movie. He wants to be the number-one man in the galaxy, but he's about number three. Obviously, he's got a couple of major impediments in Vader and the Emperor in his effort to get to the top."
>
> — **STEVE PERRY,** author,
> *Shadows of the Empire*

and the schedule of the 260-piece Scottish National Orchestra and Choir, McNeely was left with a meager three weeks to compose both the *Shadows* soundtrack and one for a major film. "It was not fun," he said. "I mean, it was fun, but it was torturous. And I finished it and I was writing *Flipper* at the same time and I went off to Scotland to record and I was still writing *Flipper* and it was really intense. And you know, I can hear that it was written in three weeks, and I know how much better it would be if I'd had six weeks or eight weeks or six months. A lot of people writing a concert piece like this would spend six months. And it wasn't the record company's fault as much as my crazy schedule. It's like anything else where you look back and think, 'I could have done this and I could have done that.' The problem is with a concert work, a symphonic composer writes the piece usually, and they get their work played, then they take their work back, they edit it, pare it down and expand some sections, but they get a first take on it and then they get to go back to the drawing board and redo it. I did it and it was what hit the paper the first time, that's what's on the record and that's what it'll be forever, so there are some things I like and some things that make me go nuts."

McNeely found inspiration in Ralph McQuarrie's paintings of the Imperial home planet Coruscant for his eight-minute "Imperial City" cue, an immense choral tone poem. "I said, 'Okay, we're starting from outer space, we're cruising in and you see it from a distance. It's like a bright glowing jewel, and the closer you get in you see the whole thing is sparkling with these spikes coming out of it and the spikes happen to be these immense buildings stretching toward the skies.' I just made up this whole scenario in my head. . . . I'm the one who gets off on it the most because I know what's going on there."

The composer got some assistance from longtime friend and *Star Wars* sound effects designer Ben Burtt, who was asked to contribute an alien language text to be sung by the orchestra's chorus. "I said, 'What if there's an ancient Imperial language previously

> **I** started to listen to the trilogy CDs and I thought, 'I have to put these away, I can't go there. John Williams did it better than anyone can ever do this, and if I start thinking about that I'll wind up in a ball and I won't be able to write anything.'"
>
> — **JOEL MCNEELY,** composer

undiscovered that only the old guys knew, and the text was either an epic battle poem or a warning? Just give me a couple of paragraphs of that,'" said McNeely, "and [Burtt] came back with the whole thing, a big text and an analysis of it. It was quite detailed and a lot of fun, and it added a whole other dimension to it. It's in keeping with the amount of detail that goes into the films. They really think these things out: George was a fanatic for detail."

In the end, *Shadows of the Empire* was a commercial success, though critically the project wasn't as well received. Former *Sci-Fi Universe* editor Mark A. Altman summed it up when he noted, "This is the stupidest idea I've ever heard. People are interested in movies, not marketing plans. This is just a crass attempt to keep the *Star Wars* juggernaut rolling in the interim between now and the release of the next *Star Wars* film."

Howard Roffman didn't agree. "We were walking a fine line because we didn't want to make it a merchandising free-for-all," he said. "That's not the idea of *Shadows*. I see it much more as a platform for a lot of creative people to express their love of *Star Wars*. I see it as a better version of what we've been doing all these years with books, comics, and games. As far as I'm concerned, if a product isn't contributing something new and creative, then it's not going to happen. You look at everything we're doing, where we are making extensions, they're all areas that allow very gifted people to bring their own creativity to bear on the *Star Wars* universe."

> **W**e were walking a fine line because we didn't want to make it a merchandising free-for-all. That's not the idea of *Shadows*. I see it much more as a platform for a lot of creative people to express their love of *Star Wars*."
>
> — **HOWARD ROFFMAN,**
> vice president of licensing,
> Lucasfilm

THE PREQUELS

Indiana Jones actually saved the *Star Wars* franchise.

Okay, maybe that's a bit of an exaggeration. Granted that the *Star Wars* franchise didn't *really* need saving, but Indy Jones — or more precisely, the *Young Indiana Jones Chronicles* TV series — nonetheless paved the way for George Lucas to finally launch the new prequel trilogy.

Writer/director Frank Darabont, the man behind the film adaptation of Stephen King's *The Shawshank Redemption* and a writer on *Young Indy,* believes Lucas's passion for that TV series grew out of a newfound liberty. In the pages of *Cinescape* magazine, he postulated that the minimogul felt that Lucasfilm and its many limbs (ILM, LucasArts, and so on) had finally reached a level of prosperity — both creatively and financially — that would allow Lucas to step back from CEO duties and concentrate on being a filmmaker again.

"I think he was coming out of 10 years worth of, 'Okay, I've got to build this empire and make sense of it. I've got to make this machinery run.' Without such guidance, companies like Lucasfilm tend to erode after a while, and it needed a steady hand on the tiller," said Darabont. "I think he was now putting on his filmmaker hat again after quite a while, and this was his means of getting his feet wet. This has been my understanding from talking to George and others during the creative process. *Young Indy* was George really hopping up on the horse, picking up the shield and sword, and saying, 'We're filmmakers again! We've been businessmen for too long!' This was his way of coming out of that period and sort of paving the way, I think, for the next *Star Wars* trilogy."

Lucas himself more or less concurred with this statement, noting that on the feature end of things it is usually very expensive to do anything. On *Young Indy,* he began by saying he wanted a couple of hundred effects shots in every hour-long episode while maintaining an F/X budget under $50,000. He wanted to experiment, and felt that they were able to produce twenty-two "feature films" in five years. "We learned a lot in the process," he told *American Cinematographer,* "and that's what I'm using now. The TV show was really a testbed for the *Star Wars* Special Editions." Simultaneously, ILM was improving digital animation, culminating in the unprecedented effects for *Jurassic Park.* That Steven Spielberg–directed film represented the moment that the company essentially "jumped the fence" and made Lucas

Young Indy was George really hopping up on the horse, picking up the shield and sword, and saying, 'We're filmmakers again! We've been businessmen for too long!' This was his way of coming out of that period and sort of paving the way, I think, for the next *Star Wars* trilogy."

— FRANK DARABONT,
screenwriter

realize just what they could accomplish. Since that time, digital animation, creating characters and being able to manipulate elements, has changed the way filmmakers think of the medium. "That's very liberating," he said. "It's a better, more efficient way of using the resources."

One question that has been raised is why would Lucas direct the first chapter in the prequel trilogy, when he has gone on the record as being so adamantly against the idea of directing?

"I've always wanted to go back and direct," he said at a recent press conference. "I've just been sidetracked by other things. I've had too many things to deal with, primarily raising kids. I feel I've finally reached the point where I can do that and direct at the same time. Also, part of it is that I wanted to make my own personal film. The new technology, the new ways of making movies are so exciting that I feel I have to help to figure out how to do this movie. And once I've figured it out, I can turn it over to somebody else and say, 'That's how to do it.' That's what I did on the first one. It would be very hard for me to work closely with the director on one of the films if I hadn't already done one myself. Just the production techniques are so unique to this particular genre that most people have had very little experience at it. I need to reeducate myself. Many of the ways of doing things have changed, and if any mistakes are made, I would like to make them myself, figure out how to do it, and this tells me how. I can tell the other directors I've been there, we don't do it that way now, we do it this way. Doing these films is very esoteric; there's nothing like *Star Wars.*"

He has also made it pretty clear that his imagination as a writer was creatively unleashed in the same way. "I'm having a good time," he said of writing the script for *Episode One.* "It's slow work, but all writing is that way I guess. It's fun to be able to get back into this universe, especially now that we have all the new technology. I can create the world more the way I envisioned it in the beginning, with more characters moving around and more kinds of things. In the

The new technology, the new ways of making movies are so exciting that I feel I have to help to figure out how to do this movie. And once I've figured it out, I can turn it over to somebody else and say, 'That's how to do it.' ➤

last films I was always struggling with certain characters who have a mind of their own and having certain characters like Yoda that couldn't walk more than three or four feet. Now I can have characters who do all kinds of things that were impossible before, so it's fun."

Also "fun" for millions of *Star Wars* fans has been trying to figure out the plot of the first film, a nearly impossible task. However, Lucas's decision to structure the middle trilogy like a classic work of Greek tragedy suggests that the first trilogy might also have the same dramatic structure. *Star Wars*, like the first act of a Greek play, provides exposition for the major characters, introduces central conflict (which will later be resolved), and ends triumphantly. *The Empire Strikes Back*, like the second act, begins "in medias res" (in the middle of the action), provides a somewhat darker vision of the central conflict, and ends with many issues left unresolved. *Return of the Jedi*, the third and final act, resolves all of the conflicts, ties up the loose ends in the denouement, and offers some form of redemption or hope.

Central to this analogy is also a tragic figure whose "hamartia" (error, transgression, or weakness of character) has caused him to fall from grace. Darth Vader, the evil Dark Lord of the Sith, is clearly this tragic figure. When he first appears in *Star Wars*, he is a most reprehensible character, capable of any abomination. But by the end of the third film, Vader is portrayed sympathetically as a pitiful old man who has made one too many mistakes in his life. He also emerges as the true hero who, by destroying the Emperor, saves not only Luke but the Rebel Alliance as well. Clearly then, his struggles as a younger man (Anakin Skywalker) with Obi-Wan Kenobi and the Emperor are

> ► That's what I did on the first one. It would be very hard for me to work closely with the director on one of the films if I hadn't already done one myself."
>
> — GEORGE LUCAS

PREQUEL TRILOGY SPECULATION

by DAN VEBBER

Shortly before George Lucas announced that he would be making the prequel trilogy, we wondered if the new set of films could live up to the existing trilogy. We collected some opinions in a series of interviews with Kevin Anderson, science fiction and Star Wars *author; renowned* Star Wars *collector and author Steve Sansweet; David "Darth Vader" Prowse; Kenny "R2-D2" Baker; Warwick "Wicket" Davis; and Jeremy "Boba Fett" Bulloch.*

Q: *One of the main reasons George Lucas gives for diving back into* Star Wars *is that computer effects have finally developed to the point that the movies can be made affordably. Do you worry that a reliance on computer effects instead of on physical models, matte paintings, and elaborate costumes will result in a slick,* Babylon 5*-esque look for the new* Star Wars *universe?*

KEVIN ANDERSON: I think all of those computer effects are basically just a tool, like a paintbrush or a sculptor's chisel. You can make really goofy-looking solid models, or you can make decent ones. I think Lucasfilm has pretty much proven that they will do things ►

with technology that you don't expect.
STEVE SANSWEET: I think the technology for something like *The Last Starfighter* has been there for the last ten years — and Lucas is very much aware of where the technology is. The problem until now was that the technology produced things that were too slick and shiny . . . and that's not the universe that Lucas created. I think he's convinced now that the technology is at a point where he could make Yoda walk or could create ten thousand stormtroopers in a battle using only one hundred extras. I don't think he's talking about everything being computer animated and digitized. I think he's talking about other techniques, such as editing and computer manipulation of real backgrounds. He's not necessarily planning to computer-render every new ship and every alien creature on the screen.

Q: Star Wars' *opening scene, in which an unimaginably huge Star Destroyer lumbered after the Rebel blockade runner, was one of the most jarring, impactful scenes in cinema history. But today, in an age when jaded audiences have seen dinosaurs brought to life on the big screen, what chance does Lucas have of creating another truly innovative and jaw-dropping sequence to open his next trilogy?*

KEVIN ANDERSON: I think Lucas's mind-set has always been to change the way cinema works. A lot of it has been behind the scenes, like the THX sound system and film transfer technology. One of the scariest things for me when I think of them working on a new trilogy is that they'll have such enormous shoes to fill. I could imagine how that might have been a part of the reluctance to doing the next movies. What can you do to top the existing trilogy? Special effects is one aspect of it, but not all. Like the opening scene of *Star Wars:* those were some nice effects, nice moving ships and everything, but I think it was the artistic eye that Lucas brought to it that made it the cinematic moment it was. Flash Gordon could have dangled a ship that kept coming and

coming and coming in front of the camera. The Star Destroyer sequence wasn't any fundamentally new technology, it was just a different way of looking at something. *Dune* was Frank Herbert's second book published. It was a fabulous book, one of the best I've ever read. He went on to a long and distinguished career, and he wrote dozens and dozens of really special books. And each time one of his big ambitious books came out, instead of readers' recognizing that it was a really good book, all they ever said was, this is good, but it's not as good as *Dune*. It's like you're cursed by doing something good. I think it's too bad that we can't just celebrate the fact that the first trilogy was monumental and look at the next one and see how good it is. Let's accept the fact that these new movies are *Star Wars* prequels, but let's also look at them as independent movies in and of themselves rather than having this predetermined attitude of "It can't possibly be as good as the first."
STEVE SANSWEET: Lucas can do another scene like that — if that's what he wants to do. He has said the next three movies will be much more character-driven, more complex in dealing with treachery. You won't know who your friends are and who your enemies are. But he's also saying

central to this tale of fall and redemption and must form the basis of the first trilogy.

Similarly, Lucas's fondness for the work of mythologist Joseph Campbell (in particular, *The Hero with a Thousand Faces*) is revealed in a common narrative thread that runs through the stories of both Luke Skywalker and his father, Anakin. Campbell wrote that heroes in every culture share a common journey that begins with a *separation* from home, family, and familiar surroundings in what he terms the "call to adventure" (some heroes refuse the call but are later forced by circumstances to take the journey anyway). And while everyone knows that "a Jedi craves not these things," these heroic figures are often called upon to undertake a dangerous journey or unknown risk. Their journey into the heart of darkness leads to an *initiation,* in which they gain valuable insight about the nature of the universe and themselves from an older mentor. That insight helps them deal with a confrontation with the dark father, wounding, and often dismemberment. Heroes who survive the ordeal are awarded great treasure (in either a physical or a spiritual sense), and *return* with their treasure to empower or control other men. The adventures of Luke Skywalker clearly follow this path.

Whereas audiences are aware of the final disposition of Darth Vader by the close of *Return of the Jedi,* Anakin Skywalker's journey as a tragic hero began much earlier. Exactly what that journey is remains shrouded in mystery, although Lucas, in an amalgamation of several interviews, has dropped a variety of hints about what audiences can expect.

As Lucas has explained it, "It's the story of how everybody [from the first trilogy] got to be where they are now, so what you've seen is sort of the last half of a series, and this is the first half. The characters are the same, but the actors obviously are not going to be the same, because it takes place when they are very young. Obi-Wan is thirtyish. In episodes two and three, Anakin is around twenty. Anakin is about the same age as Luke is in episode four, and Obi-Wan is about forty then. The second two films take place almost continuously, a couple of years in between. At the end of the third

there'll be lots of exciting stuff. I think one of the reasons we haven't seen a new trilogy until now is that Lucas knows that no matter what he does, people are going to be comparing it with their memory of the first three films. And no matter what he does, for some people it will never live up to those first three films. I think Lucas is a smart enough guy to say, "I'm not setting out to top anything. I'm setting out to continue the story. I'm going to lay it out there as best I can, and we'll let the public judge whether they like it or not."

Q: *Many people cite the Ewoks as the single greatest example of Lucas's "selling out" the trilogy, especially after his admission that he originally intended Jedi's forest battle to occur on the homeworld of the considerably less cuddly Wookiees. Did you see a trend toward increasing marketability as the first three movies progressed, and if so, do you think the integrity of future movies will be similarly corrupted?*
WARWICK DAVIS: I've never encountered any [anti-Ewok] derision, although I have heard what you're talking about from various sources. The Ewoks, if you look in the designs and how they were developed, were initially very strange, very primitive looking. Eventually, they ended up ➤

being very cuddly and very cute. I think that was a very deliberate decision by George to do that, because it really helped bring children into the movie. The adults and the fans already had something to look at.

KEVIN ANDERSON: I think *Jedi* had the cute, cuddly Ewoks not only for marketability but because Lucas was trying to play to a younger audience. What people forget is that *Jedi* had some pretty dark and grim stuff in it too, like the Emperor and Darth Vader battling, and Luke trying to kill off his own father. That was some pretty intense stuff, and maybe it was a consideration to add the Ewoks for comic relief and a much lighter story line, to balance it out. The Ewoks did seem geared toward being spun off into toys, but I never wanted any Ewok toys. I wanted a stuffed rancor.

STEVE SANSWEET: It was just as hard for the licensing arm at Lucasfilm to sell licensees on *Empire* as it was to sell them on *Star Wars,* and that was a pretty difficult sell. Despite the amount of money that they made on the first film, the licensees were dubious because there had never been a sequel made that brought in anywhere near the kind of money the first movie made. So, clearly, licensing and merchandising didn't drive *Empire*. When it came to the third movie, I think Lucas

was, in fact, looking to sort of reinvent teddy bears, but I think it was more of a personal thing than a merchandise-driven thing. He had a young daughter and he wanted to create something for her as much as anything else.

Q: *At first, Lucas said R2-D2 and C-3PO would be the only characters featured in all nine* Star Wars *movies, and even went so far as to claim that the story of* Star Wars *was really told through the droids' eyes. Now there's uncertainty whether Artoo and Threepio will be in the prequels at all [actually, it turns out they will be]. What do you think their chances are of being in the new films, and do you think leaving them out would be a mistake?*

KENNY BAKER: As far as the future movies are concerned, I haven't been approached. I don't know who has been. So whether or not I'll be in the next trilogy, I don't know as of yet [he will be]. I was used a lot in the first movie because George was directing. In the second movie, which [Irvin] Kershner directed, I was used a little less because I couldn't move fast enough. R2-D2 was okay in close-up and static scenes, where I reacted to dialogue, but not when it came to being chased or moving quickly. That's why they developed remote-controlled robots. In the third movie, Richard

Marquand told me that George Lucas wanted me to be used more, because the acting part was coming through the robot. But I still wasn't used very much in the third movie, because everything was moving quickly and there was so much action. They developed these robots, but they'll always have somebody like me in the background as backup in case the robots malfunction.

KEVIN ANDERSON: I would expect the droids will be in there and I think it would be a mistake if they weren't. But I don't know enough about what the prequels are going to be. Theoretically, Lucas could go a thousand years back in the past and not even deal with Obi-Wan and Anakin. I don't think that's going to happen, but Lucas always turns left when people expect him to turn right. If you're trying to make a series of movies, you film, Anakin is twenty-two and Ben is about forty-two, so *A New Hope* is about twenty years later when Obi-Wan is in his sixties.

"[Episode one is] a story about Ben Kenobi and Anakin Skywalker and how we got to the point where Obi-Wan Kenobi was waiting in the middle of the desert for something to happen," Lucas says. "It's also about how Darth Vader got to be who he is, and how the Emperor came to power. It starts out with the Emperor not in power, then it keeps progressing. It'll be one twelve-hour movie when it's all finished. It's bleak, but if you know the other three movies, you know everything turns out all right in the end — that the son comes back and redeems him. That's the real story. It's always about the redemption of Anakin Skywalker. It's just that it's always been told from his son's point of view. When the story of the six films is put together, it has a more interesting arc because you're actually rooting more for Darth Vader than you are for Luke. Until now, you didn't know what the problem really was, because Darth Vader is just this bad guy. You didn't realize he's actually got a problem, too."

While advances in technology are affecting the overall approach to *Star Wars* as a film franchise, they have also had an impact on the fans eagerly awaiting the new trilogy's release. In the old days (a long time ago), anyone interested in information on *Star Wars* had to wait for the newest issue of *Starlog* or the now-defunct *Fantastic Films* to find out what was going on. But today, thanks to the advent and proliferation of the Internet, fans from all over the world are united in the dissemination of facts and rumors regarding *Episode One*, supplemented by official announcements and photos from Lucasfilm itself. What follows is an Internet history of the development of the project.

> It's the story of how everybody [from the first trilogy] got to be where they are now, so what you've seen is sort of the last half of a series, and this is the first half."
>
> — GEORGE LUCAS

obviously want some sort of connecting tissue between the different series, and you're kind of limited in your options as to who can carry over in a film fifty years in the past. The droids, of course, are obvious examples, and they are *Star Wars* icons. The challenge, though, is going to be doing something significant and interesting with them rather than just having them be there for the sake of being there. I would like to see them there, but I want to see them be an important part of the story. I wouldn't presume to hold Lucas to any of his old promises, because when you're dealing with a project this huge, it really is a living and growing thing. Lucas isn't a politician who gets elected on promises, he's a creative person telling you what he thinks he'd like to do. But as twenty years go by, things should be expected to change, and I don't want Lucas to use the droids for no better reason than because he said he would in an interview with *Starlog* twenty years ago.

STEVE SANSWEET: I would hope that there would be some way to see the droids in the last movies — if Lucas ever does them. Threepio and Artoo provide a sort of continuity and warmth of recognition. And of course, their interaction is very funny. ➤

STEVE SANSWEET

Q: *The new movies will center largely on Anakin Skywalker before he became Darth Vader. How important will it be for the actor who eventually plays Anakin to base his character on the persona already created by David Prowse and James Earl Jones?*

DAVID PROWSE: I would love to play Anakin, but there's some talk about Mark Hamill filling that role, playing his own father. I don't know how they'd explain his going from his size to my size when he plays Darth Vader, though. Whoever they choose needs to be a very physical actor. He could be the greatest dramatist in the world, but without a physical presence, Vader wouldn't be worth anything.

KEVIN ANDERSON: Darth Vader is obviously where the character of Anakin has to end up. But it's like looking at only the end destination of a road map while you're trying to get there. I think people are going to have expec-

tations of Darth Vader and Anakin Skywalker, but I think it will be stronger if whoever gets picked to play the part acknowledges that his character will eventually turn into Vader but tries to provide some surprises along the way rather than doing it like everyone expects.

Q: *In all of the first trilogy, does one particular moment stand out as your favorite?*

DAVID PROWSE: My favorite moment in the trilogy is Darth Vader's entrance in *Star Wars*. I'll always remember seeing it years ago, watching it and saying, "My God, that's me up there! What an entrance!" It was the most incredible entrance anyone could wish for.

JEREMY BULLOCH: I liked the first entrance when Boba comes on. I think it's when he steps behind Darth Vader. It was just a very lovely moment, and the music really makes it. But there are lots of other moments that come to mind, as well. An awful lot of exciting stuff. In particular, I adore the Ewoks. They were just great.

KEVIN ANDERSON: When the *Falcon* first jumped into hyperspace. That's when I instantly knew this wasn't just another big-budget science fiction movie; this was truly something I had never seen before. I think I've still got

gum stuck to my chin from where it hit the floor. I had never thought of hyperspace travel before, but the moment I saw it I was instantly convinced that that's probably what it would be like.

STEVE SANSWEET: Something that really pops out was when Luke went into the heart of darkness on Dagobah, into that swampy tree to confront what turned out to be himself. I thought that was way cool.

Q: *One of the most surprising aspects of* Star Wars *has been how, in recent years, Boba Fett (who has only a few lines of dialogue in two of the movies) has developed an enormous cult following. To what do you attribute this? Does Boba Fett's recent popularity and potential for interesting back story make him likely to be a featured character in the prequels?*

JEREMY BULLOCH: I think the popularity is due in large part to the costume, which is just wonderful. I also think people are attracted to what they see as Boba's code of honor. He's ruthless. He's money-oriented. He probably was a very good soldier, but something makes him turn into a bounty hunter, something that perhaps we'll discover about the Clone Wars. His code of honor is that he'd never tread on anyone else's feet to

In September 1996 Lucas finally announced that he was going to begin preproduction on the first film of the new trilogy. However, back in November 1995 he began casting for the film, looking for actors to portray the young Anakin Skywalker and "the Queen." The audition requirements for Anakin were "Caucasian, 8–9. Anakin is a handsome young boy with extraordinary charm. He has a vulnerability and earnestness that makes him totally disarming. His amazing aptitude for things mechanical together with his quick wit and physical fitness make him a natural pilot at an early age, maturing into a fighter pilot of exceptional talent. Anakin's resourceful imagination and inventive mind already sets him apart from others. Obi-Wan Kenobi is later to recognize his innate gifts, becoming his friend and mentor, teaching him the attributes of a Jedi Knight. Anakin is a role model of the highest order, someone everybody would like to be. . . . Lead [role]."

JAKE LLOYD
(the young Anakin Skywalker)

Of the Queen, the requirements noted, "Eurasian/Latina girl 13–14. An enchanting young girl, already showing signs of blossoming into a sensual, exotic, dark-haired beauty. By contrast she has, however, the reserve, political acumen, poise and bearing of a queen and ruler, together with a natural wisdom and sensitivity that cannot be taught. A strong, spirited and highly intelligent girl, she is quick to learn the principles of justice and honor. She is a great leader and it is apparent to all. . . . Lead [role]."

In March 1996 word got out that an earlier version of the *Millennium Falcon* had been built at full size so that ILM could begin special effects testing with the ship. The rumor was that

capture a bounty. He does it his ruthless way, but he wouldn't cross anyone. As for the next movie, I get asked all the time if Boba will be in it, and I just don't know.

KEVIN ANDERSON: Boba Fett just looks cool. Darth Vader defined evil for everybody, but for me, Boba Fett defined a bounty hunter. He looked like a bounty hunter, he acted like one, he was smart, he was cold and ruthless, but he's only got three lines. I'd love to see him and I'd love to see some of his back story. I don't think he's necessarily a shoo-in for the prequels, but I think he is certain to star in a lot more sequel novels and spin-off things that pay particular attention to what the fans like.

STEVE SANSWEET: Boba Fett has the coolest costume going. Also, the whole thing around the Boba Fett action figure plays into the mysticism that surrounds the character and so on. Jeremy Bulloch carried the character very well. There was a sense of power and mystery and villainy. You wonder what Fett's background was — and because there is so little already on the canvas you can sort of come up with the colors on the palette yourself. You can make up your own stories, and in fact, some of the comics and novels have done so and resurrected him. ➤

Q: *Of the first three* Star Wars *movies, which is your favorite, and why?*

KEVIN ANDERSON: *Empire* is my favorite because it's the darkest of the three. I've found that the second installments of trilogies always feel to me to be the best ones. In the first installment, you have to spend a lot of time just getting up to speed, introducing everybody to the conflict. When the second one comes around, everything's already going at ninety miles per hour and you can just really let loose. But by the third installment, you're starting to get exhausted and it tends to slow down a bit. I liked the battles. I also really enjoy seeing the backgrounds and details about how the evil stuff works in *Empire*. There's more evil in that movie than there is in the other two.

STEVE SANSWEET: *Empire* is absolutely my favorite. It was a dark, complex, initially frustrating movie that made me think more than the other two ever did. And it was unexpected, because I had planned on seeing a thrill ride like in the first one. I wasn't expecting to put much thought into it. Suddenly, there was a whole new layer of complexity. The mysticism that Yoda added to *Empire* really made it a more adult picture that stayed with me a lot longer. ✦

ultimately the model would be transported to a film studio in England.

April brought with it the rumor that Lucas had hired Kenneth Branagh to star as the younger Obi-Wan Kenobi. Some dopey rumors that same month had Carrie Fisher fleshing out the female roles in Lucas's script (highly unlikely), with the possibility she might direct one of the entries. Even more amusing was one Website's claim that "Carol Channing [will portray] Moffina Delantreos, a whirling-dervish matriarch of House Delantreos, who controls the commercial aspects of the Old Republic." Hmm, maybe she can perform a musical number: "The Jedi are a girl's best friend!"

One *fact* that emerged a month later was that PepsiCo had signed a deal with Lucasfilm for *Star Wars* tie-ins worth an estimated $2 billion (meaning that these films have already turned a profit before a foot of film has been shot). On June 12, 1996, the title *Balance of the Force* is first bandied about — and it's a rumor that's been around for a while now. Around the same time, rumors abounded that Fox was developing an animated series called *Young Jedi Knights,* based on the novels of the same name. At the end of the month, music maestro John Williams was signed to compose the score for the new trilogy.

On July 2, the Internet reported that a new Boba Fett action figure would be equipped with a removable helmet and that his features would actually be those of Anakin Skywalker. If true, it would tie in to elements of the Clone Wars that play an integral role in the prequels.

At the beginning of August, *Star Wars* collector and Lucasfilm employee Steve Sansweet appeared on the home shopping channel QVC and mentioned that Lucas had finished writing the first draft of the screenplay. Toward the end of the month, actress Natalie Portman was approached during an interview with the rumor that she had been signed for a role in the film, but she claimed it wasn't true.

On September 6, 1996, Lucas formally announced production of the new film and noted that they would use Leavesdon Studios —

converted from a Rolls-Royce factory to a film studio by EON Productions for *GoldenEye* — for soundstages. According to the "Coming Attractions" Website, "Lucasfilm plans to utilize a technology called 'OMF' — a digital media link that allows fast data communication between the film set and the effects department; in effect, once a scene has been shot, the effects technicians can work on the scene almost immediately. This has almost always been done in the post-production phase of a movie.

In mid-September there were some rumors that Steven Spielberg had asked Lucas to consider Dreamworks as distributors for the new trilogy. Toward the end of the month, Lucas noted that he would be directing the first chapter of the prequels. Throughout the rest of the month and all of October, there were many rumors about the plot, many supposedly coming from a "spy" within Lucasfilm, but the general consensus at that time was that Lucas was purposely offering disinformation regarding the plot to throw fans off-track.

In November 1996 it was reported that ILM's Dennis Muren, John Knoll, Joe Letteri, and Alex Seiden would be handling the development of software for the film's effects. Peggy Farrell was signed as costume designer, with Doug Chiang as art director.

NATALIE PORTMAN
(the Queen)

In December actor Samuel L. Jackson appeared on a British talk show and noted, "The film I'm chasing right now is the *Star Wars* prequel. I just want to get in a room with George Lucas and tell him I'm interested. I'd be Lando Calrissian's dad, Darth Vader's dad, Luke Skywalker's slave! Anything! I just want to tell George I'll do it if he wants me." In the end, Jackson would be signed on.

In January 1997 the "Ain't It Cool News" Website announced that British actor Ewan McGregor had been signed to portray the young Obi-Wan Kenobi. On February 21 the Internet reported, "A major plotline involves the fact that only two dark lords can co-exist at one point of time. In the middle trilogy's timeframe, this would be the Emperor and Vader, which explains why in *Return of the Jedi* the Emperor wants Luke to destroy Vader and become the other dark

LIAM NEESON

lord; a team of Wookies [sic], possibly mercenaries, were mentioned as characters in the films."

On March 5 Lucas and producer Rick McCallum appeared on BBC Radio One. During that interview, McCallum noted, "The first three really deal with the fall of Anakin — you will just see the saga of a young boy, his relationship with his mother, how he grows up, who he marries, the children he has. He makes a pivotal choice in his life — a road that takes him to the dark side, and he pays the consequences of that. [In the existing trilogy] we see his children grow up and see him finally redeemed."

Added Lucas, "The fascination with doing the new movies is I've been interested in doing a lot of other things since I finished the first trilogy, which I kind of burned out after doing, but there's always been this lure about going back because the story as a whole, all twelve hours of it, is actually more interesting than what is out there now. When you actually get the whole story and see it in context, then you understand what Vader's side of the story is, what we have not heard yet, and it makes it a much more interesting drama. It's a man struggling with temptation and he loses. The big chance that I'm taking is that I am working on something that I started twenty years ago, and whether it will fit into the modern world marketing-wise, I am not sure. The first one I'm doing is very much like the first one I did before, it is kind of upbeat and fun. The first one always gets to introduce the characters and does not have all that much else to do, so it is easy. On the second one things start to go wrong and get complicated, and the third one is the dark one — it will probably fit in well with the twenty-first century."

> **W**hen you actually get the whole story and see it in context, then you understand what Vader's side of the story is, what we have not heard yet, and it makes it a much more interesting drama. It's a man struggling with temptation and he loses."
>
> — GEORGE LUCAS

April 1997 saw the first rumors that Liam Neeson was soon to sign on as a Jedi Master. A month later it seemed pretty certain that joining

Neeson would be the aforementioned Ewan McGregor as Obi-Wan, Natalie Portman as the Queen, and child-actor Jake Lloyd, costar of Arnold Schwarzenegger's *Jingle All the Way*, as Anakin Skywalker. The casting of Portman and Lloyd was made official on June 10. At the end of the month, filming actually began — at last, the first new *Star Wars* adventure in fifteen years was officially under way.

July began with the official announcement that McGregor had been signed as Kenobi. In the same issue of the *Insider*, Lucas offered, "Ewan McGregor is the perfect young Harrison Ford, but he's also a great young Alec Guinness. He's extremely relaxed and very strong. All the things that Alec Guinness is."

In an amalgamation of several interviews, McGregor exclaimed, "There's nothing cooler than being a Jedi Knight. I was six years old when *Star Wars* came out. I remember standing outside school waiting to be picked up, so excited. And my daughter's going to be six when the new *Star Wars* movies come out. That's fucking lovely in a way. I've been watching Alec Guinness movies from the fifties, like *The Card*, trying to get his voice down, but I haven't talked to him myself. What would I say? 'How'd you do it?' He's only in half the first movie, and it's a legendary performance. With all that bad dialogue, he really pulls it off. I have to get [his] accent. He's got this very specific older man's voice. It'd be great if I could trace it back to his youth and get it right. 'Yoooz the Force, Luke. Stretch out your feeeelings.'"

SAMUEL L. JACKSON

Throughout the month, Samuel L. Jackson noted on a couple of talk shows that he would have a role in the prequel. Indeed, issue 34 of the *Star Wars Insider* provided the following cast list: Pernilla August (Anakin's mother, Shmi), Frank Oz (Yoda's voice), Kenny Baker (R2-D2), Ian McDiarmid (the Emperor), as well as Jackson, Ahmed Best, Adrian Dunbar, Terence Stamp, Oliver Ford Davies, Ray Park, Jerome Blake, Warwick Davis, Hugh Quarshie, Khan Bonfils, Alan Ruscoe, Michelle Taylor, Michaela

I just want to get in a room with George Lucas and tell him I'm interested. I'd be Lando Calrissian's dad, Darth Vader's dad, Luke Skywalker's slave!"
— **SAMUEL L. JACKSON**

Cottrell, John Fensom, Liz Wilson, Christina Disilva, and Silas Carson. Readers were also told that they would see the creation of C-3PO (Anthony Daniels, reprising the role), and that Jabba the Hutt would make an appearance.

On September 14, 1997, "Corona's Coming Attractions" page featured the following "report" from an actor who spent four weeks as an extra on the film, portraying a Rebel soldier: "The Young Queen's palace is going to have a computer generated exterior. The palace walls on the set itself are only about 10 feet high and CG graphics will make up the rest so the palace will probably soar high into the heavens. The palace and the few street sets alongside are medieval themed. . . . I filmed an action scene in the hangar set where the whole area is being held by the droids. The Rebel soldiers (including me!) and pilots dart into the hangar and open fire on the droids. . . . A different scene shot on the same hangar set has some Rebel soldiers running towards the large bay doors and the doors then slide open in front of them, revealing the presence of Panaka (I believe this to be the name of the main villain). Panaka is just standing there wearing a large black cloak with a hood so you can't see his face. The Rebels turn and run away to the left and Panaka then lifts his hood, revealing his red contact lensed eyes and horned head. He unhooks his lightsaber handle from his belt, which is about a foot long, and holds it in front of him. This is the double-headed lightsaber. . . . He then spins it around him like a martial

EWAN McGREGOR
(the young Obi-Wan Kenobi)

There was a cinematic innovation in the first *Star Wars* film that made people say, 'Gee, I'd never seen that before.' I have the opportunity to do that again with the prequels."

— GEORGE LUCAS

arts weapon and runs and leaps into the hangar from the doorway, probably to face Obi-Wan." Whether or not this particular posting is true, it sounds like an intriguing sequence.

With the exception of confirming Anthony Daniels's return as C-3PO and the fact that production wrapped on September 27, Internet postings about the film became limited to discussions of character names, the question of whether Lucasfilm was giving out disinformation concerning the project, and the like. In other words, nothing too substantial. A hard-news item, however, in October, was that Lucasfilm had signed a deal with Hasbro and Galoob toys worth $600 million, bringing the prerelease take for the prequels up to $2.6 billion. Not too shabby at that.

One significant event in April 1998 was that Twentieth Century Fox, thanks to the nearly $500 million gross of the Special Edition trilogy — which Lucas gives a lot of credit to the studio for — was awarded distribution rights to the prequel trilogy.

As for what ultimately happens in *Episode One,* it's anyone's guess. One thing is for certain: the magic of *Star Wars* stands poised to capture the new millennium and, once again, a world's imagination.

"There was a cinematic innovation in the first *Star Wars* film that made people say, 'Gee, I'd never seen that before,'" Lucas told *Time.* "I have the opportunity to do that again with the prequels. The fun part for me is to say, 'You want me to come back and do that for you? I can do that. I'll do it. *Here.*"

There's nothing cooler than being a Jedi Knight. I was six years old when *Star Wars* came out. I remember standing outside my school waiting to be picked up, so excited."
— EWAN MCGREGOR

REBIRTH

THE TIME LINE

THE STAR WARS STORIES have been broken down into two separate time lines: the "real" *Star Wars* universe and the "Marvel Comics" *Star Wars* universe. The former includes the current range of novels and short stories, the newspaper comic strip, and the comic books by Dark Horse (excluding those reprinting Marvel story lines, with the exception of "The Vendelhelm Mission"), most of which were written with care to fit together as seamlessly as possible. The latter includes the comic books published by Marvel (and the three published by Blackthorne), which were never intended to fit into a larger puzzle and tend to contradict themselves and the movies in certain places.

Some of the items do not have specific dates, making their portion on the time line uncertain, so they have been placed using a best guess based on whatever references were made to other events within the story. All the stories are dated based on when they occurred in relation to the initial movie trilogy *(ANH = A New Hope, TESB = The Empire Strikes Back,* and *ROTJ = Return of the Jedi)*. There are also notations indicating which medium the story originally appeared in (M = movie, TV = TV series or special, B = book (adult or young adult), SS = short story, CB = comic book, and N = newspaper comic strip). Only the original medium is noted for stories that have been adapted in various forms (such as the movies, which were all adapted in books, comic books, and radio dramatizations). The dates provided are estimates in most cases, meaning the stories occurred during a period at that point or slightly before or after that point. Multiple stories listed in one particular year have been put in chronological order whenever possible.

THE "REAL" *STAR WARS* UNIVERSE

ANH –5000
Tales of the Jedi — The Golden Age of the Sith (nos. 0–5) (CB)

ANH –4990
Tales of the Jedi — The Fall of the Sith Empire (nos. 1–5) (CB)

ANH –4000
Tales of the Jedi — Ulic Qel-Droma and the Beast Wars of Onderon (Tales of the Jedi nos. 1–2) (CB)
The Most Dangerous Foe (main story) (SS)

ANH –3999
Tales of the Jedi — The Saga of Nomi Sunrider (Tales of the Jedi nos. 3–5) (CB)

ANH –3998
Tales of the Jedi — The Freedon Nadd Uprising (nos. 1–2) (CB)

ANH –3996
Tales of the Jedi — Dark Lords of the Sith (nos. 1–6) (CB)

ANH –3991
Tales of the Jedi — The Sith War (nos. 1–6) (CB)

ANH –3990
Tales of the Jedi — The Redemption of Ulic Qel-Droma (nos. 1–6) (CB)

ANH –32
Star Wars Episode I (M)

ANH –26
Han Solo Trilogy: Book 1 — The Paradise Snare (first flashback) (B)

ANH –25
The Last One Standing: The Tale of Boba Fett (beginning) (SS)
Mist Encounter (SS)
Dagobah (from The Illustrated Star Wars Universe) (SS)

ANH –24
Han Solo Trilogy: Book 1 — The Paradise Snare (second flashback) (B)

ANH –22
Star Wars Episode II (M)

ANH –20
Star Wars Episode III (M)
Dark Vendetta (SS)
The Last One Standing: The Tale of Boba Fett (beginning) (SS)
Han Solo Trilogy: Book 1 — The Paradise Snare (third flashback) (B)

ANH –18
Han Solo Trilogy: Book 1 — The Paradise Snare (fourth and fifth flashbacks) (B)

Droids — The Adventures of
C-3PO and R2-D2 Cycle One:
The Trigon One (episodes 1–4)
(TV)

ANH –17

Droids — The Adventures of C-
3PO and R2-D2 Cycle Two:
Mon-Julpa (episodes 5–9) (TV)

The Great Heep (TV)

ANH –16

Droids — The Adventures of C-
3PO and R2-D2 Cycle Three:
The Adventures of Mugo
Baobob (episodes 10–13) (TV)

ANH –12

The Last One Standing: The Tale
of Boba Fett (middle) (SS)

ANH –11

Payback: The Tale of Dengar
(flashback) (SS)

ANH –10

Han Solo Trilogy: Book 1 —
The Paradise Snare (main story)
(B)

Droids Welcome to Kalarba (CB)

Droids (vol. 1 nos. 1–5) (CB)

Artoo's Day Out (CB)

Droids (vol. 1 no. 6) (CB)

Jabba the Hutt — The Gar Spoon
Hit (CB)

ANH –9

Droids — Rebellion (vol. 2 nos.
1–4) (CB)

Droids — Season of Revolt (vol. 2
nos. 5–8) (CB)

Jabba the Hutt — The Hunger of
Princess Nampi (CB)

ANH –8

The Protocol Offensive (CB)

Jabba the Hutt — The Dynasty
Trap (CB)

X-Wing Rogue Squadron — The

Making of Baron Fel (no. 25)
(flashback) (CB)

ANH –7

Jabba the Hutt — Betrayal (CB)

ANH –6

X-Wing Rogue Squadron — The
Making of Baron Fel (no. 25)
(flashback) (CB)

ANH –5

X-Wing Rogue Squadron — The
Making of Baron Fel (no. 25)
(flashback) (CB)

The Breath of Gelgelar (SS)

Turning Point (SS)

Tatooine (from The Illustrated Star
Wars Universe) (SS)

Han Solo Trilogy: Book 2 — The
Hutt Gambit (chap. 1–7) (B)

Lando Calrissian and the Mindharp of Sharu (B)

This Crumb for Hire (CB)

Ewoks (TV)

ANH –4

No Disintegrations, Please (flashback) (SS)

A Hunter's Fate: Greedo's Tale (beginning) (SS)

Han Solo Trilogy: Book 2 — The
Hutt Gambit (chap. 8–16) (B)

X-Wing Rogue Squadron — The
Making of Baron Fel (no. 25)
(flashback) (CB)

Lando Calrissian and the
Flamewind of Oseon (B)

Lando Calrissian and the StarCave
of ThonBoka (B)

Han Solo Trilogy: Book 2 — The
Hutt Gambit (epilog) (B)

Do No Harm (SS)

The All-New Ewoks (TV)

Lumrunners (SS)

Ringers (SS)

THE TIME LINE

Swoop Gangs (SS)

Old Corellian: A Guide for the
Curious Scholar (SS)

Out of the Cradle (SS)

When the Domino Falls (SS)

ANH –3

Han Solo Trilogy: Book 3 — Rebel
Dawn (chap. 1–6) (B)

Darksaber (second flashback) (B)

Bespin (from The Illustrated Star
Wars Universe) (SS)

Endor (from The Illustrated Star
Wars Universe) (SS)

The Ewok Adventure — A Caravan
of Courage (TV)

ANH –2

Darksaber (third flashback) (B)

Han Solo at Stars' End — From the
Adventures of Luke Skywalker
(B)

Han Solo Trilogy: Book 3 — Rebel
Dawn (chap. 7) (B)

Han Solo's Revenge — From the
Adventures of Luke Skywalker
(B)

Han Solo Trilogy: Book 3 — Rebel
Dawn (chap. 8) (B)

Han Solo and the Lost Legacy —
From the Adventures of Luke
Skywalker (B)

Han Solo Trilogy: Book 3 — Rebel
Dawn (chap. 9–10) (B)

Darksaber (fourth flashback) (B)

A Bitter Winter (SS)

Idol Intentions (SS)

Wanderer of Worlds (SS)

The Last Hand (SS)

Ewoks — The Battle for Endor (TV)

ANH –1

Han Solo Trilogy: Book 3 — Rebel
Dawn (chap. 11–13) (B)

The Great Herdship Heist (SS)

The Draw (SS)

The Final Exit (SS)

Imperial Center Coruscant
(from The Illustrated Star Wars
Universe) (SS)

Laughter after Dark (flashback)
(SS)

Darksaber (fifth flashback) (B)

A Hunter's Fate: Greedo's Tale
(middle) (SS)

X-Wing Rogue Squadron —
The Making of Baron Fel (no.
25) (flashback) (CB)

A Boy and His Monster:
The Rancor Keeper's Tale (beginning) (SS)

ANH –0.5

Han Solo Trilogy: Book 3 —
Rebel Dawn (chap. 14–15) (B)

Darksaber (sixth flashback) (B)

X-Wing: The Farlander Papers —
From the Chronicles of the
Rebel Alliance (B)

Tinnian of Trial (SS)

Dark Forces: Soldier for the Empire (B)

The Adventures of Dannen Life-
hold: Breaking Free (SS)

Drawing the Maps of Peace: The
Moisture Farmer's Tale (day 1
through day 32, during *ANH*)
(SS)

The Adventures of Dannen Life-
hold: Changing the Odds (beginning, during *ANH*) (SS)

Han Solo Trilogy: Book 3 — Rebel
Dawn (chap. 16) (B)

ANH

Star Wars Episode IV: A New Hope
(M)

Passages (beginning, during *ANH*)
(SS)

Han Solo Trilogy: Book 3 —
   Rebel Dawn (epilog, during
   ANH) (B)
We Don't Do Weddings: The
   Band's Tale (during *ANH*) (SS)
Empire Blues: The Devaronian's
   Tale (during *ANH*) (SS)
Drawing the Maps of Peace: The
   Moisture Farmer's Tale (day 50,
   during *ANH*) (SS)
One Last Night in the Mos Eisley
   Cantina: The Tale of the Wolf-
   man and the Lamproid (first
   and last flashbacks, during
   ANH) (SS)
A Hunter's Fate: Greedo's Tale
   (end, during *ANH*) (SS)
Be Still My Heart: The Bartender's
   Tale (during *ANH*) (SS)
Soup's On: The Pipe Smoker's Tale
   (during *ANH*) (SS)
Nightlily: The Lovers' Tale (during
   ANH) (SS)
Swap Meet: The Jawa's Tale (dur-
   ing *ANH*) (SS)
Trade Winds: The Ranat's Tale
   (during *ANH*) (SS)
When the Desert Wind Turns: The
   Stormtrooper's Tale (during
   ANH) (SS)
Play It Again, Figrin D'an: The Tale
   of Muftak and Kabe (during
   ANH) (SS)
The Sand Tender: The Hammer-
   head's Tale (during *ANH*) (SS)
At the Crossroads: The Spacer's
   Tale (during *ANH*) (SS)
Hammertong: The Tale of the
   "Tonnika Sisters" (during *ANH*)
   (SS)
Spare Parts (SS)
The Adventures of Dannen Life-

hold: Changing the Odds (end-
   ing, during *ANH*) (SS)
A Certain Point of View (during
   ANH) (SS)
Tales from Mos Eisley — Light
   Duty (during *ANH*) (CB)
Tales from Mos Eisley — Mostly
   Automatic (during *ANH*) (CB)
Tales from Mos Eisley — Hegg's
   Tale (during *ANH*) (CB)
X-Wing: Rogue Squadron #1/2
   (during *ANH*) (CB)
X-Wing Rogue Squadron — The
   Making of Baron Fel (no. 25)
   (flashback) (CB)

ANH + (immediately after *ANH*)
Darksaber (first flashback) (B)
Vader's Quest (nos. 1–4) (CB)
Boba Fett — Enemy of the Empire
   (nos. 1–4)
Passages (ending) (SS)
To Fight Another Day (SS)
Only Droids Serve the Maker (SS)
Droid Trouble (SS)

ANH +0.5
River of Chaos (CB)
Doctor Death: The Tale of Dr.
   Evazan and Ponda Baba (SS)
Combat Moon (SS)
Sandound on Tatooine (SS)
Priority: X (SS)
Alderaan (from The Illustrated
   Star Wars Universe) (SS)
Chessa's Doom (flashback) (SS)
Galaxy of Fear: Book 1 — Eaten
   Alive (B)
Galaxy of Fear: Book 2 — City of
   the Dead (B)
Galaxy of Fear: Book 3 — Planet
   Plague (B)
Galaxy of Fear: Book 4 —
   The Nightmare Machine (B)

Galaxy of Fear: Book 5 — Ghost of the Jedi (B)

Galaxy of Fear: Book 6 — Army of Terror (B)

Galaxy of Fear: Book 7 — The Brain Spiders (B)

Galaxy of Fear: Book 8 — The Swarm (B)

Galaxy of Fear: Book 9 — Spore (B)

Galaxy of Fear: Book 10 — The Doomsday Ship (B)

Galaxy of Fear: Book 11 — Clones (B)

Galaxy of Fear: Book 12 (B)

Command Decision (SS)

ANH +1

Splinter of the Mind's Eye — From the Adventures of Luke Skywalker (B)

Newspaper comic strip story 1 (untitled) (N)

Newspaper comic strip story 2 (untitled) (N)

Newspaper comic strip story 3 (untitled —"Gambler's World") (N)

Tatooine Sojourn — From the Adventures of Luke Skywalker (N)

Princess Leia, Imperial Servant — From the Adventures of Luke Skywalker (N)

The Second Kessel Run — From the Adventures of Luke Skywalker (N)

Bring Me the Children — From the Adventures of Luke Skywalker (N)

As Long As We Live — From the Adventures of Luke Skywalker (N)

The Frozen World of Ota — From the Adventures of Luke Skywalker (N)

Planet of Kadril (N)

X-Wing Rogue Squadron — The Making of Baron Fel (no. 25) (flashback) (CB)

The Capture of Imperial Hazard (SS)

A Bad Feeling: The Tale of EV-9D9 (beginning) (SS)

ANH +2

A Boy and His Monster: The Rancor Keeper's Tale (middle) (SS)

The Bounty Hunter of Ord Mantell! (N)

Darth Vader Strikes (N)

The Serpent Masters! (N)

Deadly Reunion! (N)

Traitor's Gambit! (N)

The Night Beast! (N)

The Return of Ben Kenobi (N)

Small Favors (SS)

Shape-Shifters (SS)

Special Ops: Ship Jackers (SS)

Special Ops: Drop Points (SS)

Finder's Fee (SS)

The Occupation of Rhamalai (SS)

Therefore I Am: The Tale of IG-88 (beginning) (SS)

Big Quince (flashback) (SS)

Explosive Development (flashback) (SS)

Starter's Tale (flashback — or some version of these events) (SS)

ANH +2.5

The Power Gem! (N)

Iceworld! (N)

Newspaper comic strip story 21 (untitled) (N)

Doom Mission! (N)

Race for Survival! (N)

The Most Dangerous Foe
(framing story) (SS)

The Paradise Detour! (N)

A New Beginning (N)

Showdown (N)

The Final Trap! (N)

The Bounty Hunter Wars:
Book 1 — The Mandalorian
Armor (B)

The Bounty Hunter Wars:
Book 2 — The Slave Ship (B)

The Bounty Hunter Wars: Book 3
Crimson Bounty (SS)

X-Wing Rogue Squadron —
The Making of Baron Fel (no.
25) (flashback) (CB)

Side Trip Part One (SS)

Side Trip Part Two (SS)

Side Trip Part Three (SS)

Side Trip Part Four (SS)

X-Wing Rogue Squadron — The
Making of Baron Fel (no. 25)
(flashback) (CB)

Double Cross on Ord Mantell (SS)

Payback: The Tale of Dengar (beginning) (SS)

TESB (ANH +3)

Star Wars Episode V: The Empire
Strikes Back (M)

One Last Night in the Mos Eisley
Cantina: The Tale of the Wolfman and the Lamproid (second
flashback, during *TESB*) (SS)

Hunting the Hunters (during
TESB) (SS)

Therefore I Am: The Tale of IG-88
(middle, during *TESB*) (SS)

Payback: The Tale of Dengar (middle, during *TESB*) (SS)

The Prize Pelt: The Tale of Bossk
(during *TESB*) (SS)

The Last One Standing: The Tale
of Boba Fett (middle, during
TESB) (SS)

Of Possible Futures: The Tale of
Zuckuss and 4-LOM (during
TESB) (SS)

Shadows of the Empire (prologue)
(B,CB)

TESB + (immediately after *TESB*)

The Emperor's Trophy" (SS)

Hoth (from The Illustrated Star
Wars Universe) (SS)

TESB +0.5

TIE Fighter: The Stele Chronicles
(B)

Firepower (SS)

Desperate Measures (SS)

Slaying Dragons (SS)

The Longest Fall (SS)

Shadows of the Empire (main
story) (B,CB)

A Barve Like That: The Tale
of Boba Fett (flashback,
during Shadows of the Empire)
(SS)

Therefore I Am: The Tale of IG-88
(middle, during Shadows of the
Empire) (SS)

Payback: The Tale of Dengar
(middle, during Shadows of
the Empire) (SS)

Shadow Stalker (CB)

Uhl Eharl Khoehng (SS)

Mara Jade — By the Emperor's
Hand (nos. 1–6) (CB)

A Barve Like That: The Tale of
Boba Fett (flashback, immediately before *ROTJ*) (SS)

A Time to Mourn, a Time to
Dance: Oola's Tale (flashback,
immediately before *ROTJ*) (SS)

ROTJ (TESB +1 or ANH +4)

Star Wars Episode VI: Return of the Jedi (M)

That's Entertainment: The Tale of Salacious Crumb (during *ROTJ*) (SS)

Payback: The Tale of Dengar (middle, during *ROTJ*) (SS)

A Time to Mourn, a Time to Dance: Oola's Tale (during *ROTJ*) (SS)

Let Us Prey: The Whipid's Tale (during *ROTJ*) (SS)

A Boy and His Monster: The Rancor Keeper's Tale (ending, during *ROTJ*) (SS)

The Last One Standing: The Tale of Boba Fett (middle, during *ROTJ*) (SS)

Taster's Choice: The Tale of Jabba's Chef (during *ROTJ*) (SS)

And Then There Were Some: The Gamorrean Guard's Tale (during *ROTJ*) (SS)

Old Friends: Ephant Mon's Tale (during *ROTJ*) (SS)

Out of the Closet: The Assassin's Tale (during *ROTJ*) (SS)

Sleight of Hand: The Tale of Mara Jade (during *ROTJ*) (SS)

Shaara and the Sarlacc: The Skiff Guard's Tale (during *ROTJ*) (SS)

Goatgrass: The Tale of Ree-Yees (during *ROTJ*) (SS)

The Great God Quay: The Tale of Barada and the Weequays (during *ROTJ*) (SS)

And the Band Played On: The Band's Tale (during *ROTJ*) (SS)

A Bad Feeling: The Tale of EV-9D9 (ending, during *ROTJ*) (SS)

Skin Deep: The Fat Dancer's Tale (during *ROTJ*) (SS)

Of the Day's Annoyances: Bib Fortuna's Tale (during *ROTJ*) (SS)

Tongue-Tied: Bubo's Tale (during *ROTJ*) (SS)

A Free Quarren in the Palace: Tessek's Tale (main story, during *ROTJ*) (SS)

Epilogue: Whatever Became Of . . . ? (during *ROTJ* and covering many years after) (SS)

Therefore I Am: The Tale of IG-88 (end, during *ROTJ*) (SS)

One Last Night in the Mos Eisley Cantina: The Tale of the Wolfman and the Lamproid (framing story and last flashback, during *ROTJ*) (SS)

Escape from Balis-Baurgh (flashback, during *ROTJ*) (SS)

ROTJ +(immediately after ROTJ)

The Truce at Bakura (B)

X-Wing: Rogue Squadron Special (CB)

A Barve Like That: The Tale of Boba Fett (main story, shortly after *ROTJ*) (SS)

Payback: The Tale of Dengar (end, shortly after *ROTJ*) (SS)

Yavin 4 (from The Illustrated Star Wars Universe) (SS)

ROTJ +0.5

The Jabba Tape (CB)

The Vandelhelm Mission (CB)

X-Wing Rogue Squadron — The Rebel Opposition (nos. 1–4) (CB)

X-Wing Rogue Squadron — The Phantom Affair (nos. 5–8) (CB)

Junior Jedi Knights — Vader's
Fortress (B)

Junior Jedi Knights — Kenobi's
Blade (B)

Young Jedi Knights — Heirs of the
Force (B)

Young Jedi Knights — Shadow
Academy (B)

Young Jedi Knights — The Lost
Ones (B)

Young Jedi Knights — Lightsabers
(B)

Young Jedi Knights — Darkest
Knight (B)

Young Jedi Knights — Jedi under
Siege (B)

ROTJ +19

Young Jedi Knights — Shards of
Alderaan (B)

Young Jedi Knights — Diversity Alliance (B)

Young Jedi Knights — Delusions
of Grandeur (B)

Young Jedi Knights — Jedi Bounty
(B)

Young Jedi Knights — The Emperor's Plague (B)

Young Jedi Knights — Return to
Ord Mantell (B)

Young Jedi Knights — Trouble on
Cloud City (B)

Young Jedi Knights — Crisis of
Crystal reef (B)

No Disintegrations, Please (framing story) (SS)

ROTJ +21

The Star Wars Chronology (B)

Boba Fett — The Vader Job (CB)

THE "MARVEL COMICS"
STAR WARS UNIVERSE

ANH −32

Star Wars Episode I (M)

ANH −25

Star Wars (no. 24) (back story) (CB)

ANH −22

Star Wars Episode II (M)

ANH −20

Star Wars Episode III (M)

ANH −18

Droids — The Adventures of C-
3PO and R2-D2 Cycle One: The
Trigon One (episodes 1–4) (TV)

ANH −17

Droids — The Adventures of C-

3PO and R2-D2 Cycle Two:
Mon-Julpa (episodes. 5–9) (TV)

The Great Heep (TV)

ANH −16

Droids — The Adventures of C-
3PO and R2-D2 Cycle Three:
The Adventures of Mugo
Baobob (episodes 10–13) (TV)

ANH −5

Flight of the Falcon (CB)

Droids (nos. 1–5)

Ewoks (nos. 1–9)

Droids (no. 5)

Ewoks (nos. 10–14)

THE TIME LINE

Ewoks (TV)

ANH −4

Star Wars Annual 2 (back story)
(CB)

The All-New Ewoks (TV)

ANH −3

Star Wars Annual 2 (flashback) (CB)

The Weapons Master! (back story)
(CB)

The Ewok Adventure — A Caravan
of Courage (TV)

ANH −2

Ewoks — The Battle for Endor (TV)

ANH −1

The Way of the Wookie! (CB)

Star Wars (no. 17) (back story) (CB)

ANH

Star Wars Episode IV: A New Hope
(M)

ANH +

The Day after the Death Star! (CB)

ANH +1

Pizzazz (nos. 1–16) (CB)

War on Ice! (CB)

Star Wars 3-D (no. 1) (CB)

Star Wars (nos. 7–15) (CB)

Star Wars (no. 24) (framing story)
(CB)

Star Wars (no. 16) (CB)

ANH +2

Star Wars (no. 17) (framing story)
(CB)

Star Wars (nos. 18–23) (CB)

Star Wars (nos. 25–30) (CB)

Star Wars Annual 1 (CB)

Star Wars (no. 38) (CB)

Star Wars (nos. 31–34) (CB)

Tilotny Throws a Shape (CB)

Star Wars (nos. 35–37) (CB)

Star Wars (no. 70) (back story)

Weapon's Master (framing story)
(CB)

Pandora Effect (CB)

World of Fire (CB)

Star Wars 3-D (nos. 2–3) (CB)

TESB (ANH +3)

Star Wars Episode V: The Empire
Strikes Back (M)

TESB +1

Star Wars (nos. 45–50) (CB)

Star Wars (no. 86) (CB)

Star Wars (no. 55) (CB)

Star Wars (no. 78) (CB)

Star Wars (no. 83) (CB)

Star Wars (nos. 56–65) (CB)

Star Wars Annual 2 (framing story)
(CB)

Star Wars (nos. 66–69) (CB)

Star Wars (no. 70) (framing story)
(CB)

Star Wars (nos. 71–77) (CB)

Star Wars Annual 3 (CB)

Star Wars (nos. 79–80) (CB)

Death Masque

Dark Knight's Devilry

Dark Lord's Conscience

Rust Never Sleeps

Blind Fury

ROTJ (TESB +1 or ANH +4)

Star Wars Episode VI: Return of
the Jedi (M)

ROTJ +1

Star Wars (nos. 81–82) (CB)

Star Wars (nos. 84–85) (CB)

Star Wars (nos. 87–91) (CB)

Star Wars (no. 98) (CB)

Star Wars (nos. 92–97) (CB)

Star Wars (no. 101) (CB)

Star Wars (nos. 99–100) (CB)

Star Wars (nos. 102–107) (CB)

FIFTY REASONS WHY JEDI SUCKS

BY DAN VEBBER AND DANA GOULD

ON ITS OWN, *Return of the Jedi* has a lot of problems. But compared with *Star Wars* and *The Empire Strikes Back,* it's just plain bad. Search your feelings — you know it to be true. Like most of you out there, we love *Star Wars* more than words can say and will always respect and thank George Lucas for providing a generation of moviegoers with the most significant mythos of the last twenty-five years.

But also, like most of you out there, whenever we watch the trilogy, the awed reverence with which we watch *Wars* and *Empire* is replaced during *Jedi* by laughing, moaning, and shouted insults that make *MST3K* look tame by comparison. Fifteen years after its release, it's become sadly evident that *Jedi* hasn't aged well at all, while *Wars* and *Empire* increasingly gain acceptance as cinema classics. (We could just as easily have made a list of one hundred reasons *Star Wars* and *The Empire Strikes Back* are two of the greatest films ever made, but where's the fun in that?)

It would be easy to put the blame for *Jedi*'s failure squarely on the shoulders of its director, the late Richard Marquand. But while few would argue that Marquand was the greatest choice to inherit the franchise, the fact remains that it was executive producer George Lucas who hired him, who told him how to handle the material, and who always had the final say. So we'll let Marquand rest in peace; chances are he did the best he could.

What Lucas was thinking is another story. Whether *Jedi*'s faults are a result of his sincere artistic vision or of something more sinister (read: "marketable") may never truly be known. But by comparing the genesis of each of the three films, we can make a pretty good educated guess. When *Star Wars* was conceived, no one had any idea how much money it would eventually pull in. *Empire* was still a risk, as successful sequels were rare at that point. When it came time to do *Jedi,* however, the machinery was fully in place to sell it to the hilt. Lucas knew he could make far more money from merchandise than from theater grosses, so it's likely that the question "How easily will this translate into a Kenner toy?" figured more prominently in many of his *Jedi* decisions than it did in those that formed the first two *Star Wars* films. (And honestly, who can blame him? If we had the chance to build a ranch estate and media empire as vast as those owned by Lucas, we'd sell out in less time than it takes to shut one of those pressure doors on the Death Star.)

There are plenty of fervent fans who argue that by the mere fact of its being part of the trilogy, *Jedi* should be above criticism. We'd ask those people whose initial response to this list is one of anger to apply the fifty points below to their next *Jedi* viewing and join us in hoping that *Jedi* was a freak occurrence and not the beginning of a downward trend that will continue into the new films.

1 ▪ EWOKS, EWOKS, EWOKS: One of the miracles of the *Star Wars* trilogy is that Lucas's bizarre and ever present fascination with little people didn't hurt the first two films. The Jawas were cool. But George had to push his luck. The Ewoks are not cool. Period. In circles of die-hard *Star Wars* fans, to say you hate the Ewoks is like saying you enjoy breathing air. The Ewoks are *the* primary example of many of the points on this list: their unapologetic cuddliness is uncharacteristic and unwelcome; they look fake; they engage in constant physical comedy; their teddy bear design is wholly uninteresting; they live in boring surroundings; several of the film's dumbest scenes revolve around them; they were originally supposed to have been Wookiees; and they sing that damn song at the end (well, at least until the Special Edition). But aside from what we see on-screen, the Ewoks are miserable little creatures for a completely different reason: they are the single clearest example of Lucas's willingness to compromise the integrity of his trilogy in favor of merchandising dollars. How intensely were the Ewoks marketed? Consider this: *Ewok* is a household word, despite the fact that it's never once spoken in the film.

2 ▪ THE TONE IS INCONSISTENT: The Rebellion is in ruins, Darth Vader is Luke's father, and Han is frozen. Why Lucas decided to smother these ambitious plot elements under a load of feel-good clichés and textbook plot structure is anyone's guess (it's our theory that he was infected with the same mania that caused Spielberg to make *Hook* eight years later). *Jedi* never has any idea of what it's trying to be. Throughout, the mood and pacing is herky-jerked back and forth between dramatic and lighthearted. The scenes with Vader look and feel like they're taking place in a different film from those with our heroes, and no amount of special effects or nostalgia for *Wars* and *Empire* can make the pieces fit together. Lacking any consistent driving force (pun intended), *Jedi* is impossible to take seriously and has little to none of the mythic, transporting feel of its predecessors. We're always aware we're watching a big-budget movie.

3 ▪ THE LOOK IS ALL WRONG: After the second film, did the Empire celebrate its trouncing of the Rebellion by going through the galaxy with a big bottle of Windex? Everything in *Jedi* looks clean and polished, from the ships to the costumes to the backgrounds. One of the triumphs of the first two films was the fact that it was next to impossible to imagine they were filmed right here on Earth. In contrast, *Jedi*'s sets look like sets. We can picture cameras, plywood, and the key grip eating a sandwich just out of the frame. Marquand never seems to know where to put the camera and is constrained by the space his scenes inhabit instead of inspired by it. In the end, it's surprising that *Jedi* doesn't have any cardboard tombstones falling over or a brief appearance by Vampira as the ghoul's wife.

4 ▪ IT'S JUST A BUNCH OF MUPPETS!: Admittedly, *Wars* had its share of fake-looking aliens in the Mos Eisley cantina scene, but many of them were genuinely innovative at the time (Hammerhead is still impressive) and none of them crossed the not-so-thin line between costume and (shudder) Muppet. Even Yoda in *Empire* was constructed, filmed, and voiced well enough that we never thought to look for the hand up his rear. Don't get us wrong — we love Muppets, just not in the *Star Wars* universe. And *Jedi*'s Gamorrean guards (only slightly less realistic than a Tor Johnson Halloween mask), Salacious Crumb (it's good to see the Great Gonzo is still getting work) and Max Rebo (the blue piano-playing elephant with the oft-visible wire controlling his trunk) are proof that you can take the Henson studio out of *Sesame Street* but you can't take *Sesame Street* out of the Henson studio. Will the Criterion Edition laser disc include the deleted footage of Statler and Waldorf cracking wise from the balcony?

5 ▪ PAINFUL LACK OF INNOVATION: When it comes to scavenging, Lucas could teach even the Jawas a thing or two. *Jedi* borrows from *Wars* on levels ranging from conceptual to minute. There's another opening scene with a Star Destroyer (though this time it isn't even permitted to finish its awesome crawl across the top of the screen). There's another Imperial stronghold to infiltrate and another energy beam to turn off. And of course, there's another Death Star to blow up for the film's climax (though at least the Emperor had enough brains to plug up that pesky exhaust port). Most of the creatures and droids seen on Tatooine in *Wars* make background appearances in Jabba's court — even Greedo's alive and well! (Okay, maybe it's a different Rodian. They all look the same to us). Finally, little thought seems to have been given to developing or maturing any of the main characters in a realistic manner. Han and Threepio suffer most, coming across as catch-phrase-spouting caricatures of their previous selves.

6 ▪ WITTY BANTER: Note to writer Lawrence Kasdan: If you must fill your script with witty banter, at least try to make it, well, witty. With one or two exceptions, the humor in *Wars* and *Empire* was subtle, based around throwaway lines and the personality quirks of well-written characters. *Jedi's* overly contrived "humor" too often seems inspired by the setup–to–punch line wordplay found in a typical episode of *Three's Company*. In what is probably the film's single most painful moment, Solo requests Threepio to do a number of chores. After continually tapping him on the shoulder and preventing him from leaving to complete his duties, Solo quips, "Hurry up, will ya? I haven't got all day." Har-dee-har-har. Based on witticisms like that, it's amazing that Luke never rebuked the Emperor by stating "Up your nose with a rubber hose."

7 ▪ PHYSICAL COMEDY: This is a galactic rebellion, for heaven's sake! Yet an Ewok clocks himself with his own slingshot. Threepio's legs point skyward after he falls off the skiff into the sand. Countless adorable Muppets zanily cover their eyes or flip-duck off their perches when faced with tense situations. Worst of all, there are two solid instances where burps are used for cheap laughs. Burps! And where are the fart jokes? Well, maybe in the next film. *Jedi* is as good a parody of the trilogy as one could hope for; there was really no need for Mel Brooks to make *Spaceballs*.

8 ▪ UNINTERESTING LOCALES: *Wars* and *Empire* took us to locales that many of us have never been to in real life, namely a vast desert, a run-down spaceport, an enormous space battle station, a planet of ice and snow, a dense, slithering swamp, and a floating cloud city. *Jedi* just rehashes what we've already seen (though *Jedi's* Tatooine looks significantly less exotic than it did in *Wars,* having been filmed in California instead of Tunisia), adding only one new biome: the woods (oh, so *that's* what trees look like). If this pattern continues, expect the next *Star Wars* film to be set on the mysterious planet of sidewalks and suburban ranch homes.

9 ▪ THE FOREST BATTLE ON ENDOR: If we wanted to see improbable jungle shenanigans, we'd have rented *Battle for the Planet of the Apes*. The myriad traps and offensive weapons constructed by the Ewoks (apparently over the course of one night) work with such predictable precision against the Imperials that the "battle" is little more than scene after predictable scene of sticks and stones taking

out high-tech weaponry and forest-trained stormtroopers. *Jedi* may be a fantasy film, but the Ewoks' victory still flies in the face of all reason, logic, and precedent. It's a cute little war in which dozens of human stormtroopers are beaten to death and we're treated to only one dead Ewok. Happily, audiences have always responded to the stupidity of this imbalance: in screening after screening, the Ewok's groaning demise is typically met with more cheers and applause than the destruction of the Death Star.

10 ▪ SOLO: In *Empire,* Threepio states that the carbonite would keep Solo safe, provided he survived the freezing process. Safe, yes, but Threepio said nothing about the side effects. Namely, that people in carbon-freeze gain twenty pounds and take on the demeanor of Ward Cleaver on Quaaludes. *Wars* and *Empire* established Solo as a braggart, pirate, and all-around scoundrel. In *Jedi,* he's just a good-hearted, slack-jawed simp whose comments and actions are almost exclusively played for laughs. In not a single scene does Solo have the same acerbic edge he possessed in the previous films. Harrison Ford does nothing to help the situation (perhaps to his credit), acting with a boredom rarely paralleled as he kills time waiting for another Indiana Jones installment.

11 ▪ MUSIC: The soundtrack to *Wars* is an unquestioned classic. *Empire*'s soundtrack gave us the trilogy's best piece of music: "The Imperial March." What does *Jedi* have to offer? Some playful *Peter and the Wolf*–esque Ewok tunes and Jabba's foam-and-latex band. The song "Lapti Nek" was translated into English for an MTV video, and we learned that "Lapti Nek" actually means "workin' out." That whole *Flashdance* craze was certainly popular back in 1983, but now it's just embarrassing. Jabba's band is a pale imitation of *Wars'* cantina musicians. The Muppets look fake, and the music they play is truly wretched. (Yet one of the scenes added to the Special Edition *Jedi* is *another* song by the band!) Even more insipid, though, is the Ewoks' celebratory "Yub-yub" number at the end (now cut from the Special Edition), which sounds suspiciously as if it's sung not by Ewoks but by humans. The theme to the *Alien Nation* TV show sounded more authentic.

12 ▪ THREEPIO: Threepio was bearable in *Wars* because he and Artoo played an integral role in the unfolding of the plot. He got on our nerves in *Empire*, but we could at least sympathize with the human characters, who were more or less stuck with him and expressed their irritation. In *Jedi*, Threepio's along by choice, and everyone just loves chuckling at the way he screws everything up. They decide to bring him along to Endor for no good reason, and we're all forced to endure another barrage of predictable outbursts highlighting the shiny droid's cowardice, ego, and annoying verbosity. Shut him up or shut him down!

13 ▪ OBI-WAN'S APPEARANCE TO LUKE: In case you missed the first two films, Obi-Wan Kenobi is supposed to be dead. In *Wars* and *Empire*, he made himself known to Luke through an occasional voice in the head or in a floating vision. In *Jedi*, all of Obi-Wan's street credibility as a wizened spiritual guide is thrown out the window when he appears on Dagobah and shuffles around like Fred G. Sanford in a coat of glow paint. Rather than floating in one place, he fades in twenty feet away and walks up to Luke, eventually resting his noncorporeal butt on a rock. The ensuing two-way conversation scrambles to tie up too many loose ends at once, made worse by the fact that the character saying it all shouldn't even be there on such a literal level. And unlike his similarly flawed Dagobah appearance in *Empire*, Obi-Wan never fades back into oblivion once his message is delivered in *Jedi*. For all we know, he and Luke could have spent hours hanging out and gossiping like housewives.

14 ▪ LUKE: We like Mark Hamill, really. But though he was perfectly cast as the wet-behind-the-ears student in the first two films, he simply lacks the dignity to pull off a believable Jedi Knight. To top things off, he has Aunt Beru's haircut from the first film. We forget — was *Jedi* released before or after the advent of the Supercuts salon chain?

15 ▪ SURPRISE! THEY'RE BROTHER AND SISTER: After *Jedi* came out, Lucas would routinely go on record stating that in his mind, *Star Wars* was always first and foremost a story about a brother and a sister. Does anybody really buy this? *Wars* and *Empire* both had sexu-

TEN REASONS WHY JEDI DOESN'T TOTALLY SUCK

1 ▪ LUKE'S GANGPLANK WALK:
The suspense leading up to Luke's jump-off and bounce-back on the skiff still gets us biting our nails, and the first seven or eight seconds of the ensuing battle are actually pretty exciting. Too bad the rest of the melee deteriorates into slapstick.

2 ▪ THE EMPEROR'S ARRIVAL AT THE DEATH STAR:
One of the best examples of the power and importance of the Emperor is the hundreds of TIE fighters ceremoniously swarming like bees around the docking bay that receives him. The following interior shot is backed by the trilogy's loudest, scariest, and best use of the "Imperial March" theme.

3 ▪ THE SPEEDER BIKE CHASE:
The only time the forests of Endor don't look boring is during the speeder bike chase — primarily because most of us have never seen trees zipping by our heads at 200 mph.

4 ▪ THE EMPEROR:
It was wise to cast human Ian McDiarmid, and not another damn Muppet, as the Emperor. He exudes pure, seductive evil, and the scenes with him are the best in the film. A couple are even among the best in the trilogy. ➤

5 • WEDGE'S PROMOTION:

Wedge Antilles would have been number one on our list of side characters, but he appears in all three films, so we consider him one of the main bunch. In *Jedi* he's deservedly been promoted to Red Leader and gets to fire the decisive shot that leads to the second Death Star's explosion. Good shooting, Wedge!

6 • THE AT-STS:

The scout walkers may blow up too easily and resemble rampaging chickens, but they're still wonderfully designed and are animated inside a complex environment more or less flawlessly. If only they'd stepped on a few more Ewoks (Have we mentioned we hate Ewoks?).

7 • THE FINAL SPACE BATTLE:

No space combat before or since has taken such consistent advantage of all three axes of movement. The scenes are exceptionally well choreographed, and it's always clear what's going on — compare *Jedi*'s battle to the confusing mess of planes and spaceships that zip around aimlessly in the final scenes of *ID4*.

8 • OUTRUNNING THE DEATH STAR EXPLOSION:

Setting aside the fact that Lando really should have died, the *Falcon* outrunning the explosive wave is always impressive. Nowadays, every

ally charged scenes that play significantly creepier when watched with the knowledge that Luke and Leia are siblings. It seems unlikely that Lucas would have included those scenes if he knew that one day people would be seeing them from such a different perspective. What seems likely, however, is that when *Jedi* came around, Lucas was grasping at straws, searching desperately for a plot revelation to equal *Empire*'s classic father/son moment. Oh well — even if Lucas is telling the truth (Yoda did, after all, say in *Empire* that there was "another"), the issue could have been handled in a less clumsy manner. Having Luke and Leia learn about their relationship through means other than spur-of-the-moment (albeit Force-guided) guesses would have been a start.

16 • UNFORGIVABLE DIALOGUE: Threepio approaching Jabba's palace: "I have a bad feeling about this"; Han Solo, when confronted by Ewoks: "I have a bad feeling about this"; Leia, after releasing Solo from carbon freeze: "I gotta get you outta here"; Leia, after being freed from Jabba's chains: "We gotta get outta here"; Leia, after she and an Ewok are ambushed on Endor: "Let's get outta here." With dialogue like this, it seems Lucas finally put that "million monkeys at a million typewriters" theory to the test.

17 • HORRIBLE EXPOSITION: "Artoo, look! It's Captain Solo — and he's still in carbonite!" Lines like this are for those people who somehow missed the first two movies. Threepio is the main offender throughout, even going so far as to offer a long, Ewokese summary of the trilogy's plot thus far (with sound effects, no less). Of course, Lucas would probably say that scene was to show "the entrancing magic of storytelling." Call us cynical, but entrancing magic makes us want to puke.

18 • JABBA THE MUPPET: Er — Hutt. Jabba isn't all that scary. It seems Lucas became so enamored of his technology that he forgot humans are far more ominous than any shop-built alien life-form could ever hope to be. Remember Grand Moff Tarkin? Now *there* was a creepy villain. We're so busy trying to figure out where all the puppeteers were hiding beneath Jabba's frame that we're never able to accept him as a living, breathing character. And no matter how you cut it, his eyelids still look fake. If only they hadn't lost the phone number of that fat Irish guy who originally played him in that deleted *Wars* scene.

19 ▪ STUPID COINCIDENCES: "We have been without an interpreter since our master got angry with our last protocol droid and disintegrated him." Pan over to said droid being pulled apart in a machine, to allow for a startled reaction shot by Threepio. Numerous scenes like this further damage *Jedi*'s ability to convince us this stuff is really happening. Jabba and his minions sit silently behind the *Let's Make a Deal* curtain, and the fact that the escape skiff just happens to have two magnetic retrieval devices to pluck the fallen droids out of the sand are further examples of this problem. None of these scenes needed to center around such ridiculous leaps in logic; more often than not they're simply indicative of lazy screenwriting or are inserted for excessive rim-shot-ready moments.

20 ▪ BOBA FETT'S DEATH: It's inexcusable that such an imposing figure as Boba Fett — the one bounty hunter good enough to capture Solo — flies clumsily to his death in the Sarlacc pit while screaming like Shemp from the Three Stooges. Any *Star Wars* geek worth his weight in trading cards will tell you that Boba Fett is the trilogy's most underused character. His brief but badass appearance in *Empire* had us all anxiously awaiting the next film, assuming his role would be greatly expanded by the events surrounding what we then thought would be an incredible escape by Han. Not only does Fett have nothing to do in *Jedi,* but in the ultimate indignity, he's killed off without ceremony or honor for no better reason than another damn burp joke. According to the novels and comics, Fett survived. But that's not what's implied in the film itself, and it doesn't make the scene any less shameful.

21 ▪ TERRIBLE, TERRIBLE POSTPRODUCTION LOOPING: In about half of *Jedi*'s scenes, little attempt is made to match the dialogue with the characters' lip movements — it's almost like watching a Mothra flick. If Lucas were smart, he'd blame this on the film's being dubbed from its original language. You know — the one they spoke a long time ago in a galaxy far, far away.

action film made seems to have a shot like this. Problem is, movies like *The Long Kiss Goodnight* expect us to believe that not only spaceships but people on foot can outrun explosions. Yeah, right.

9 ▪ THE AT-AT ON ENDOR:
Seeing an AT-AT emerge from the forests of Endor at night adds a welcome dark and moody touch to the film. When it delivers Luke to Vader, *Jedi* almost feels like *Empire* for a few wonderful seconds.

10 ▪ VADER'S SKELETON:
If you have a laser disc player or a good enough videotape, you can pause and see Vader's insides lit up by lightning as he hoists the Emperor above his head. Someone at Lucasfilm took the time to make those fleeting shots count, designing a skeleton for the Dark Lord that is mostly human but partially bionic. Little things do, indeed, mean a lot. ✦

22 ▪ SUBPAR SPECIAL EFFECTS: It's strange that the film that gave us sci-fi's most intricate and well-choreographed space battle to date also gave us so many effects that look just plain silly. The rancor aside (see below), consider Han's light-streaming release from the carbonite, the seemingly Magic Markered shadow under Jabba's sail barge, and the explosion of the shield generator on Endor (in which Han and his team, about twenty feet from the bunker, aren't affected in the slightest by an explosion that, from our viewpoint, engulfs several square miles of forest).

23 ▪ THE RANCOR EFFECTS: In quite probably the worst use of a blue screen in the history of big-budget film, the rancor looks so awful it deserves its own separate mention. Planning this sequence, the ILM team seems to have been inspired by old episodes of *Lidsville,* as the admittedly well-designed puppet appears at all times either flat or two-dimensional or surrounded by an unearthly glow. This is one effect we won't mind seeing cleaned up.

24 ▪ LEIA AND HAN'S RELATIONSHIP: It's A Galaxy Far, Far Away 90210! The subtle, repressed passion of *Empire* is simplified to high school relationship levels in *Jedi.* They kiss, they say "I love you," Han throws a hissy fit and gets jealous of Luke. The couple play off each other in such obvious ways that we're reminded of the Screenwriting 101 rule of "show, don't tell." Han and Leia never look or act like two adults in love — and no amount of gushy language can cover up that fact.

25 ▪ CARRIE FISHER'S "ACTING": Han: "Who are you?" Leia: "Someone who LOVES you." When Carrie Fisher isn't staring vacantly into space, she's emoting to degrees previously seen only in Mexican soap operas. At least today she's cool enough to admit that she was zoned out on coke the entire time.

26 ▪ OBVIOUS MISSED OPPORTUNITIES: Putting aside the fact that the entire movie is a missed opportunity in the context of the trilogy, *Jedi* has specific missed opportunities too numerous to count within its own structure. These range from major (Lucas's throwaway admission that he had originally intended Endor to be a planet of Wookiees, and the fact that Lando doesn't die in the Death

Star assault, as *Jedi*'s original script dictated) to picayune (when the Alliance fleet suddenly realizes the Death Star's shield is still functional, it would have been nice to see one or two X-Wings crash into said shield and explode, having not had enough time to pull up).

27 ▪ YODA: In *Empire,* Yoda was a sagacious sprite who brought to mind Gaelic legend. In *Jedi,* he's an annoying toad who sounds like Super Grover (thanks to Frank Oz's forgetting how to do the voice) and looks about as realistic as his Kenner action-figure likeness (thanks to bad, overlit cinematography; see point 3). Like the movie he's stuck in, *Jedi*'s Yoda is lacking in wisdom and festering with cuteness. Get out your laser discs (okay, or your videotapes) and compare the two Yodas head-to-head. You'll be surprised.

28 ▪ THE OPENING TEXT CRAWL: Let's compare the opening text crawl in which we are given our first taste of each of the three films, shall we: *Star Wars:* "It is a period of civil war. . . ." *Empire:* "It is a dark time for the Rebellion. . . ." *Jedi:* "Luke Skywalker has returned to his home planet of Tatooine in an attempt to rescue his friend Han Solo from the clutches of the vile gangster Jabba the Hutt. Charo guest stars." Okay, we threw in the part about Charo. But the point is, we're talking mythic tracts versus a blurb from *TV Guide.* The first sentence in *Jedi* centers around the word *friend.* Well, that's just peachy, but we much prefer the first two films' implications that we're about to see something a bit larger than a buddy picture.

29 ▪ IMPERIAL TECHNOLOGY: Imperial engineers should really figure out a way to keep their vehicles from blowing up so easily, both in space and on the ground. In *Jedi,* not only does a single crashed A-Wing take out an entire eight-kilometer Super Star Destroyer, but several scout walkers explode like Pintos whenever something taps them a little too hard. (True, the Imperial walkers in *Empire* could be tripped up a bit easily, but at least they didn't burst into fireballs until hit by Rebel blaster fire.) It seems strange that the Rebels even bothered procuring spaceships and blasters — based on what *Jedi* shows us, the Empire could have been defeated with a couple of well-placed safety pins.

30 ▪ JABBA'S DROID TORTURE ROOM: First of all, torturing droids is

stupid on a purely conceptual level, seeing as how they're machines and all. But what on earth was going through Lucas and Marquand's heads when they decided to play the scene in Jabba's droid room for laughs? *Wars* and *Empire* both have torture scenes. They're pretty unsettling. Know why? BECAUSE THEY'RE TORTURE SCENES, FOR CHRIST'S SAKE! Torture's not supposed to be funny — no one wants to laugh at a screaming power droid as a bad steam effect shoots out of its feet to simulate the application of intense heat. But to the makers of *Jedi*, there's nothing like a little humor at the expense of torture victims, even if they are mechanical. Following the release of *Jedi*, Amnesty International must have logged hundreds of reports of people flogging their waffle irons and blenders.

31 ▪ USE OF EARTH SLANG AND POP CULTURE: We were almost willing to forgive the fact that an Ewok exclaims "Yahoo," or that Threepio uses the supposedly Ewokese word *boom*, until we saw the abominable scene where an Ewok swings from a vine and lets out a note-for-note copy of Tarzan's famous yell. Have we mentioned that we hate the Ewoks?

32 ▪ JEDI AFTERLIFE: The Jedi apparently have a lot in common with the Catholics. You can screw up your entire life, strangle scores of people, and oversee the construction of a planet-destroying battle station, but as long as you repent with your last breath, you get to party with Yoda and Ben in the netherworld. Speaking of that, Yoda seems to have gotten the short end of the afterlife stick — why does Anakin's ghost get to regrow his hair and get all spiffed up and nice looking, while Yoda, who managed to resist the dark side all his nine-hundred-plus years, still looks like a crumpled old salamander?

33 ▪ UNREALISTIC, BORING FIGHT SEQUENCES: Why stage an elaborate hand-to-hand fight with a scout trooper when you can just have Solo use the old "shoulder tap" trick? Or when you can throw a duffel bag at an Imperial guard and he'll backflip over a railing and into the shield generator's energy core? Not since Charlton Heston took out a gorilla bare-handed have we been asked to swallow such nonsense.

34 ▪ STORMTROOPERS HAVE BECOME PUSSIES: "Look out — teddy bear creatures! And they've got primitive handmade weapons! Let's forget our years of intense military training, put down our high-tech weaponry, and run away!"

35 ▪ VADER'S REAL FACE: You know, Darth, that scar will never heal unless you stop scratching it. But enough with the clever bons mots — it should have been David Prowse under that helmet. Period. He deserved at least that much, and probably would have been willing to shave his head. Sebastian Whatsisname [Shaw] delivers an acceptable acting job (actually, one of *Jedi*'s only acceptable acting jobs), but that pudgy head just doesn't match up with the body we see on Vader throughout the rest of the trilogy.

36 ▪ BAD EDITING: It seems that the folks at Supercuts were hired by Lucasfilm not only to style the actors' coils but to hack and splice the film as well. That *Jedi* has problems with its editing is largely a subjective opinion and hard to quantify, but we base our belief on the fact that certain scenes just plain lack the punch and pacing we know they could and should have had (though whether this is the director's fault or the editor's isn't always clear).

37 ▪ THE ALIEN LANGUAGES ARE POORLY PRESENTED: Bib Fortuna repeatedly lapses from Huttese into English for no apparent reason, and we learn from Leia's bounty hunter alter ego that at least one translation of "Thirty thousand, no less" is "Yoto. Yoto." Huh? And while we're on the subject, if Threepio is Jabba's translator, why does he translate what others are saying into English rather than Huttese? The precedent is there to employ subtitles, but they're only rarely used to suggest some iota of realism.

38 ▪ INCONSISTENCY WITHIN THE ESTABLISHED UNIVERSE: It can always be argued that the *Star Wars* universe contains a wide array of peoples and languages. Still, it strikes us as sloppy that codes on *Jedi*'s computer screens are in alien gobbledygook language, while the tractor beam controls in *Wars* were in English. And speaking of English, almost all the Imperials in *Wars* and *Empire* have an English accent. *Jedi* doesn't continue this trend — unfortunately, because as everyone knows, the British are inherently terrifying.

39 ▪ YODA'S DEATH SEQUENCE: Yoda says, "Soon will I rest. Yes, forever sleep." Less than four minutes later — *bam!* He's a goner. And what does Luke do while his beloved master lies choking and gasping for his final breaths? Well, he just sort of sits there like a doofus and watches him writhe in pain. Not that dialing 911 is an option on Dagobah, but a simple, "Hey, Master — you okay?" would have been a nice gesture.

40 ▪ THE ALLIANCE BRIEFING: In *Wars,* the briefing before the attack on the Death Star had the feel of a serious military operation. In *Jedi,* the briefing is a forum for witty repartee, attended by chuckling, smirking buddies and a medical droid who has no business being there other than to fill a vacant seat. It's no wonder the Rebels got their asses kicked in *Empire* if this is how their top military leaders conduct themselves when the galaxy is at stake. Eventually, Luke barges in unannounced and the "meeting" breaks up with all the parliamentary procedure of porno night at the Elks Club.

41 ▪ PARADOXICAL LESSONS IN THE FORCE: Yoda says the only way Luke can become a Jedi is to face Vader. Minutes later, he says it's unfortunate that Luke rushes to face Vader. This is in addition to Yoda's assertion in *Empire* that if Luke faces Vader, he'll become an agent of evil. So he needs to face Vader to become a Jedi, but he can't face Vader or else he'll become a slave to the dark side. This is a paradox on a par with the one Kirk used to confuse and blow up Nomad.

42 ▪ VADER'S NOT-SO-SPECIAL SHUTTLE: When we first saw Vader's shuttle with its clean lines and sleek, triwing design, it seemed a fitting vessel to transport a leader of his stature. But later we find out that apparently every Imperial shuttle — even the ones that transport supplies to work sites — looks just like Vader's. One explanation: after Vader damaged that fancy bent-wing TIE fighter they gave him in *Wars,* he lost his special-ship privileges. The more likely explanation: someone at Lucasfilm was too lazy or cheap just to design and build a model for a different style of shuttlecraft.

43 ▪ SLOPPY CONTINUITY ERRORS: In quick cuts between two different views of a character, it's a good bet that his or her expression and/or stance will be jarringly inconsistent. Check out Bib Fortuna in the scene where Jabba refers to the newly defrosted Solo as bantha fodder. Our favorite slip, however, is the star field behind the Emperor's throne, which in every shot consists of the same group of stars crawling slowly toward the left of the screen.

44 ▪ THAT SCENE WITH THE EWOK ON THE SPEEDER BIKE: This scene doesn't really exemplify any of the larger points in this article, but we hate it so much that we couldn't just ignore it. If *Jedi* weren't so darned cutesy, that Ewok would have been splattered into tree pizza and we'd have been a lot happier. Have we mentioned we hate Ewoks?

45 ▪ GENERALLY DUMB DIALOGUE: Vader, upon seeing that Luke has constructed a lightsaber: "Your skills are complete. Indeed, you are powerful, as the Emperor has foreseen." (Wait a second — all because he read a Time/Life book on electronics and soldered together some transistors? Does this mean Tim Allen is a Jedi?) Yoda, near death, to Luke: "Remember: a Jedi's strength flows from the Force." (That's more of a first-day lesson, isn't it, Yoda? Something tells us that Luke had that particular bit of wisdom written on a Post-it note and stuck to his W-Wing cockpit long ago.)

46 ▪ ADMIRAL ACKBAR: Sure, Admiral Ackbar looks neat, but he's quite the wishy-washy leader, judging from how Lando continually questions, ignores, and overrides his orders. Dumbest of all (though never actually mentioned in the film), Admiral Ackbar's fishlike race is called the Mon Calamari. Ha, ha, ha! (The joke isn't quite so funny when you realize that there are more fish people in *Jedi* than there are black people or female people.)

47 ▪ DUMB RESOLUTION OF PROBLEMS: The most pathetic example of facile problem solving is the "secret back door" on the shield generator base, which means our team won't have to be bothered with devising an interesting way to break in. Luckily for them, the base is apparently staffed by the one garrison in the Empire commanded by Colonel Klink.

48 ▪ ARTOO: Of all the main characters, Artoo is the only one who isn't handled in a totally embarrassing fashion, but there are still some inconsistencies in the presentation of his personality. He's supposed to be the brave, assured one to Threepio's sissy-boy, but in a couple of scenes he whimsically shakes and shivers with fear like Scooby-Doo. Is he into this whole Rebellion thing or not?

49 ▪ THE WIZARD OF OZ HOMAGE AT JABBA'S FRONT DOOR: Anyone who's ever seen MGM's seminal musical fantasy experiences more than a little déjà vu when Threepio knocks on Jabba's door and asks the whimsical attendant to admit him to the Emerald City — er — rusty palace. Had there been a precedent of scene-specific homage in *Wars* or *Empire,* we might have been more forgiving on this point, but the scene as presented in *Jedi* sticks out and degrades the overall integrity of the mythos established in the first two films. (Sure, *Wars* mimicked Kurosawa's *The Hidden Fortress* almost scene for scene, but only socially maladapted film geeks noticed that.)

50 ▪ THE SARLACC PIT AS FREUD'S *VAGINA DENTATA*: Come on, like it never occurred to you.

INDEX